WAR ON THE SILVER SCREEN

War on the Silver Screen

SHAPING AMERICA'S PERCEPTION OF HISTORY

GLEN JEANSONNE AND DAVID LUHRSSEN

 Potomac Books | *An imprint of the University of Nebraska Press*

Library of Congress
Cataloging-in-Publication Data

Jeansonne, Glen, 1946–
War on the silver screen: shaping America's
perception of history / Glen Jeansonne and
David Luhrssen.
pages   cm
Includes bibliographical references.
ISBN 978-1-61234-641-0 (pbk.: alk. paper)
ISBN 978-1-61234-642-7 (pdf)
1. War films—United States—History and
criticism. 2. History in motion pictures.
I. Luhrssen, David. II. Title.
PN1995.9.W3J35 2014
791.43'6581—dc23
2014025858

Set in Garamond Premier
by Renni Johnson.
Designed by N. Putens.

Contents

Acknowledgments   *vii*

Introduction   *ix*

1. World War I (1914–1918)   *1*

All Quiet on the Western Front (1930)

Paths of Glory (1957)

Lawrence of Arabia (1962)

Gallipoli (1981)

2. World War II (1939–1945)   *28*

Casablanca (1942)

Saboteur (1942) and *The
Best Years of Our Lives* (1946)

Twelve O'Clock High (1949)

Patton (1970)

Schindler's List (1993)

Flags of Our Fathers (2006)
and *Letters from Iwo Jima* (2006)

3. The Cold War (1947–1991), including
the Korean War (1950–1953) and
the Vietnam War (1955–1975)   *82*

The Manchurian Candidate (1962)

From Russia with Love (1963)

*Dr. Strangelove, Or: How I Learned
to Stop Worrying and Love the
Bomb* (1964) and *Fail-Safe* (1964)

Apocalypse Now (1979)

Charlie Wilson's War (2007)

4. The War on Terror (2001–)   *143*

United 93 (2006)

The Hurt Locker (2008)
and *Zero Dark Thirty* (2012)

Notes   *165*

Bibliography   *179*

Acknowledgments

The authors gratefully acknowledge Elizabeth Demmers, our original editor at Potomac Books, for believing in the project. Paul McComas, Mary Manion, and Steve Spice shared movies and ideas during the writing of the book. John Jahn was tireless with editorial as well as copyediting suggestions. Earlier versions of the essays on *Charlie Wilson's War*, *United 93*, and *Zero Dark Thirty* originally appeared in Milwaukee's weekly newspaper the *Shepherd Express* and are used with permission.

Introduction

Movies about wars have done more to stamp the wars' images in the American psyche than the reality of those wars themselves. Who can ponder the moral consequences of neutrality in the face of Nazism without remembering *Casablanca*, the heroism of bomber crews without *Twelve O'Clock High*, or the morass of Vietnam without *Apocalypse Now*? This book examines the often indelible impressions left by the fictional stories told on film. For better or worse the movies have shaped the American imagination more profoundly than the printed word.

Since 1917 the United States has almost constantly been at war or anxious over the prospect of war. Wars, past and present, have seldom been far from the minds of Americans, and movies have often helped define the public's attitudes toward them. Some of these wars have seemed straightforward, with clear objectives such as "making the world safe for democracy," ridding the world of dictators, or repelling imminent threats to the homeland. Some have been more muddled and have provoked mixed emotions because their goals were ambiguous and their resolutions less definitive. For nearly a half-century the United States fought a Cold War, punctuated intermittently by the eruption of "limited" hot wars in Vietnam and Korea. The nation fought proxy wars, propaganda wars, and a war on terror.

Movies have registered the public's varied feelings about these conflicts and have defined the ways we remember them. *All Quiet on the Western Front* captured the futility with which many Americans regarded World War I, and most films on the subject since then have registered unease. World War II, on the other hand, has been characterized as a period of unity, heroism, and prosperity in almost every American cinematic depiction. It was the "Good War" that drew Americans together and banished the Great Depression. That firm sense of common purpose inspired Alfred Hitchcock, a filmmaker not ordinarily interested in war movies, to dramatize the significance of ordinary Americans in *Saboteur*. Other wars, especially those that ended less successfully, have been represented as lessons in folly, over-extension, and poor judgment, even imperialism, and are haunted by resentment and cynicism. Vietnam is the prime example. By placing viewers in the boots of combat infantrymen, Oliver Stone's *Platoon* dramatized the confusion of that conflict for those who fought.

Ironically, for citizens of a nation that became the world's pre-eminent superpower after 1917, Americans tend to regard themselves as peace-loving people. But sometimes, as with the attack on Pearl Harbor or those on 9/11, wars have come to them. Under such circumstances the slate is wiped clean of ambiguity, and the bloodshed is honored and accepted. In other wars American lives seem to have been wasted because the nation did not achieve its full objective or because its purpose was messy or confused.

American culture also retains an isolationist streak as a legacy of the Republic's earliest years and encapsulated in the popular imagination by George Washington's warning against "foreign entanglements." Americans tend to be impatient with inconclusive wars of long duration, preferring quick, decisive, unequivocal victories. Yet by cultural tradition they dislike compromising their democratic ideals and would like to see these values take root throughout the world. Their belief in a combination of democracy, capitalism, and Christianity has compelled many Americans to want these values strengthened at home and spread abroad. Yet the world is a dangerous, changing place, and no ideals, however noble, inevitably survive the cauldron of war completely intact. Wars involve killing or being killed.

There is, or at least there has been, among many Americans a type of innocence, even naïveté, that does not exist in older civilizations that have experienced greater bloodshed over longer periods. At times Americans overlook, or forget, the relative youthfulness of its civilization and its ideals. In comparison with the once-dominant civilizations of Egypt, India, Persia, China, Greece, and Rome, even Great Britain and France, the United States is a newcomer to the role of world leader that recent generations sometimes take for granted. Americans are, in a relative sense, almost novices to bloodshed on a grand scale, much less to barbarian invasions. It is sobering to consider that in none of its twentieth-century wars were U.S. casualties comparable to those of its major allies or of its enemies. And the stories told by Hollywood have generally overlooked the disparity in suffering.

Much of what Americans remember about the nation's wars, even those within living memory, rely less on factual data than on fictional accounts, whose appeals to emotion are grist for box office success. The emotion evoked might be grim, shocking, romantic, heroic, or simply dramatic, but the strength of the emotion is great in the movies we remember best. Wars naturally lend themselves to intense drama. This book is about the movies that have done the most to shape our memories and impressions of the nation's wars. Our feelings about wars are often generated less by what we read or hear in lectures than by visual images, complemented by powerful dialogue, that make them unforgettable. Books work on the mind, on the intellectual side of human nature, while motion pictures operate at the visceral, emotional level, which is locked into our electrical, chemical, and cellular memories. Books may be read and absorbed at intervals, but films are compressed, intense, and immediate. Reading is a solitary experience; moviegoing, even watching DVDs at home, is usually a collective experience. War movies play a role in national bonding, even when their portrayal is inexact and their narrative structure necessarily distorts true events, compressing them into a beginning, a middle, and an end. The conventions of Hollywood demand a happy ending, though the horror and ambiguity of warfare sometimes trump conventions.

As humans, we like to think of ourselves as rational, thinking beings, yet much of what we do is emotionally driven: whom we fall in love with; whom we hate intensely—emotion defines our friends and lovers as well as our foes. We may not know at an intellectual level why we like or love some people more than others, why we prefer football to baseball, or why we like chocolate but reject caviar. Emotion often rules our choices on Election Day, the books we enjoy, the movies we like, when we tune in to a sitcom and when we turn the chatter off. Films are potent in shaping our views of the past, in establishing our heroes and our villains, and in determining how we feel about ourselves, individually and collectively, and about our history as inhabitants of a nation. We identify with actors and occasionally with directors. We glamorize them, and they become role models.

The combination of war and film is extremely powerful, sometimes overpowering. Who could be unmoved by *Schindler's List*, forget George C. Scott in *Patton*, or resist feelings of nationalism when watching the bombing of Pearl Harbor or the landings on D-Day? Although memories generated by motion pictures might distort reality—consider *Gone with the Wind* and *Titanic*—the same is true of human communication generally and certainly for such classic works as *The Iliad* and the Norse sagas.

There have been numerous films made long after the fact on the subject the United States's early wars, whether the Revolution that resulted in the nation's independence, the conflicts with American Indians, or the Civil War that tore the country apart. This book, however, begins with World War I, the conflagration that coincided with the birth of Hollywood. It was the first war of the cinematic age and the first instance in which movies competed with the experience of participants in molding the public's memory of the conflict. Real wars, moreover, are seldom entertaining for participants, but the principal purpose of most films is to entertain, and if they are meant to deliver an overt message, as war movies often do, they must be dramatized with memorable characters and storytelling. It does not matter whether the characters ever really existed or that elements of the story were trimmed or altered to fit the popular conventions of Hollywood.

This text is arranged chronologically. Every chapter addresses a particular American conflict, beginning with World War I and concluding with the twenty-first-century war on terror, and focuses on films that have helped determine the way the war is remembered and understood. Each chapter identifies ideas about American wars originating in cinema that have endured or, in the case of the war on terror, are likely to continue to influence popular perceptions. Introducing each chapter is an overview describing the important events of the war in question and placing that conflict in its historical context. Understanding how the war developed and was fought to its conclusion provides a foundation for appreciating the depiction of the war in film. Equally important, the battlefront is integrated with the home front, including the mood of the nation and the role of the media. Wars and the movies that depict them do not operate in a cultural or political vacuum.

The historical test of art or entertainment is separate, however, from any contemporary success, which while perhaps lucrative might be short-lived. What matters is how it endures. Shakespeare's greatness is due partly to the fact that his work still speaks to us and remains relevant to our internal and external worlds. It is easier to judge the historical significance of any work of fiction at a distance. Proximity can be a disadvantage. Popularity might fade. The films discussed here are enduring signal films that continue to direct the dialogue over American wars in the academy and among the general public. After a century of living with motion pictures, human consciousness has come to accommodate this relatively new form of cultural production; we often process reality like a director in the editing room, viewing social reality as it appears in the movies. The longevity of certain films and the messages and images they convey thus have continued relevance for our time.

CHAPTER ONE

World War I (1914–1918)

By the end of the summer of 1914 the world had shifted on its axis, and Europeans remembered those final balmy months before the war with a peculiar melancholy. *Limelight* (1952), Charlie Chaplin's bittersweet story of a stage performer's last days, was set in that summer, as if the sad, spent figure he portrayed represented a society about to slip away forever into what Henry James called "an abyss of blood and darkness."

The "Great War," as the conflagration was initially called, was the bloodiest conflict the world had yet endured. While the outcome was decided in western and eastern Europe and on the North Atlantic, the results of the Near East campaign continue to define the boundaries of global conflict a century later. The Far East, the Pacific, Africa, and the South Atlantic were settings for sideshow battles, yet Britain and France pressed the manpower and resources of India, Africa, and the Antipodes into service, contributing greatly to the Allied victory. The scope was not as wide as World War II, but in some ways it was the more terrible conflict, at least in Europe, where massed armies hurtled in medieval charges against modern weapons or bogged down for long stretches in the dank stalemate of the trenches. The casualties of trench warfare are almost unimaginable in the twenty-first century, when the United States's decade-long war in Afghanistan claimed only 3,000 American lives. On a single day, August 23, 1914, the French lost 130,000 dead or wounded at Charleroi. The death toll from this early and little remembered battle would soon be eclipsed by more terrible carnage.

The flashpoint for war was the June 28, 1914, assassination of the archduke Franz Ferdinand, heir to the throne of the troubled Austro-Hungarian Empire, but the dry tinder had been gathering for decades. The nationalism that flared into virulence during the nineteenth century made the old multiethnic Turkish and Austrian empires increasingly untenable. Nationalism spurred the forcible unification of the historically divided lands of Italy and Germany, late arrivals in the scramble for overseas colonies and itching to compete for prestige and economic advantage with the established global empires of France and Great Britain. The Continent was engaged in an expensive arms race, especially after Germany began building a fleet with the stated objective of challenging British dominance of the seas. Germany came into being after the crushing of France in the Franco-Prussian War and French nationalists sought revenge. A set of treaties bound the principal powers of Europe to the alliance system that triggered war in August 1914.

The archduke's assassin was a fanatical nationalist who sought to unite the Serbs of the Austro-Hungarian Empire with the independent Serbian kingdom. Austria blamed the Serbian government and issued a harsh ultimatum; coupled with Serbia by their shared Eastern Orthodox religion and Slavic ethnicity, Russia's Tsar Nicholas II stood by his little Balkan brother as Germany's ruler, Kaiser Wilhelm II, recklessly encouraged his German-speaking Austrian ally. By August 1, when Russia and Austria went to war, Germany was drawn in through its defense treaty with Austria, and France entered the fray through its pact with Russia. Seeking to outflank French defenses, Germany invaded neutral Belgium. Britain, obliged to defend Belgium by treaty and hoping to protect France, declared against Germany. The Great War was under way.

Only the most prescient, or the most cautious, worried about the duration and outcome as Europe mobilized its armies. "The European masses, stoked with xenophobic nationalism, went willingly, even gaily, to a conflict which their leaders, imbued with a perverse combination of arrogance and fatalism, believed they could control."[1] Generations of Europeans understood war in the romantic terms of the era's popular fiction and the stirring iconography of imperialism; most thinkers dismissed a long, destructive war between the "civilized powers" as impossible because of the economic ties of an increasingly global economy.[2] The population of every combatant nation greeted the declaration of war as a respite from the monotony of everyday life at a time when popular culture offered relatively few diversions. It was a break from boredom for the upper and middle classes, a holiday from long hours of toil for the working class, and a glorious opportunity for everyone. "I am not ashamed today to say that, overwhelmed by impassionate enthusiasm, I had fallen on my knees and thanked Heaven out of my overflowing heart that it had granted me the good fortune of being allowed to live in these times," Adolf Hitler recalled.[3] Millions of men in Great Britain, France, Germany, Austria-Hungary, and Russia shared an eagerness to serve their nation on the battlefield. The British poet Siegfried Sassoon, whose verses would later condemn the carnage, signed up for the Royal Army on August 1, 1914. He called his training "a picnic in perfect weather" and nurtured "serious aspirations to heroism in the field."[4]

The anticipated war of rapid movement, with its swift victories, never materialized. The elaborate strategies devised before the war, especially the German Schlieffen Plan and the French Plan XVII, bogged down as the western front sank into a bloody deadlock. French, British, and Belgian armies faced the Germans across six hundred miles of trenches. On the eastern front the Russians defeated the Austrians but were gradually pushed back by the Germans, enduring enormous losses and straining the empire's fragile social and economic system. Italy, ostensibly bound by treaty to the Central Powers of Germany, Austria-Hungary, and Turkey, sought territorial gains at Austria's expense and entered the war in 1915 on the side of the British, French, and Russian Allies. The Turkish Empire crumbled during the war under pressure from British and Russian armies and an Arab revolt encouraged by T. E. Lawrence.

Disillusion set in among frontline troops on all sides, even as their governments propped up home front morale through rigorous censorship and propaganda campaigns, employing posters depicting the enemy in lurid colors and the homeland in valorous hues. The reality of massive casualties proved as impossible to conceal, however, as the unexpected duration of the war and the shortages of food and other necessities. Opportunities for adventure and daring usually occurred at the periphery. The war would not be won in the air by the era's primitive aircraft, but their pilots — especially fighter aces such as France's René Fonck, Germany's Baron Manfred von Richthofen, Canada's Billy Bishop, and America's Eddie Rickenbacker — were lionized as the aerial cavalry of the mechanized age. A German naval squadron under Count von Spee made a heroic dash for home across the Pacific from its base in China at the start of the war, beating the British off the coast of Chile but succumbing to defeat at the Falkland Islands. In East Africa the German commander Paul von Lettow-Vorbeck fought a brilliant guerrilla campaign with integrated black and white units against numerically superior British and South African forces. Perhaps alone among the officers of any combatant in World War I, Lettow-Vorbeck declared, "The better man will always outwit the inferior, and the color of his skin doesn't matter."[5] He surrendered only after the Armistice was signed in 1918.

The German admiralty hoped to defeat Britain by starving the island kingdom through a naval blockade enforced by U-boats. The submarine campaign took a toll on British shipping, yet Germany never possessed a U-boat fleet sufficient to sever traffic to the British Isles entirely, and the submarine attacks threatened to draw the United States into the war. Although neutral and initially unwilling to involve itself in a foreign conflict, the United States was one of Britain's principal trading partners; American business and financial interests were invested in a British victory. When Germany declared that its U-boats would sink all ships entering British waters in February 1915, U.S. president Woodrow Wilson warned that Germany would be held accountable for any loss of American lives. The torpedoing of the British liner *Lusitania* and other ships carrying American passengers tested patience in the United States. Congress finally declared war in April 1917 and authorized conscription for the American Expeditionary Force, which joined the Allies on the western front a year later.

Americans marched to war to the tune of George M. Cohan's "Over There," whose rousing chorus, "We won't be back until it's over, over there!" supplanted the sentiment of a song popular only two years earlier, "I Didn't Raise My Boy to Be a Soldier." The United States contributed to the Allied victory by injecting fresh columns of troops against the tired Germans, lifting the morale of the exhausted Allies, and throwing the full weight of its industrial and naval might against the Central Powers. By the time Germany signed the Armistice on November 11, 1918, the Austro-Hungarian and Turkish empires had collapsed, the Tsar had been deposed, and Russia was sliding into civil war, which the Communists under Vladimir Lenin would win.

The United States emerged as the world's leading financial power by war's end, the only participant whose economy benefited from the conflict. The idealistic Wilson hoped to leverage the nation's newly won influence by reordering world politics on the principles of democracy and self-determination, but his ambitious goals proved to be in vain. In the end the Versailles Peace Conference of 1919 resulted in more problems than solutions. The delegates of many would-be nations, encouraged by Wilson's call for self-determination, were barred from deliberations; Japan, which had seized German possessions in China as Britain's ally, was humiliated by the conference's refusal to recognize racial equality; and pushed by French president Georges Clemenceau, Versailles imposed a punitive peace on Germany. The terms may have been understandable, given Germany's plans for

Europe in the event of its victory, but Versailles stoked resentments that would be exploited by Hitler and helped precipitate World War II.

In 1914 the young American film industry welcomed the coming of war, which closed the U.S. market to French and Italian studios, whose epic productions competed for American audiences in the era when silent pictures were a universal visual medium.[6] With Europe largely cut off by naval blockades, U.S. studios consolidated into a few large firms whose brand names remain familiar a century later. They proceeded to turn movies into one of the country's leading exports. When the United States entered World War I in 1917, the film industry eagerly volunteered to help the Wilson administration convey its messages to the public, and stars such as Mary Pickford and Charlie Chaplin helped finance the war by promoting the sale of Liberty Bonds.[7] The industry's eagerness paralleled the war effort by studios in belligerent European nations. Like their overseas counterparts, Hollywood altered the course of its production practices by only a few degrees and devoted but a small percentage of its output to outright propaganda. War movies released by Hollywood in 1917 and 1918 included overheated titles such as *The Hun Within* and *The Kaiser: The Beast of Berlin*. Other more prestigious pictures featured love stories interrupted by the war, notably D. W. Griffith's *Hearts of the World*, starring Lillian Gish, and Cecil B. DeMille's *The Little American*, with Mary Pickford in the lead role.

In the war's final years outdoor cinemas were rigged up on the back of trucks to bring entertainment to frontline troops. Propaganda designed for home front audiences had little appeal, so wide was the chasm between combat as imagined by civilians and the reality experienced by soldiers. On the front line the favorite star was Charlie Chaplin.[8] The consummate silent comic even spoofed the war in his 1918 comedy *Shoulder Arms*, in which the Little Tramp bungled his way into heroism.

Shoulder Arms was popular, providing relief from the bleakness of a war that claimed over nine million combat deaths. The fighting brutalized much of Europe; the psychological damage ignited massive postwar violence, especially in Germany and Russia, and opened opportunities for Hitler, Stalin, and Mussolini. In the United States, where casualties were a relatively modest 53,000 dead and 200,000 wounded, the war regenerated a spirit of isolationism, catalyzing the U.S. Senate's rejection of the League of Nations. In many victorious nations large elements of the population vowed "never again" and turned a blind eye to Hitler and other dangerous actors until it was too late.

ALL QUIET ON THE WESTERN FRONT (1930)

Movies glorifying the Great War were rare once the conflict ended. The tone was set in 1919 by French filmmaker Abel Gance, whose *J'Accuse* includes footage shot at the front as well as one of the most dramatic scenes from the early years of cinema, a parade of the dead looking back in mute accusation at the folly of this world. Filmed using soldiers on leave in 1918, most of the actors died before the war was over.[9] Exceptions to the gloom include director William Wellman's Oscar-winning *Wings* (1927), Howard Hawks's *The Dawn Patrol* (1930), and Howard Hughes's *Hell's Angels* (1930), which capitalized on the heroism of the air war. Even those entertaining pictures contained negative elements, including the death of most of the lead characters. *Hell's Angels* had an unexpected legacy. America's most notorious motorcycle gang, founded after World War II by army air force veterans, took its name from the movie.

All Quiet on the Western Front (1930), Hollywood's greatest World War I film, was made when the conflict was fresh in memory and public revulsion against the war remained visceral. The pacifist viewpoint was conveyed by a sympathetic portrayal of soldiers who had been America's enemy a decade earlier. "Death is not an adventure to those who stand face to face with it," proclaimed a caption at the film's opening. *All Quiet on the Western Front* was no celebration of combat but, rather, a harrowing story of wasted sacrifice. Nevertheless, its battle scenes are thrilling and set a precedent for later films. Film historian Andrew Sarris worried that contemporary pacifists might find *All Quiet* "self-defeating in that the orgasmic violence of war is celebrated as much as it is condemned."[10] *Celebrated* is too strong a word; the film choreographs the violence artistically without obscuring its message that this war should never have been fought. The movie was based on the international best seller by Erich Maria Remarque. While not a frontline soldier like the characters in his novel, Remarque served near the front in the German infantry, was wounded by grenade fragments, and drew upon his wartime experiences.[11] The novel, published in Germany in 1929 as *Im Western nichts Neues*, struck a nerve by expressing the feelings of millions of readers across the world. Although Remarque claimed *All Quiet* was "unpolitical,"[12] it became a prominent target in the ideological war waged by the rising Nazi Party, whose publicists angrily chastised the novel for denigrating Germany's war aims and the sacrifice of its soldiers. When the movie adaptation opened in Berlin, Joseph Goebbels, the future propaganda minister of Nazi Germany, disrupted the premiere by planting stink bombs and releasing white mice in the cinema. After the Nazis took power, the book was burned in public bonfires, and Remarque fled abroad, arriving in the United States in 1939, aided by the American ambassador in London, Joseph Kennedy.[13]

Capitalizing on the worldwide success of the inflammatory novel, Universal Studios purchased film rights to *All Quiet on the Western Front* and assigned it to director Lewis Milestone. A Russian Jewish immigrant, Milestone had enlisted in the Signal Corps in 1917 and gained experience editing combat footage. Afterward he went to Hollywood, where he worked as an editor and screenwriter before turning to directing. One of his silent movies, *Two Arabian Knights* (1927), a comedy about a pair of American POWs who escape Germany disguised as Arabs, won an Oscar at the first Academy Awards.[14]

All Quiet on the Western Front constituted a far more serious undertaking. At two hours and twenty minutes, it ran slightly longer than the average feature film of its time. It is the only pre–World War II Hollywood movie about World War I that continues to find a significant audience; the drama is persuasive, the gritty realism remained unsurpassed for decades, and the perspective remains timely. Almost every subsequent screen depiction of the war draws from this classic. Milestone and his primary screenwriter, the famous playwright Maxwell Anderson, carefully transposed the novel's themes and characters to the screen while respecting the author's intentions. It earned Oscars for Best Film and Best Director.

All Quiet opens in a provincial German town during the first days of the war with crowds cheering reservists as they march to the railroad station. As the parade passes under a classroom window, the schoolmaster, echoing popular opinion across Europe, proclaims, "I believe it will be a quick war with few losses." Urging his students to enlist before the fighting is over, he adds, "Sweet and fitting it is to die for the Fatherland." The cult of death for one's country took root among all the combatants as a modern analog to Christian martyrdom. Attractive as martyrdom might be for the young, however, the students, including the protagonist Paul Bäumer, appear oblivious to any real danger. Close-ups of the teacher's face reveal a demonic fanatic, while close-ups of the students show only gullible naïveté. Bursting into a rousing demonstration, singing "Wacht am Rhein," a patriotic song later sung by the Nazis in one of *Casablanca*'s most memorable scenes, the students felt liberated by the coming of war to cut loose. Ironically, their spontaneous release from school brought them to the even more regimented society of Germany's imperial army. The war would not be the short vacation they were promised.

Milestone's cameraman, Karl Freund, a master of German expressionist cinema who arrived in the United States the year Remarque's novel was published, visually established the boys' initiation into the military without words. An ominously weighty gate swings open, introducing Paul and his friends to the parade ground where they will train. An aerial view juxtaposes the immensity of the camp with their own insignificance. Inside the barracks the boys encounter a reassuringly familiar figure from their hometown but are startled to find their amicable postman transformed by rank and uniform into a petty tyrant. He becomes their drill sergeant, obsessed with hammering the recruits into soldiers — even if it kills them.

Harsh as it was, their training could not prepare them for the terrible reality of trench warfare. The cameras hug the ground to show the men dropping to avoid exploding shells; rain, mud, and the cries of the wounded from the dark compound the misery. *All Quiet* depicts the shock of seeing the first dead bodies. Death would soon become the soldiers' constant companion. After a while some of Paul's comrades eagerly go over the top to face enemy machine guns, preferring that danger to the anxiety of waiting to die.

The battles are precisely staged with cameras tracking along with the charging and retreating troops. Depicted is an ebb and flow of advance and withdrawal, a rhythm of attack and respite, masses of troops and lonely individuals on a denuded no-man's-land pockmarked by shell holes. The scenes of close combat between Germans and French are graphic.

Yet combat is only one problem confronting Paul and his company. Lice are everywhere. The shelling deprives the men of sleep. Soldiers fight over meager food, and rats infest the dugouts. The quest for food introduces a fellow soldier, Katczinsky, a rough-hewn but good-hearted peasant and prototype for the gruff sergeant familiar from later war movies. "Kat" teaches the recruits tricks to prolong their survival, such as foraging for pigs in the rubble. As the war drags on endlessly, some men fake mental illness. Others actually lose their sanity. Shell shock, as combat stress reaction was then called, was a ubiquitous facet of the war in all countries. By the end disobedience and shirking became common. A field hospital housed inside a ruined church, dominated by a looming German expressionist crucifix, swarmed with casualties.

It is easy to sympathize with the principal characters and to become absorbed in their lives. For American audiences *All Quiet* forced audiences to identify with the German side and fostered the insight that the war appeared similar from both sides of the trenches. The rationale for the war was questioned and condemned by the characters. Who wanted this war? they wondered. Was it the arms merchants? "Every full-grown emperor needs a war to make him famous," offers one soldier. Another suggests that the generals and cabinet ministers fight it out on an open field, stripped to their underwear. Such sentiments pervaded many depictions of the conflict, including the other enduring World War I film from between the world wars, Jean Renoir's *The Grand Illusion* (1937), inspired by the wartime experience of Capt. Charles de Gaulle and his comrades, who devised increasingly elaborate and futile plans of escape from German POW camps.[15] At least in *The Grand Illusion*, two of the three protagonists live through the final reel. In *All Quiet* no one survives.

If there is sentimentality in *All Quiet on the Western Front*, the emotion is well earned. The acting is superb. Then little known, Lew Ayres was cast as Paul Bäumer. Afterward Ayres became familiar as mild-mannered Dr. Kildare in a series of B movies. In a case of life inspired by art, Ayres declared himself a conscientious objector in 1941 as America girded for the next war. The movie industry retaliated by shunning him. Exhibitors refused to show his movies. After the United States entered World War II, Ayres volunteered as a medic and earned the respect of fellow soldiers for bravery under fire.[16]

The controversy over Ayres's refusal to bear arms coincided with the release of a movie all but designed to counter *All Quiet*, Howard Hawks's *Sergeant York* (1941), based on the true story of Alvin York, a conscientious objector at the start of World War I who became one of the war's most decorated GIs. Although *Sergeant York* was popular in its time and featured a solid, Oscar-winning lead performance by laconic Gary Cooper, the film reduced trench warfare to a relatively simple exercise. *Sergeant York* was less a representation of World War I than a preparation for World War II.

PATHS OF GLORY (1957)

Paths of Glory opens by contrasting war as experienced by the men who orchestrate it and the men who fight it. In scene 1 a pair of French generals meets in an elegant chateau to discuss strategy for breaking the German defenses. Meanwhile, their soldiers face the enemy from weather-beaten, mud-splattered trenches. When the divisional commander, General Mireau (George Macready), and his obsequious adjutant inspect the front line, their uniforms are pressed and immaculate. The infantry manning the trenches are clad in shabby overcoats; many stagger past badly bandaged. The martinet Mireau repeats his drumhead greeting at every turn. "Hello there, soldier," he says. "Ready to kill more Germans?"

When one soldier responds incoherently and his sergeant apologizes for the man's shell shock, Mireau explodes. "There is no such thing as shell shock!" he shouts, slapping the soldier hard across the face. "I won't have our brave men contaminated by him." The casualty of combat stress reaction is sent to the rear, an unintended blessing from an uncaring commander. The regiment will suffer heavy losses the next day as a result of his orders.

Like *All Quiet on the Western Front*, *Paths of Glory* was adapted from fiction. Yet Humphrey Cobb's 1935 novel, which the film's director, Stanley Kubrick, read as a child in his father's library, was not an international sensation. Although a theatrical adaptation played on Broadway play in 1938, *Paths of Glory* was forgotten by the time Kubrick developed a screenplay along with pulp writer Jim Thompson, whose crime novel *The Grifters* would become a popular film, and novelist Calder Willingham, who later wrote the screenplay for *The Graduate*. "Nobody wanted to do it," Kubrick recalled, but the project interested Kirk Douglas, a star with influence in Hollywood. Douglas claimed he "cajoled" United Artists into financing *Paths of Glory*. The budget was relatively low, Kubrick was known in Hollywood only for the modest film noir *The Killing* (1955), and the lion's share went for Douglas's fee for playing the protagonist, Colonel Dax. The picture was shot economically near Munich, with German policemen portraying the nameless French soldiers who died in the movie's assault on the "Ant Hill," a fortified German emplacement whose capture was deemed vital by the French sector commander, General Broulard (Adolphe Menjou).[17] *Paths of Glory* builds from the precedent of *All Quiet on the Western Front* in its ravaged depiction of frontline combat but benefits from the greater mobility of cameras and other technical advances during the nearly thirty years separating the films.

A *New York Times* article inspired Cobb's novel on the aftermath of the "Maupas Affair." Théophile Maupas was one of four French corporals, from a regiment decimated by combat, executed in 1915 for disobeying orders to attack. The controversial incident was only one example of the French high command's draconian response to the collapse of discipline and morale in units pushed beyond endurance by suicidal assaults on German positions. In 1917 officers selected men from their units to stand trial for mutiny or cowardice after a spectacular protest in which entire units refused to move forward. Sixty-eight divisions totaling over a half-million men were affected. Most of the striking soldiers were neither pacifists nor unpatriotic. They were prepared to defend their lines against German attack but refused to commit mass suicide in ill-conceived military operations and protested for better living conditions. Courts-martial ordered the execution of 554 men and the imprisonment of many more. The crisis abated with the replacement in May 1917 of Gen. Robert Nivelle, an advocate of attack without regard for casualties, by Marshal Henri-Philippe Pétain, an officer who was parsimonious with the lives of his troops. Pétain commuted all but forty-nine death sentences. The respect he earned for his mercy from the French public helped sustain his collaborationist regime at Vichy after France fell to Germany in 1940.[18] Although Kubrick derived his story from a fictionalized account of one particular incident, *Paths of Glory* represents the crumbling endurance through the middle years of the war by frontline soldiers and the determination by some officers to punish their men for failing to carry out impossible orders.

Paths of Glory was only a modest success at box offices upon its release in 1957, but the critical acclaim it earned positioned Kubrick for his ascent as one of the most admired directors of the twentieth century. A photographer for *Look* before turning to movies, Kubrick was already a great visual artist. The luminous black-and-white film stock proved an ideal medium for representing trench warfare, starkly highlighting key points and, drained of all but a limited spectrum of colors, leaving the grisliest horror to the shadows and the imagination.

When a French night patrol conducts reconnaissance on the Ant Hill, the three men crawl across the cratered, lunar landscape of no-man's-land, encountering surrealism in the form of a German biplane rising nose up from the field. The dawn attack on the Ant Hill is masterfully staged, starting with the bombardment by French 75-mm artillery, intended to soften enemy positions but hurling mud and debris into the French trenches. Drawing his pistol and blowing furiously into his whistle, Dax jumps over the top of the forward trench and leads his men in a futile charge as shells shriek overhead. Soon enough, the heavy rattle of German machine guns is heard, and soldiers begin to drop. "This materializes as one of the great movie attack scenes ever done, with astonishing tracking shots craning over a landscape already shattered by prior disasters," writes film historian Dave Thomson. Kubrick hand-held a camera during that scene.[19]

General Mireau and his staff calmly watch the onset of battle through binoculars from a rear command post, sipping cognac and sharing a toast. "To France," they concur. Mireau's mood darkens when he notices one of his companies stalled in the face of withering enemy fire. "Miserable cowards!" he shouts. "Why are they not advancing?" Mireau orders his captain to phone the artillery with instructions to push the company forward by bombarding the shirkers. The captain hesitates before calling the battery, whose commander refuses to obey unless he receives the order in writing. Conscience mingles with a suspicion that the general is breaching regulations and a determination to avoid responsibility. Mireau vows to punish the failure of his men to perform the impossible. "If those little sweethearts won't face German bullets, they'll face French ones," he sputters.

Kubrick reshaped Cobb's novel cinematically as well as to accommodate the star, Kirk Douglas, who insisted on a heroic role on the battlefield and in the courtroom for his character, Colonel Dax.[20] *Paths of Glory* is as much a courtroom drama as a war movie. After the battle the focus shifts to the prosecution and execution of enlisted men for their failure to seize the Ant Hill. Mireau wants to try ten men from each company for cowardice in a kangaroo court, which would amount to the execution of thirty soldiers. "They're scum, Colonel," he tells Dax, who angrily offers himself as a substitute. "Suppose we don't overdo this thing," General Broulard intervenes. The wily Broulard might not possess better moral judgment than Mireau, but like Machiavelli's Prince, he values the appearance of morality, especially when answering to politicians and pundits. He suggests a compromise. Only one soldier from each company, chosen by their commanders, will stand trial.

Kubrick's protagonists have seldom been so unabashedly heroic, so unproblematic, as Douglas's Colonel Dax. Steel helmeted, dirty faced, and blowing "Avant!" on his whistle as he hurls himself against the enemy, Dax fills the screen with an unforgettable image of frontline combat. Unlike many future conflicts, in World War I officers below the rank of general actually led their men into battle. "On both sides, officers were far more likely to be killed than the men to whom they led over the parapets of trenches and into machine-gun fire."[21]

Dax's valor is not confined to the battlefield. Physical bravery is only one path to glory; the courage of conviction is another. Dax, one of France's greatest criminal attorneys before the war, volunteers to defend the three soldiers before a court-martial in the cavernous hall of the chateau, its checkered floor suggesting a giant chessboard of war and justice. His task is hopeless. The judges refuse to allow due process and tolerate the presence of a defense counsel only to preserve the bare outline of legality.

The three soldiers — Paris (Ralph Meeker), Ferol (Timothy Carey), and Arnauld (Joseph Turkel) — are guilty of nothing but bad luck. They are ceremoniously marched to a carefully groomed killing field and put before a firing squad. The orderliness of the execution, a deadly parade staged for Mireau's pleasure, stands in contrast to the chaos of battle the men had survived. After the trial Mireau is dismissed when Dax produces evidence of the general's order to shell his own troops; Dax gets the final world, calling the suavely unconcerned Broulard "a degenerate, sadistic old man," but to no avail. In the final scene Dax learns he had been ordered back to the front. He marches toward the horizon as THE END appears on screen.

Although the battle for the Ant Hill and the trial of the three soldiers are fiction, they dramatize many similar events that actually occurred during World War I. *Paths of Glory* remains a powerful memorial to that war's frontline troops and an indictment of commanders in any war who play with their soldiers' lives as if they are pawns. *Paths of Glory* ruffled feathers in France and alarmed authorities elsewhere. It was banned in France until 1974, and the U.S. military prohibited screenings on its European bases.[22]

LAWRENCE OF ARABIA (1962)

Lawrence of Arabia begins at the end of T. E. Lawrence's life, with the retired war hero racing his prized motorcycle down the narrow English country roads where he crashed and died in 1935. His death during the film's first minutes is a reminder of the adventurous spirit that animated his campaign against the Turks at the head of an Arab liberation army. The narrative arc is a long flashback beginning in 1916 in Cairo, where Lawrence toils in an army map room and a fellow clerk comments that the heat and dust are preferable to the trenches. The real Lawrence would have agreed. War in the Near East bore little resemblance to the static battlefields of western Europe. Cavalry had room to maneuver in the Syrian desert and on the plains of Palestine, those lands of the imagination rooted in biblical stories and vividly depicted as places of refuge from modernity in Orientalist paintings and literature. The struggle for the Arab world was in motion, and no one better represented the dash and duplicity of that campaign than T. E. Lawrence.

A celebrity whose story captivated newspaper reporters and their readers, Lawrence mythologized himself through his memoir, *The Seven Pillars of Wisdom* (1926), and a popular abridgment on his military campaign, *Revolt in the Desert* (1927). Like Rudolph Valentino's "white sheik," Lawrence embodied the West's romantic fascination with the exotic East. He was among the small band of heroes who emerged from a war generally regarded as sordid; he retained the old values of chivalry "because the circumstances of the Arabian campaign allowed it."[23] Unlike the western front, with its mechanized slaughter, Arabia was a realm where knightly combat, the clank of Damascus steel against the lance, was still possible, even if dynamite was Lawrence's most potent weapon. His story was destined to inspire the imagination.

Although David Lean was the first director to dramatize that story, he followed a long line of contenders. Lawrence proposed a movie version of his story as early as 1926; producer-director Rex Ingram (*Ben-Hur*) was interested but never committed himself. Alexander Korda, who produced such celebrations of the British Empire as *The Four Feathers* and *That Hamilton Woman*, purchased rights to *Revolt in the Desert* in 1934, secured director Lewis Milestone of *All Quiet on the Western Front*, and tapped Leslie Howard to play Lawrence. Concerned about a "Hollywood treatment" with a tacked-on love story, Lawrence insisted on stipulations that Lean fulfilled nearly thirty years later: having a British director and no female characters. After Lawrence's death the project underwent a raft of directors, screenwriters, casts, studios, and delays. Unrest in Palestine repeatedly thwarted the planned location shoots. The British Foreign Office worried about the screenplay's inclusion of Britain's "alleged promises" to Arab leaders, and Turkey complained about "aspersions on Turkish history and national character." World War II and postwar budget constraints stalled prospects for filming Lawrence's life, even as playwright Terence Rattigan dramatized Lawrence in the popular play *Ross* (1960), a production that almost became the basis for a movie version.[24]

The assignment of turning Lawrence's life into a fictionalized movie finally fell to David Lean, who had idolized his subject as a child. "He was to English boys the last word in exotic heroes," he recalled. "But then Lawrence is an enigma and I've always been fond of enigmas. I like 'flawed heroes.' Perfect heroes are dull."[25] Lean had just completed his World War II epic, *Bridge on the River Kwai*, and was intrigued by the connection he saw between *Kwai*'s protagonist, Colonel Nicholson, and Lawrence. Both were Englishmen of the old school, rugged gentlemen in alien settings faced with enormous challenges. Marlon

Brando was originally chosen as Lawrence, but Lean was relieved when the actor bowed out in favor of *Mutiny on the Bounty*. Peter O'Toole, the director felt, was more amenable to the psychological study he had in mind.[26] Lean was not alone in his awe for the hero of the Arab Revolt. Lawrence was lionized from the war years through the 1950s, inspiring literature as well as idealistic young men dreaming of finding purpose in faraway places. Lean's epic rapidly subsumed and defined Lawrence's reputation in the popular imagination. Because of the movie, which won seven Oscars, including Best Picture and Best Director, "Lawrence of Arabia" is a name universally recognized in the twenty-first century, even by people who never actually watched the entire four-hour production.

Thomas Edward Lawrence was born in Wales in 1888. While studying history at Oxford, he embarked on a journey to Syria and Palestine, writing his thesis on Crusader castles. He was beaten, robbed, and left for dead by Kurds; suffered malaria and dysentery; was roughed up by Turkish police; and learned to dress like an Arab and understand their language and customs. He worked on an archaeological dig in Syria and acted as arbiter in disputes among the Arab workmen. Early in 1914 Lawrence joined an archaeological expedition in the Sinai, a border province of the Turkish Empire, as cover for a Royal Army reconnaissance mission. When the war came, a man of Lawrence's interests had no trouble gaining commission as a lieutenant in military intelligence and a posting to Cairo.[27] In 1916 he joined forces with the Emir Feisal, a prince of the Hashemite dynasty, whose descent from the Prophet Muhammad accorded him honor among the Bedouin tribes. Lawrence's hit-and-run strategy against the Turks, eloquently depicted in *The Seven Pillars of Wisdom*, became a model for modern guerrilla warfare. He was a shy man who loved the spotlight, a poet of action. "We watched her hungrily as she approached our mine," Lawrence said, describing a Turkish locomotive on a railroad line he had rigged with explosives, "and when she was on it there came a soft cloud of dust and a report and she stood still."[28]

Lawrence was a curious figure, a conservative rebel fomenting upheaval to buttress the British Empire, yet the rebel side of his character defined him in popular consciousness and established expectations for the film. Played by Peter O'Toole, the cinematic Lawrence was probably more insouciant than the real man. O'Toole depicts him as continually challenging authority. He neglects to salute his superiors until reprimanded. With the encouragement of the wily political agent Dryden (Claude Rains, echoing his duplicitous role in *Casablanca*), Lawrence's officious commander sends him to Arabia, more to get rid of the upstart than from any expectation of success. "It's going to be fun," the movie Lawrence insists before departing.

Fun is a not word associated with the real Lawrence. "It will be an adventure and a trial of the will" might have captured his sensibility more accurately. "We were a self-centred army without parade or gesture," Lawrence said, recalling his Bedouin comrades in *Seven Pillars*, "devoted to freedom, the second of man's creeds, a purpose so ravenous that it devoured all our strength."[29]

To shape the complexity of history into mythology, and for compelling storytelling, Lean and principal screenwriter Robert Bolt condensed events and suspended chronology. In *Lawrence of Arabia* the British hero proves himself to the skeptical Arab warriors by leading a surprise attack on the Red Sea port of Aqaba. The epic march across hundreds of miles of trackless desert really occurred, and caught the Turks unaware, yet the battle unfolded differently than in the movie, and the assault happened months after Lawrence and his Bedouin allies had begun their raids against the Turks. The film never gives the political context of great power intrigue on the Arabian Peninsula starting nearly a decade before the war. Britain had other agents in the desert, and Germany also dispatched scholar-adventurers to the Arabs. The Germans tried, among other things, to bribe the Bedouins to attack the Suez Canal. Feisal's father was Hussein, the sherif of Mecca, an important player in everyone's scheme. As hereditary protector of Islam's holy places, the sherif represented a potential rival in the Muslim world to the Turkish sultans, who since the sixteenth century had claimed the title of caliph, or commander of the faithful. The uneasy relations between caliph and sherif fractured when the British poured arms, gold, and promises into the desert, outspending their German rivals. Lawrence was never the only foreign agitator in the Bedouin ranks but was the most successful and the most famous. While he was the right man for the job, his mission would have been impossible without the largesse of the British government and the logistical difficulties of his German rivals. Germany was unable to offer the Arabs as many incentives.[30]

The greatest misrepresentation in *Lawrence of Arabia* is the implication that Lawrence was the principal agent of Turkey's defeat. The real story began in 1914 with the Anglo-Indian invasion of Mesopotamia and continued in 1916 as Gen. Edmund Allenby, a minor character in the movie, led British forces in the push through Gaza into Palestine and Syria. Lawrence stood at Allenby's side when Jerusalem and Damascus fell, but although he played no direct role in defeating Turkey's field army, the public remembers Lawrence, while Allenby is forgotten. The Lawrence legend, fostered by his success as an author, began with his embrace by the news media in the colorful reporting of Lowell Thomas, represented in the film by a fictional American reporter in search of a hero whose magnetism would draw the United States into alliance with Britain. The legend is sustained even today by the enduring reputation of Lean's film.

Lawrence of Arabia is a powerful work of imagination; its desert setting is no mere backdrop but is as integral to the story as any of its characters. At dawn, when the orange band of the rising sun outlines the horizon between the empty space of pale sand and the dark infinity of the heavens, the desert is like a Marc Rothko painting. The awesome scale of this boundless land is enthralling. O'Toole's outstanding performance captures Lawrence's erratic nature, which included cold courage and regret, dark nights of the soul and a messianic streak. His relationships with Auda Abu Tayi (Anthony Quinn) and Sherif Ali (Omar Sharif, making his debut in world cinema) register some of the difficult camaraderie Lawrence achieved with his Bedouin companions.

Many of the movie's Arab characters were real or composed from real people; likewise, Lawrence's raids on Turkish trains are accurately depicted. By tying down Turkish troops in desert garrisons along rail lines, Lawrence contributed to the Allied victory in the Near East. "The Arab war was geographical, and the Turkish army an accident," Lawrence wrote in his epigrammatic style. He encouraged the undisciplined but tough, mobile Bedouin to strike across great distances, seldom holding any position but forcing the Turks to disperse their forces to hold their supply lines. "Consequently, we must extend our front to its maximum, to impose on the Turks the longest possible passive defense, since that was, materially, their most costly form of war."[31] His strategy, which inspired guerrilla commanders across the globe, is well portrayed in the film.

Lawrence of Arabia climaxes with Britain's betrayal of Arab independence and Lawrence's subsequent disillusionment. The movie references the Sykes-Picot Agreement, in which Britain and France secretly agreed to carve up the Arab provinces of the Turkish Empire, and depicts Arab disunity after victory. Sykes-Picot was only one of several conflicting British commitments. The Balfour Declaration promised Jews a national homeland in Palestine, whose inhabitants were mostly Arab. British negotiators made contradictory offers to Hussein, the sherif of Mecca, and the desert chieftain Ibn Saud, setting the stage for civil war on the Arabian Peninsula. Saud won by 1932 and established the nation that bears his name, Saudi Arabia. The conflict between Jews and Arabs over Palestine remains unresolved a century later. Despite Britain's duplicity, its Arab allies were not entirely abandoned. Hussein's son Abdullah was given the throne of Transjordan, a British protectorate that achieved independence as the Hashemite Kingdom of Jordan. Abdullah's great-grandson and namesake rules Jordan today. Hussein's other son, Feisal, was crowned king of Iraq, as Mesopotamia was renamed. His heir was killed in the 1958 revolution that precipitated the rise of Saddam Hussein.

The disappointment O'Toole's Lawrence feels at the film's conclusion is drawn from truth, but in reality the desert fighter moved on.

He accompanied Feisal to the Versailles peace conference; became an advisor in the Colonial Office to Winston Churchill, an architect of the "Eastern policy" Lawrence helped execute during the war; wrote an essay on guerrilla warfare for Encyclopedia Britannica; and enlisted in the Royal Air Force. Airman Lawrence was posted to the unruly northwestern frontier of the Indian Empire, nowadays a Taliban stronghold in Pakistan. Lawrence fought in faraway lands only to die, as the movie depicts, in an accident a short way from home.

GALLIPOLI (1981)

A half-million Allied and Turkish soldiers died at Gallipoli, the rocky peninsula on the European edge of the Dardanelles. The narrow straits led from the Aegean Sea to the Sea of Marmara and the imperial capital of Constantinople straddling the Bosporus on the way to the Black Sea. The strategic waterway was the gateway to the Russian Empire to the north and the lynchpin of Europe and Asia. On April 25, 1915, Allied forces landed on Gallipoli to secure the Dardanelles. The chief advocate of the operation was the voluble Winston Churchill, who at age thirty-nine was the youngest man ever to hold office as first lord of the Admiralty. Churchill gambled that success on the shores near the fabled city of Troy would open supply lines to Russia, force the collapse of the Turkish Empire, and provide a morale-lifting break from the stalemate of trench warfare on the western front. Eight and a half months later the Allies evacuated their beachheads in defeat, albeit in a brilliant evacuation conducted with such stealth that the Turks awakened to find the beaches empty save for camouflage and decoys. *Gallipoli* became a watchword for strategic overreach and military disaster. Churchill resigned as sea lord in the aftermath and retreated to the backbenches of British politics. He reemerged only when his resolute opposition to Hitler proved prophetic. Although remembered as the great war leader who saved Britain during the darkest hours of World War II, Churchill's record was indelibly stained by Gallipoli. It remains an entry in the debit column of his accomplishments.

Historians continue to argue whether Gallipoli was sheer madness or a matter of ambition outrunning technology.[32] After all, successful amphibious assaults of comparable scale were carried out at Normandy during World War II and Inchon during the Korean Conflict by forces equipped with specialized landing craft, air cover, and more sophisticated communication and fire control for naval support. Contemporary observers did not dismiss the strategy behind the failed tactics of Gallipoli. "Had the Allied fleets once passed the defenses of the straits, the administration of the Young Turks would have come to a bloody end," wrote the U.S. ambassador to Turkey, Henry Morgenthau.[33] The debate continues in academia, but the public remembers Gallipoli from the film of that name by Australian director Peter Weir.

Gallipoli was released worldwide by Paramount Studio and drew popular audiences on the strength of Mel Gibson, already a rising star after his apocalyptic cult movie *Mad Max* (1979). *Gallipoli* was responsible for "elevating the blooding of the Australian military (in the service of the British Empire) to the level of myth."[34] It fashioned a foundational legend for Australia, one of the world's youngest nations as World War I began. According to Weir, his generation of Australians knew of Gallipoli only through the rather perfunctory observation of the annual Anzac (Australian New Zealand Army Corps) Day holiday. It was ancient history to them. American born but Australian reared, Mel Gibson recalls reading barely a paragraph or two about the battle in high school history texts. Inspired by *All Quiet on the Western Front* and *Paths of Glory*, Weir was determined to show the tragedy of young manhood wasted in senseless combat. For him Anzac's heroism at Gallipoli is "the great Australian story" and marked the birth of his nation's identity. "In our country, we had no Wilfred Owens, no Robert Graves, no Sassoon, no great war poets who could tell us about the lost generation," he remarked.[35] He was determined to tell their story through the poetry of cinema.

Gallipoli played to audiences well beyond Australia and left an unforgettable impression everywhere. Rather than present a panorama of Australia at war, Weir endowed his film with universal appeal through the odd couple story at *Gallipoli*'s heart, the friendship of two very different yet complementary young men from Australia's outback. The idealistic dreamer Archie Hamilton (Mark Lee) and the cynical Frank Dunne (Gibson) seem to share only two things: they are competitive runners graced with great speed, seeking adventure in the world beyond the cattle stations and dusty railroad towns of Western Australia. Before long they fall into the sort of abiding friendship most commonly found among young people, unburdened by responsibility in the summer of their lives. These fictional characters embody aspects of the Australian character, of "mateship," and yet their train-hopping hoboes' journey from the heartland to the big city crosses physical and psychological terrain comparable to that of the American experience. For much of its running time *Gallipoli* is a road picture, not a war movie. Archie and Frank are youths in search of their destiny; tragically, their destination is a rocky spit of land half a world away and raked by enemy gunfire. With a dramatic irony that strengthens *Gallipoli*'s emotional power, the audience watches the innocents marching naively into slaughter.

When Australia went to war alongside its British mother country in 1914, the new nation's volunteer army had no difficulty filling the ranks. Weir's film shows newspapers flush with accounts of Australian gallantry in a "baptism of fire" at Gallipoli and the boys eager to join the fray. Frank is the holdout among his mates. "It's an English war. It has nothing to do with us," he insists, proud of his Irish heritage. And yet social encouragement for enlisting is found at every turn and becomes hard even for Frank to resist. The girls love to see the young men riding off in uniform, especially if they wear the smart tunics and plumed bush hats of the Light Horse, Australia's elite formation. Some brigades actually had the opportunity to fight on horseback in General Allenby's thrust through Palestine; those troopers were the subjects of a less well-known Australian film that followed in *Gallipoli*'s wake, *The Lighthorsemen* (1987). Archie and Frank found themselves in one of the brigades shipped without their mounts to Gallipoli.

Weir portrays their arrival on the narrow strand below the rising hills, where the front lines cling precariously, as a picnic. The sound of nearby gunfire and the bursting shells overhead provide the excitement the boys crave. Archie, Frank, and their mates swim playfully in the Dardanelles, their unreal calm accurately reflecting the Light Horse troops' cavalier attitude before they advanced to the front. "The Lighthorsemen were undismayed by the appalling task before them," according to British historian Robert Rhodes James, whose uncle had served at Gallipoli. "They were young, enthusiastic, aggressive and bored."[36]

In *Gallipoli*'s climactic scene the Light Horsemen charge on foot with fixed bayonets against heights commanded by the machine guns of "Johnny Turk." The artillery bombardment expected to soften enemy lines halted earlier than promised, and when the Light Horse commander, Major Barton (Bill Hunter), peers over the parapet with his periscope, he sees Turkish troops returning to their positions little worse for the shelling. Barton pleads that attack is suicide, but an ice-cold British superior is adamant, ordering the Australians forward over his field telephone. "Come on lads — steady lads," Barton encourages, before blowing his whistle, like Colonel Dax in *Paths of Glory*, to signal charge. Weir and screenwriter David Williamson, one of Australia's outstanding playwrights, interviewed surviving veterans of the battle and poured over the chronicle of Anzac's official historian, C.E.W. Bean, whose description of the charge of the Light Horse tallies with *Gallipoli*'s account. "Except those wounded whom bullets had knocked back into the trench . . . almost the whole line fell dead or dying within the first ten yards," Bean wrote.[37]

The battleground in *Gallipoli* was filmed on the cliff-edged coast of South Australia, where the sweep of the bluffs closely resembles the Anzac Cove on the Dardanelles. Australian army troops served as extras. The project was financed in part by media mogul Rupert Murdoch, whose father, Keith Murdoch, had been a pith-helmeted journalist covering Gallipoli for the Australian press and bristling under wartime censorship. Determined to expose the carnage he witnessed, he composed an angry letter to Australian prime minister Andrew Fisher, describing the incompetence of the British command and the bravery of Anzac. Fisher forwarded Murdoch's letter to Britain's war cabinet, which reacted by dismissing Sir Ian Hamilton, the Allied commander at Gallipoli, who was unfairly singled out for many of the mission's problems. By then the mission was probably beyond saving.[38]

Although Weir took pains to re-create his settings accurately, he presented history cropped on all edges, leaving a narrow picture of the events at the Dardanelles. By giving the impression that the only combatants were Australians under British command pitted against Turks, *Gallipoli* entirely excises the campaign's international character. Even the New Zealanders in Anzac are overlooked in the film. In reality British casualties outnumbered the Australian dead and included men from an Irish regiment. The British-officered Indian army was also well represented. France contributed a sizable contingent, including knife-wielding Senegalese regiments. The Zion Mule Corps, recruited by the British from Russian Jews who had fled Palestine for Egypt during the war, carried supplies.[39] The Turkish Fifth Army on the Dardanelles was commanded by a German, Liman von Sanders. German advisors and Austro-Hungarian artillery assisted in the defense of Gallipoli, albeit the brunt fell to Lt. Col. Mustapha Kemal, who crafted his own legend out of the Allied defeat. As Kemal Ataturk, he became the father of the Turkish Republic after war's end.

Gallipoli's most enduring image comes in its final moments. Archie, still radiant as a Renaissance cherub, races uphill against Turkish gunfire on his impossible final run. Struck by bullets, his body is suspended in a freeze-frame before the screen goes dark. The unforgettable picture of naïveté sacrificed has become an enduring symbol of World War I, a conflict of doubtful ends exacerbated by terrible means.

The movies that shape World War I in popular memory were released by Hollywood studios and, except for *Lawrence of Arabia* and *Gallipoli*, directed by Americans, yet none refer to America's role in the war. One reason may be that the stories of other nations seem more compelling and representative than any U.S. account. Even the most memorable American novel of the war, Ernest Hemingway's twice-filmed *A Farewell to Arms*, concerns an American who volunteers as an ambulance driver on the Italian front while the United States remains neutral. America arrived late to the war, and its troops entered combat only in the last stages. While the conflict impacted America less than other nations, it left bad memories on all sides.

World War II was a different story altogether. Not only did the United States largely eclipse its Allies in cinematic memory, but the war continues to be recalled as a time when the nation came together against common enemies. America's opponents in World War II posed an existential threat not only to the country's independence but to its essential values as a nation. Anything less than victory would have meant the end of the American experiment in representative democracy and the ideals of the nation's Bill of Rights.

CHAPTER TWO

World War II (1939–1945)

Most Americans, including survivors of the era, think of World War II as a golden age. It was the "Good War," fought by the "Greatest Generation," whose moral purpose was so clear that only an ardent Nazi sympathizer could have wished for a different outcome. "This was the film age, and the script could have been written in Hollywood," said historian Michael C. C. Adams. He added that "the bad guys," at least the Nazi SS and the Italian Fascist militia, even dressed for their parts in black hats.[1] Americans remember the war in the three-act structure of classic Hollywood. In act 1 the nation enjoys peace in its splendid isolation, aloof from the global conflict; in act 2 the United States suffers defeat in the Pacific and peril on all fronts; by the conclusion of act 3 a hard-fought series of campaigns results in unconditional victory. Once the United States was pulled into war by Japan's attack on Pearl Harbor, an event dramatized in such popular films as the Oscar-winning *From Here to Eternity* (1953) and *Pearl Harbor* (2001), the movie metaphor of wagons circled against the enemy came into play. Americans generally regard World War II as a time when parties, races, and classes set aside their differences, united in common cause against encirclement by foes bent on destroying the nation's way of life.

The reality was more complicated. The Roosevelt administration seized forty plants and, briefly, the national railroad system to prevent strikes from disrupting the war economy. Race riots requiring military intervention broke out in Detroit and Harlem, while in Southern California, off-duty sailors and soldiers clashed with Chicano youth in the "Zoot Suit Riots." Tens of thousands of U.S. citizens of Japanese heritage were interned in "war relocation centers" in response to public anxiety over the loyalty of Japanese Americans and fears of sabotage on the West Coast.

The amber glow of nostalgia is seldom darkened by recollections of the bad news from the war years. The discord heard alongside the chorus of national unity has always been muffled in popular culture. The most popular movie about the home front made during the war, the melodramatic *Since You Went Away* (1944), which transformed housing shortages into adventure, barely alluded to profiteering and focused on the emotional loss of separation and death. Labor unrest and race riots have never been themes for movies on World War II. The anti-Chicano violence was the subject of an independently distributed film by Mexican American director Luis Valdez, *Zoot Suit* (1981); the Japanese internment figured in at least one Hollywood movie, *Snow Falling on Cedars* (1999); but neither film left a widespread impression. The nation's segregated military, especially the challenges of African American servicemen fighting for democracy while being relegated to second class, has, however, been addressed by Hollywood in recent years. The George Lucas–produced *Red Tails* (2012) lionizes the 332nd Fighter Group (known as the Tuskegee Airmen), and Spike Lee's *Miracle at St. Anna* (2008) chronicles the experiences of black infantrymen on the Italian front.

The paradoxes of World War II are evident. The United States, where racism was endemic, was combating the racist ideology of Nazism; Great Britain was a global empire fighting to prevent the emergence of a new German empire in Europe; and the murderous regime of Joseph Stalin struggled for survival against another mass murderer, Adolf Hitler. And yet the larger moral issues are clear. The United States and Britain provided better political and social models and their shortcomings were more amenable to reform than their opponents; Anglo-American ideals promoted the dignity rather than the degradation of humanity.

Once again, the United States was a latecomer; the nation's traditional isolationism, coupled with negative memories of the previous world war, dampened support for intervening in an overseas conflict that began in Asia with Japan's conquest of Manchuria (1932) and had its European dress rehearsal with the Spanish Civil War (1936–39). Militant nationalism in Japan, Germany, and Italy, along with the global ambitions of the Soviet Union, made international relations tense even before Italy conquered Ethiopia (1936), Germany reoccupied the demilitarized Rhineland (1936), Japan began its protracted assault on the Chinese interior (1937), and Germany annexed Austria (1938). U.S. president Franklin D. Roosevelt stood on the sidelines, limited by the Neutrality Acts and the public mood, as Britain's prime minister, Neville Chamberlain, tried to forestall a European war. Reflecting the widespread sentiment that Germany had been ill treated by the Treaty of Versailles, Chamberlain sought to appease Hitler by acceding to Nazi demands to unify German-speaking central Europe.

With war imminent, Chamberlain and his French counterpart, Edouard Daladier, met with Hitler and his Italian ally, Benito Mussolini, at Munich (1938), seeking a compromise that would leave Europe's balance of power undisturbed. At Munich, Czechoslovakia's predominantly ethnic German border province, the Sudetenland, was handed to Hitler, stripping the Czechs of a defensible border. Chamberlain returned from Munich promising "peace in our time." Hitler, however, had other plans.

In September 1939 German troops rolled into Poland, triggering an alliance system that brought Britain and France into their second war with Germany in a generation. This time the scope of German ambitions was wider and more sinister. Hitler intended to dominate Continental Europe, subjugate Russia, and annihilate the Jews. Nazi ideology was based on a hierarchy of races and the notion that two races were in contest for world domination. In Hitler's mind the northern European Aryans had to destroy the Jews or face their own destruction. Unresolved resentments over the outcome of the last war strengthened the hands of Hitler, Mussolini, and the Japanese military, all of them eager to redraw the map of the world. Chamberlain would soon step down in favor of a more vigorous leader. Winston Churchill was determined to stand against German aggression and gambled on the eventual support of the United States.

World War II was the most far-ranging conflict in history, fought on every continent save South America and Antarctica and on every ocean. It was the first war in which airpower was significant, and among the combatants only the continental United States was invulnerable to air attack. From 1939 through 1945, 19.5 million soldiers, sailors, and airmen died, and an additional 20 million civilians perished from malnutrition caused by little remembered disruptions in the world economy resulting from the war. "Death by famine lacks drama," as British journalist Ian Stephens commented on the war-related starvation in Bengal, which claimed 3 million Indians.[2] Movies have not been made from the crisis of calories that gripped much of the globe during World War II. The total death toll among soldiers and civilians from combat, air raids, starvation, and other causes has been put at 50 to 70 million.[3]

The war proceeded along many avenues and assumed many forms. Denmark fell to Germany in 1940 within hours, after a few skirmishes with only 300 casualties in one of history's swiftest conquests. By contrast, the Nazi assault on the Soviet Union one year later was the largest operation in military history, involving 4 million invading troops; by the end of the first week, 600,000 Soviet troops were killed, missing, or captured. In Poland the Nazi occupiers launched a concerted campaign to extinguish the national culture and economy. In France cooperation and outright collaboration with the Germans and the Vichy regime among artists, intellectuals, businessmen, and ordinary people was common until the tide of war shifted. The reality was more nuanced than the cinematic images of brave resistance.[4] While the Nazis hurried to exterminate the Jews even as Allied victory became inevitable, the execution of the Holocaust did not run smoothly in all sectors of occupied Europe. The Vichy French regime under Marshal Pétain and Pierre Laval deported 65,000 Jews to the death camps, eagerly in the case of foreign Jews, whereas Germany's reluctant Balkan ally, Tsar Boris III of Bulgaria, frustrated all attempts to deport his country's Jews.[5] The carpet bombing of German and British cities was brutal, indiscriminate, and intended to terrorize civilian populations. Other operations were conducted with the clockwork precision worthy of a Hollywood movie. In 1943 Waffen-SS commandos, landing in gliders on a mountaintop resort, freed Mussolini, who had been arrested on orders of Italy's king, Victor Emmanuel III, and spirited him to safety in an airplane waiting nearby.[6]

In some respects World War II resembled World War I, especially Germany's U-boat blockade of Great Britain and its thrust against France through neutral Belgium; for a second time a neutral United States helped arm Britain before finally committing to the Allies. Yet in many respects these were very different conflicts. In World War I fellow citizens seldom turned on each other, while World War II devolved into civil war as Communist partisans clashed with Fascist militia in Italy, France, and Yugoslavia. Technology has been crucial to winning wars since the first spear was hurled, yet advanced science had never played so key a role as in World War II. Radar helped the British defeat the Luftwaffe and enabled the growth of postwar commercial aviation. Germany's V-2 rocket, which struck London and other cities late in the war, made ballistic missiles and the space program possible; Germany deployed jet fighters, too late and too few to alter the course of the air war but setting the bar for air wars to come. The earth seemed to shift with the incineration of Hiroshima and Nagasaki by atomic bombs, yet computer technology, growing out of Britain's code-breaking program at Bletchley Park, had far greater long-range significance to everyday life despite being little noticed at war's end.

As in World War I, the United States was the one nation to benefit economically and politically from the conflict, and this time the American ascent was far more dramatic. The United States ended the war as the predominant global power, the only combatant whose homeland was touched only marginally by fighting. France, China, Italy, and Soviet Russia had been battlefields; Britain's cities were bombed to rubble; Germany and Japan were in ruins. The United States suffered light casualties relative to other warring nations, losing 300,000 dead to Germany's 5.6 million and the Soviet Union's 20 million. America's enemies were broken and its allies bankrupt. The widespread destruction of friend and foe afforded the United States an opportunity to invest in the future by helping rebuild the economies of Western Europe and Japan through the Marshall Plan, an economic aid program, unprecedented in scale, proposed by U.S. secretary of state George Marshall (1947). Marshall money was even offered to the Soviet bloc, but Stalin stubbornly refused capitalist economic assistance, even though he was willing to accept capitalist military aid during the war.

There was ample reason for Americans to feel good about the war, and the tendency to accentuate the positive began with government censorship of the news as well as the patriotism of Hollywood. When Walter Cronkite, then a foreign correspondent for United Press, filed a story on the U.S. Eighth Air Force's practice of bombing through cloud cover, contradicting official claims of "pin-point accurate" air raids, his report was blocked by the military. "This was a media generation; it had come of age with talking pictures and radio: and the military was careful to polish its messages with a Hollywood glow."[7] The famous image of Gen. Douglas MacArthur wading ashore upon returning to the Philippines was filmed many times, with the care of a Hollywood production, to get the angle just right.

The army's Bureau of Public Relations regulated the flow of information to the American public, and its Information and Education

Division (I&ED) produced movies to indoctrinate troops with the war's objectives and the character of the enemy. Maj. Frank Capra, who in peacetime had directed *Mr. Smith Goes to Washington*, supervised a series of seven "information" films for I&ED called *Why We Fight*. Although intended for the military, they were released to civilian audiences in the United States and Europe. Capra was given his own unit, the 834th Signal Photo Group, and was granted wide scope by his commander, Brig. Gen. Frederick Osborn, a wealthy friend of President Roosevelt. While some career officers objected to training films made in Hollywood, Osborn understood the value of entertainment in education.[8]

Hollywood went to war along with the rest of the nation, supplying movies to the military for entertaining servicemen overseas. It was "the only industry that made its product available to the government free of charge." Several studio heads were granted commissions as officers, and the studios and their stars were active in promoting bond drives to finance the war. Bette Davis ran the famous Hollywood Canteen to provide dancing and dinner for servicemen in Los Angeles, and several stars, including Jimmy Stewart, Clark Gable, and Tyrone Power, enlisted, even though the Roosevelt administration had declared the movie industry "essential" to the war effort, providing easy deferments to studio employees. Support for the war was so great that many enlisted, even if, like Gable, they were already too old to be drafted.[9]

The war was also fought in other sectors of the entertainment industry. Radio, a popular medium for drama in the 1930s and 1940s, was the original home of *Captain Midnight and His Secret Squadron*, a popular show on the Mutual Broadcasting System among young listeners, who purchased "Code-o-Graphs" to decode secret messages included in the broadcasts. After Pearl Harbor, Captain Midnight turned his attention from ordinary evildoers to the Axis; he made the transition to comic books, a syndicated comic strip, young adult novels, and a movie serial. The comic book character Captain America's 1940 debut heralded mounting anxiety over the war. He was the result of a government experiment. When the 4F Steve Rogers was injected with a serum by a scientist, he was transformed into the red, white, and blue-clad superhero, "the first major comic book hero to take a stand against fascism."[10] Captain America outlasted the war; an enduring fixture in the comic book subculture, he was the protagonist of the World War II adventure *Captain America: The First Avenger* (2011). The cinematic battle against Nazism, which survives as a potent representation of evil, continues unabated in the twenty-first century. As Ralph J. Gleason remembered the war in an essay on *Casablanca*, "Those were times when things were so much simpler; the good guys and the bad guys so much more clearly defined and the struggle itself, the moral imperative for man, so much more easily seen."[11]

CASABLANCA (1942)

Hollywood produced as many as four hundred military-themed movies during World War II, a comparatively modest percentage of the industry's overall output of seventeen hundred movies from 1942 to 1945.[12] In this endeavor Hollywood operated along lines parallel to Germany's state-run film industry. Nazi propaganda minister Joseph Goebbels decreed that 80 percent of German film production should be dedicated to "good, high-quality entertainment," with only the remaining 20 percent reserved for films of "national political character."[13] Most of the war movies made in America during the duration of the war were individually unremarkable but constituted, as a whole, one of the storehouses of memory for those years.

Hollywood strove to represent every branch of the service. *Action in the North Atlantic* (1943), starring Humphrey Bogart and Raymond Massey, celebrates the dangerous convoy missions of the Merchant Marine and was used, despite stagy battle scenes, as a training film. *Air Force* (1943), starring John Garfield and directed by Howard Hawks, concerns the crew of a B-17 Flying Fortress that arrived at Hawaii's Hickham Field hours after Pearl Harbor was bombed. The army air force loaned Hawks one of its bombers to enhance the production's realism. *The Fighting Sullivans* (1944) was based on the true story of the five Sullivan brothers from Waterloo, Iowa, who enlisted in the navy after Pearl Harbor and died together when a Japanese submarine torpedoed their cruiser, the USS *Juneau*, off Guadalcanal.[14]

Perhaps the most representative wartime combat movie, *Bataan* (1943), starred Robert Taylor as a sergeant whose hastily assembled squad fights a desperate rearguard action against the Japanese during the war's opening weeks. The squad is drawn from all services and is a microcosm of America, representing city and country, WASP, Jewish, Hispanic, black, and Filipino servicemen. The Japanese are depicted as hateful, almost subhuman, and the Americans are noble in bravery and sacrifice. The title was especially meaningful for contemporary audiences; at Bataan, the fortified peninsula guarding Manila Bay, U.S. and Filipino forces made their final stand against the Japanese invasion of the Philippines in 1942. Several months after the movie's release, Americans became aware of the "Bataan Death March," during which thousands of POWs were murdered and abused by the victorious Japanese.

War movies shot during the war were never in color, even though popular films such as *Gone with the Wind* and *The Wizard of Oz* had already taken advantage of the newly perfected Technicolor process. Color seemed more suitable for musicals, fantasies, and even war pictures set safely in the past. The threat to America's existence as a nation called for the sober newsreel tones of black-and-white.

The most important war film from those years was made in black-and-white; guns are seldom fired, and only two men die on camera. *Casablanca*, the wartime war movie most familiar to general audiences in the twenty-first century, is as much a love story as a profile in courage, yet as film critic Roger Ebert said, "The great break between *Casablanca* and almost all Hollywood love stories — even wartime romances — is that it does not believe love can, or should, conquer all."[15] Sacrifice for the greater cause of human dignity and freedom, with America as its beacon, trumps romantic love. "It doesn't take much to see that the problems of three little people don't amount to a hill of beans in this crazy world," concludes the protagonist, Rick Blaine (Humphrey Bogart) in one of that movie's dozen unforgettable lines.

Casablanca was one of several Hollywood films, including the Bogart vehicles *To Have and Have Not* and *Passage to Marseilles*, concerning the neutral yet Fascist-leaning Vichy French and set in the months before Pearl Harbor. The time frame was meant as a painful reminder of the naïveté of isolationism in a dangerous world, and the Vichy regime served as a warning of what the United States might become if it lost the war. "I'll bet they're asleep all over America," Rick muses, having seen fascism close-up from running guns to Ethiopia and fighting with the Loyalists in the Spanish Civil War. A disgruntled idealist, Rick has retreated to Casablanca in French Morocco, where he owns the polyglot city's swankiest nightclub, Rick's Café Américain, a mecca for refugees and those who prey on them. Vichy commanders and underground leaders are welcome. Outwardly, Rick is disdainful of political commitment. "You'll excuse me, gentlemen. Your business is politics. Mine is running a saloon," he tells the visiting Gestapo officer, Major Strasser (Conrad Veidt), and the Vichy police prefect, Captain Renault (Claude Rains).

Rick will be thrust back into politics, however, by the unexpected arrival of the lost love of his life, Ilsa Lund (Ingrid Bergman), accompanying her husband, the fugitive resistance leader Victor Laszlo (Paul Henreid). Laszlo seeks the letters of transit stolen from murdered German couriers that would enable him to exit French Morocco with Ilsa. They would flee to neutral Portugal and fly from Lisbon to New York on the Pan American Clipper, where he could continue his struggle against Nazism. The man who stole those letters, the duplicitous Ugarte (Peter Lorre), handed them to Rick before his arrest by Renault's men; giving them to Laszlo means losing sight of Ilsa but aiding the fight against fascism. Rick would rather keep Ilsa in Casablanca. He wants to hurt her, and he also wants to open his own wound and feel the pain of losing her.

Casablanca's tone is romantic; its purpose was to support the war effort through a moving love story. It was not the only Hollywood movie conceived along those lines but is the only one to achieve universal and enduring recognition. *Casablanca* was composed from a series of happy accidents and became something larger than any of its contributors could have imagined. It originated as *Everybody Comes to Rick's*, a stage play by Murray Bennett and Joan Alison inspired by Bennett's 1938 vacation on the French Riviera, where he encountered a café of refugees from Nazi Germany. *Everybody Comes to Rick's* never found its way to Broadway, but Warner Brothers purchased screen rights as fodder for a timely romantic thriller in an exotic setting. *Casablanca* was slated as an "A-List" film but barely. It was expected to fare well enough at box offices before disappearing from memory. No one understood that they were constructing a classic.

By some reports three directors turned down the picture before it fell to Hungarian émigré Michael Curtiz, whose reputation for hard work (he had directed over sixty films since coming to Hollywood in 1926) ensured that the project would be assembled efficiently, without overruns in time or money. The studio suggested that leading roles might go to Ronald Reagan and Ann Sheridan, but Bogart was on the rise as a sensitive outlaw after a pair of great films in 1941, *High Sierra* and *The Maltese Falcon*, and Lt. Col. Jack Warner, the studio chief-cum–Signal Corps officer, deciding he wanted a fresh face for the female lead, borrowed Bergman from rival mogul David O. Selznick. Bergman, who debuted in her native Sweden and made one movie in Nazi Germany on her way to Hollywood, was perfectly cast as an unsentimental romantic idealist. Her European accent and manner added authenticity, but Ilsa's emotional indecision over Rick and Laszlo might have resulted less from great acting than the improvised circumstances of the production.

Six weeks before shooting began, the screenplay remained an outline about a café in Casablanca and a bitter American expatriate named Rick. A week later two of the original screenwriters, Julius and Philip Epstein, were called to Washington DC to work on Frank Capra's *Why We Fight* series. Howard Koch, who penned the Mercury Theatre's adaptation of *War of the Worlds* for Orson Welles, was left to complete the task, delivering freshly typed pages of the screenplay to the set each morning. Bergman had no idea whether Ilsa would exit Casablanca with Rick or Laszlo until the shooting was well under way.

"I remind myself to play down the melodrama," Koch said, recalling the scene in which Ugarte was arrested at Rick's Café, "letting the incident cause a minimum of commotion in the club — to give the impression that violence is endemic to wartime Casablanca." To his astonishment the screenplay "seemed to be building, creating its own tensions." Although annoyed at the time with Curtiz for reworking the script, he later conceded that the Hungarian infused geopolitical reality into the romance. "Perhaps it was partly this tug-of-war between Curtiz and me that gave the film a certain balance."[16]

The intangibles of chemistry ignite the acting in virtually every scene. Bogart, Lorre, and Sidney Greenstreet as Ferrari, Casablanca's criminal boss, had already played together with great charm in *The Maltese Falcon*. Bergman was an immigrant by choice, but most of the cast were — like the people they played — refugees from across Europe. Henreid, Lorre, and S. Z. Sakall (as Rick's lovable headwaiter) had all fled the Nazis for America. German actor Conrad Veidt ended his distinguished career in exile playing Hollywood Nazis; the sinister humorlessness of Strasser was deeply felt. Casablanca's portrayal of blacks and women transcended the era's stereotypes. Sam (Dooley Wilson) may have been a faithful sidekick, the Jim to Rick's Huck Finn, but he was endowed with dignity and autonomy; Ilsa was neither wallflower nor femme fatale but possessed agency and a full emotional life. With a ringmaster's skill Curtiz kept all the characters moving in the right circles at deliberate speed. *Casablanca* is a movie without a wasted or superfluous second.

Although *Casablanca* is a beautiful dream woven on the back lot of the Warner Brothers studio, it draws power from its connection to contemporary reality.[17] The idea anchoring the story — Casablanca as a way station for refugees on their way to the New World via Lisbon — was correct. As the stentorian narrator announces in the opening scene, most of the displaced who made their way to the Moroccan city had to "wait and wait and wait" for visas or other travel documents. Money to complete the perilous journey was often short. Many refugees fleeing the Nazis found their way to "Unoccupied

France," where Germany's reach was limited by the terms of the armistice with the defeated French regime that had abandoned Paris for the resort town of Vichy, with its many comfortable hotels. The Vichy administration continued to govern French North Africa, where Jewish relief agencies and U.S. consular officials — welcomed by Vichy as a counterweight to the Germans — conspired with easily corrupted local officials to provide a precarious haven, more Limbo than Paradise, for the refugees. From Casablanca the next step on the trail of exile was Lisbon, the capital of neutral Portugal, where U.S. merchant ships called and the PanAm Clipper, a giant Boeing 314 seaplane, provided luxury transatlantic service three times a week. It was the only commercial flight between the United States and Europe.

The letters of transit prominent in *Casablanca*'s plot are also drawn from reality. Called "laissez-passer" in diplomatic parlance, such letters are issued by governments in lieu of passports to provide passage for refugees or for other purposes. Aware that possession of these stolen letters could permit Laszlo to escape, Major Strasser is determined to recover the letters and keep the resistance leader penned up in Casablanca. He may assume that Vichy would frustrate Germany's desire to extradite this dangerous fugitive; perhaps he is considering having Laszlo assassinated. *Casablanca*'s major historical faux pas is Ugarte's assertion that Gen. Charles de Gaulle signed the letters. The problem is that Vichy regarded de Gaulle as a traitor for establishing the "Free French" government-in-exile in London and calling on Frenchmen to continue the fight against Germany. The only door de Gaulle's signature could have opened in French Morocco would have led the bearer to a jail cell. De Gaulle's symbol, the double-barred Cross of Lorraine, is covertly flashed to Laszlo by an underground leader in Rick's Café as a sign that he is among friends. Renault would have arrested anyone seen displaying that symbol.

The atmosphere in North Africa was tense, and not only because of the Free French. Worried that the powerful French fleet, the world's fourth largest, would fall into German hands and enable the Nazis to challenge British sea power and invade the British Isles, the Royal Navy engaged in an undeclared war against Vichy. Britain seized merchant as well as warships and attacked the French naval base at Mers el Kebir in Algeria, killing fourteen hundred sailors. Vichy responded with an air raid on British installations at Gibraltar and braced for more attacks. Casablanca was subject to blackouts and alerts; the battleship *Jean Bart* guarded the harbor; the Foreign Legion manned the defenses; and warplanes operated out of the city's airfield, represented in the movie by Los Angeles Airport. Military personnel from all branches are seen in the background of many scenes from *Casablanca* wearing accurate uniforms. Warner Brothers, whose wardrobe department produced the uniform Lt. Colonel Warner wore to work after the war began, took greater pains than most other Hollywood studios in getting the small details right. Among those greeting Major Strasser's arrival at the airport is the Italian Captain Toneli, brushed aside by Vichy and Nazi officials alike. Italy's poor performance in the war became a joke on both sides of the conflict, with the Nazis forced to rescue their floundering ally in Greece and Libya. Later, at Rick's Café, one of Renault's men harangues Toneli over Italy's inability to win a battle without German assistance. As a comic opera Italian, Toneli embodies the general sentiment on his country's doubtful contributions to the war. *Casablanca's* famous conclusion, when Renault suggests to Rick that they make for the Free French garrison at Brazzaville, also reflects reality. De Gaulle's chief headquarters outside London was in Brazzaville, capital of French Equatorial Africa, the sprawling colony encompassing the postindependence nations of Chad, Cameroon, Gabon, the Republic of Congo, and the Central African Republic.

History overtook *Casablanca* just weeks before its November 26, 1942, New York premiere. On November 8 U.S. troops under Maj. Gen. George S. Patton landed in French Morocco as part of Operation Torch, the Allied occupation of French North Africa. It was the amphibious assault that prepared the way for the invasion of Sicily in Operation Husky (1943); the landings on the Italian mainland later that year at Salerno, Calabria, and Taranto; and the D-Day invasion at Normandy (1944). Suddenly Casablanca was above the top fold of every newspaper, and as industry insiders chuckled, even Warner Brothers could never have staged such publicity. "It is difficult to see how exhibitors can fail to clean up on so screaming a subject," insisted one of the trade papers.[18]

Worried about the powerful guns of the French navy, the United States avoided a direct assault on Casablanca, landing instead at points north and south of the city. Operation Torch was the one time when two of the world's elite combat forces, the U.S. Marines and the French Foreign Legion, met in combat. The United States enjoyed superiority in numbers and resolve. With the British landing simultaneously in Algeria, Vichy officials quickly decided that the prevailing wind had shifted to the Allied side.

Afterward the political atmosphere at Casablanca was as murky as that depicted in the movie, with the Roosevelt administration preferring to negotiate with Vichy and the British backing the Free French. As *Casablanca* was released more widely across the United States in January 1943, the film enjoyed another round of publicity from world events, when Roosevelt and Churchill met in Morocco at the "Casablanca Conference," which was actually held at the nearby resort town of Fedala. The Allied leaders discussed strategy and announced that they would accept nothing less than "unconditional surrender" from Germany. Some historians believe that the declaration prolonged the war by dimming the prospects for moderate Germans to negotiate a settlement.[19] Ironically, because one of the objectives of the unconditional surrender proclamation was reassuring Stalin that there would be no separate peace between the West and Germany, the Soviet leader chose this moment to extend peace feelers to the Nazis in neutral Sweden and to organize a government-in-exile among captured German officers.[20]

The cinematic *Casablanca* was a hit upon its release. Nominated for eight Oscars, it won for Best Picture, Best Director, and Best Screenplay at the March 2, 1944, Academy Awards. The win at Oscar night mirrored audience response at the time of its release but cannot explain its enduring popularity. After Warner Brothers sold *Casablanca* into syndication in the 1950s, the movie became a mainstay for local television stations. Of course, many old Hollywood movies went into syndication, sliced in pieces to make room for commercials, and yet more than two decades after its first appearance on TV, a 1977 *TV Guide* poll named *Casablanca* the most popular and frequently shown film on television.

Casablanca cemented the reputation of its protagonist, Humphrey Bogart, and some of its posthumous popularity is linked to Bogart's emergence as a cultural touchstone. Alistair Cooke summed up his appeal, calling him "a touchy man who found the world more corrupt than he had hoped," the carrier of a "rather shameful secret, in the realistic world we inhabit, of being a gallant man and an idealist."[21] To the aspiring gangster in *Breathless* (1960), the classic bellwether of French new-wave cinema, Bogart was simply the embodiment of cool. A generation of American college students agreed, such as the patrons of the Brattle Theatre near Harvard, who turned up regularly during *Casablanca*'s annual three-week run during the 1960s. Foreshadowing the phenomena surrounding *The Rocky Horror Picture Show* (1975) and other cult classics, the audience "arrived in costume, complete with trench coats and snap-brim hats, and reciting Rick's dialogue with him."[22]

Bogart's hard-edged idealism is integral to the movie's success but cannot entirely explain it. Bogart starred in thirty films after *Casablanca*, yet none achieved the same place in cultural memory. Perhaps *Casablanca*'s standing was the result of the many fortuitous accidents that lifted it beyond the ordinary run of Hollywood productions, but maybe it also resulted from the story's higher stakes. The denouement of the war teetered in the balance as *Casablanca* was being shot, and the cast and crew were as uncertain of its outcome as Ilsa was unsure of where her heart would lead her. These tensions remain palpable in *Casablanca* seventy years later.

SABOTEUR (1942) AND THE BEST YEARS OF OUR LIVES (1946)

World War II was won on the assembly line as well as the front line, with American industry outproducing the nation's enemies and sustaining its allies. In the propaganda sheets the United States dropped by the tens of thousands over France and Germany, as many words were devoted to production figures for tanks and planes as to military victories.[23]

Saboteur opens in a defense plant, a fighter plane factory in Los Angeles manned by an army of workers; noticeable among them are women, whose contribution became prevalent as the war progressed and was symbolized by Rosie the Riveter, sleeves rolled up and wrench or welding torch in hand. *Saboteur*, however, is less concerned with who works on the line than the threat to American industry by the "Fifth Column," a network of traitors plotting sabotage and fomenting a Fascist regime, named after conspirators in the Spanish Civil War who undermined the Loyalist regime from within.

Directed by Alfred Hitchcock, *Saboteur* was one of the filmmaker's two major contributions to the war effort. His other war film, *Lifeboat* (1944), was disturbing in its depiction of the ultimate triumph of a rather hapless, self-involved cast of Allied civilians trapped in a lifeboat with a shrewder, better-disciplined U-boat commander. *Saboteur* presents a more conventional hero in Barry Kane (Robert Cummings), a defense worker accused of setting the fire that gutted his aircraft factory and killed his best friend. Convinced that the culprit is a saturnine coworker called Fry (Norman Lloyd), Barry embarks on a transcontinental odyssey, fleeing the police while chasing Fry and his paymasters. *Saboteur* revolves around a classic Hitchcock "wrong man" plot but keyed to the world situation. Barry seeks not only to clear his own name but also to apprehend Fry, lest the conspiracy against America's war economy continue.

The synapses of *Saboteur*'s plot deteriorate upon close scrutiny. As *New York Times* critic Bosley Crowther put it at the time of its release, "So fast, indeed, is the action and so abundant the breathless events that one might forget, in the hubbub, that there is no logic in this wild-goose chase."[24] *Saboteur* is a B movie but a B picture composed of many unforgettable scenes, including the shootout between Fry and police at Radio City Music Hall (where the film had its premiere screening); Fry wrestling for a detonator with Barry, his finger touching the button seconds too late to destroy a battleship on its launch ramp at the Brooklyn Navy Yard; and the climactic scene at the top of the Statue of Liberty, when Fry slips from Lady Liberty's hand to his death, the seam of his jacket tearing as Barry tries to hold him by the cuff.

An affable everyman who risks his life at a dizzying height trying to save his worst enemy, Barry is ethical and determined. His journey across the United States both affirms the good character of the American people and casts suspicion that traitors are hidden everywhere and in plain sight. Strangers help Barry along the way. Among them are a gregarious truck driver, a blind philosopher-pianist (who calls hitchhiking "the surest test of the American heart"), and especially the pianist's niece Pat Martin (Priscilla Lane), who must overcome her reluctance to believe Barry's story in the face of contrary police and media reports before becoming his romantic partner. The "freaks" in a circus caravan decide to shelter Barry and Pat from the police but only after taking a vote. In keeping with *Saboteur*'s unsettling subtext, the balloting produces a close call with one abstention, two votes for turning the couple in and three for hiding them. The abstaining fat lady is unconcerned with the outside world, one half of the Siamese twins is an irritable contrarian, and the dwarf with the Hitler mustache is a Fascist. Perhaps Dorothy Parker, the *New Yorker* satirist and Algonquin Round Table raconteur who cowrote the screenplay and was responsible for this scene, feared that democracy would win in America by only a slender majority.

The Fifth Columnists are an odd lot. Fry is in it for the money, while the others appear motivated by belief. Most are family men, albeit the oddly named Freeman (Alan Baxter), who occupies a middle rung in the conspiratorial hierarchy, conveys a queer impression. A Nevada sheriff is part of their ring, as is a cantankerous old cowboy straight from a western movie who complains about "the big boys back east." The ringleader, Charles Tobin (Otto Kruger), is a prominent attorney, doting grandfather, and suave bon vivant who circles comfortably in his swallowtail coat around the summit of power. Chilling in his easy charm, Tobin, when confronted by the patriotic Barry, scoffs at "people that plod along without asking questions, the moron millions," adding, "There are a few of us who are clever enough to see a more profitable type of government." He concludes that "the competence of totalitarian nations is much higher than ours," to which Barry replies, "We'll win no matter what you guys do." In *Saboteur* the villain is assigned the best lines and is played by the more sophisticated actor. Hitchcock later complained of the blandly competent Cummings, "His features don't convey an anguish."[25]

Tobin's partner in conspiracy, Mrs. Van Sutton (Alma Kruger), is a bejeweled dowager at the center of New York society. In one of *Saboteur*'s most unnerving scenes, Barry and Pat are trapped inside the vast ballroom of her Manhattan mansion, the setting for a charity dance attended by the city's elite families and high-ranking officers from all branches of the service. Tobin and Van Sutton are familiar with the famous guests, yet as in a nightmare the heroes have no idea whom to turn to for help. Every smiling face might conceal a conspirator.

Saboteur's popularity upon release in May 1942 tapped anxiety about America's internal enemies. The Roosevelt administration authorized military authorities to intern all residents of Japanese descent, including citizens, as potential threats to security. "There is no way to determine their loyalty," Lt. Gen. John L. DeWitt told Congress.[26] Race and outrage over Pearl Harbor were the determining factors in a mass roundup of Japanese, which began just as *Saboteur* debuted in American theaters; individual suspects of German or Italian background were ordered to move from "exclusion zones" but not entire German or Italian communities.

There was little evidence to support the fear that Japanese residents might engage in sabotage or espionage against the United States. A more realistic threat came from Americans of northern European heritage, like the Fifth Columnists in *Saboteur*. Father Charles E. Coughlin preached anti-Semitism, isolationism, and Fascist-like ideas to a coast-to-coast radio audience of millions until the Roman Catholic Church silenced him in May 1942. Several uniformed American Fascist groups were organized in the 1930s, including the Silver Shirts under William Dudley Pelley. Pelley was arrested for sedition in April 1942 and indicted with other extreme right-wing leaders for "conspiring to impair the morale and the loyalty of the armed forces." Their trial was protracted, and in the end the Justice Department failed to prove its assertion that Pelley and two dozen other defendants were Nazi agents plotting to establish a puppet regime after a German victory. On trial were a loose association of rightist agitators, including Elizabeth Dilling, an anti-Semitic, anti-Communist, pro-German leader of the isolationist "Mothers' Movement." Among others indicted for conspiracy were Gerhard Wilhelm Kunze, August Klaprott, Herman Max Schwinn, and Hans Diebel, leaders of the largest group of Nazi sympathizers in the United States, the German American Bund.

The Bund numbered as many as twenty thousand members, largely German Americans. With their brown shirts, Hitler salutes, and swastika armbands, the Bund modeled itself on the German Nazis but added a few American touches, including an invocation of George Washington as the "First Fascist." The Bund maintained training camps in New York, New Jersey, Pennsylvania, and Wisconsin; its rallies in public auditoriums often led to clashes with Communist protestors. Although the Bund disbanded after the United States declared war on Germany in 1941, many of its leaders were prosecuted or forced to relocate away from coastlines under military regulations.

The most publicized act of apparent sabotage was the February 1942 fire that badly damaged the famed French ocean liner *Normandie*, recently seized in the port of New York by the U.S. Navy and renamed the uss *Lafayette*. Over objections from military authorities, Hitchcock inserted a glimpse of the *Lafayette* capsized at its pier, standing in for the battleship damaged but not sunk by Fry's bombs.[27] A congressional investigation later determined that the fire was not sabotage but was caused by the carelessness of workmen converting the liner into a troopship. The Fifth Column many Americans feared, and the sort of conspiracy featured in *Saboteur*, never materialized, and the U.S. war economy became the arsenal and machine shop of the world.

The protagonists of *The Best Years of Our Lives*, a trio of discharged veterans, encounter the scale of U.S. war production upon landing on their hometown airfield, covered as far as the eye can see by B-17 bombers that never saw combat. This is the air armada's final stop before the scrapyard. American industry produced enough military material from 1942 through 1945 to clad the entire world in steel.

America's veterans returned to a nation changed by the conflict. In Boone City, the representative middle-American city where *The Best Years* is set, the airport is new, and a favorite bar, Butch's, has a new neon sign. The most profound changes, however, were not immediately discernible in bricks and mortar. Gross national product rose 60 percent during the war; prices climbed 30 percent; earnings doubled. The national debt quintupled, but corporate profits were up 68 percent. The war helped lift the nation out of the Great Depression, and the massive spending by the federal government trickled down to the growing middle class.[28] Over fifteen million civilians moved during the war, especially black and white southerners seeking employment in northern factory towns. "And while the war brought good times for many, it put strain on the family and on ethnic, gender, and class relations," historian Michael C. C. Adams wrote. The divorce rate rose from 16 percent in 1940 to 27 percent in 1944, and many wartime marriages cracked once couples separated by military service were reunited.[29] The gap between generations widened alarmingly, and more women than ever found paid jobs outside the home.

The Best Years of Our Lives addresses most of these issues during its nearly three-hour running time, an unusual length for a Hollywood movie and indicative of the importance given to its topic. The protagonists represent three socioeconomic groups and branches of the service. Al Stephenson (Fredric March), an upper-class banker called to the army, lives in Boone City's grandest apartment house, staffed with a concierge and an elevator operator; Homer Parrish (Harold Russell), a middle-class boy who joined the navy, returns to his parents' bungalow in a neighborhood of narrow lawns and modest dwellings; Fred Derry (Dana Andrews) is lower-class, a bombardier whose parents dwell in a shack beneath a viaduct. As a taxi takes them into town from the airport, they share their apprehensions over their homecoming. Al compares his return to a military assault. "It feels like I'm going to hit a beach," he tells his companions in the cab. His wife (Myrna Loy) and children (Teresa Wright and Michael Hall) are overjoyed to see him, yet he is unready for intimacy with his wife and senses a divide between himself and his offspring. Al's son lectures him about the danger of atomic weapons; his daughter worked for two years in a hospital and "knows the facts of life." Al resorts to alcohol, becoming a jolly drunk.

Homer has a special problem. He lost both hands when his carrier sank during the Battle of Leyte Gulf (October 1944), and his arms end in hooks. The reference is to the USS *Princeton*, struck during the battle by an armor-piercing bomb dropped by a Japanese dive bomber and engulfed in fire after the sprinkler system failed. *The Best Years* is frank in its depiction of the physical injuries of war and helped begin a shift in public perceptions toward the disabled. Director William Wyler coaxed a remarkable performance from first-time actor Harold Russell, an army veteran who had lost his hands after a bomb exploded during training. The dialogue crystallizes his experience in the accident's aftermath. "They took care of me fine," Homer says of the care he received. "They even taught me to use these things," and he demonstrates the skill he learned in a naval hospital by signing his name and lighting a cigarette. Fortunately for Homer, his worst apprehensions are not realized. Despite many awkward moments, his parents and the girl he left behind care for him and accept his disability.

The changes the war brought to gender relations strike Fred especially hard. Fred met his wife while in basic training in Texas; like many wartime romances, the couple barely knew each other before he was sent overseas. Fred is surprised to learn that she no longer lives with his parents but has rented her own apartment downtown. "She took a job?" he asks angrily when his father breaks the news. "Where?" To Fred having a working wife is an offense against his manhood, an implication that he is incapable of supporting his family. Fred is unable to adjust to his wife's living arrangements and is annoyed by her romanticized perception of him as a returning war hero. Unlike civilians who followed the war through sanitized dispatches and newsreels, Fred was in combat. He still awakens from nightmares of nighttime bombing raids.

Her advice to him, "Snap out of it!" echoes the unsympathetic attitudes of many Americans unfamiliar with post-combat stress disorders. The psychological damage of combat found its way into other films, often subtly in such films noir as *The Blue Dahlia* (1946) and *In a Lonely Place* (1950), in which "returning GIs . . . seem to be walking around in their own nightmares."[30] In those dark crime dramas a few veterans return home tightly tense and even homicidal, a cycle that would be repeated in many depictions of Vietnam veterans in the 1970s and 1980s.

The issue of finding work for veterans is prominent in *The Best Years*. Although Al returns to the bank and is promoted to vice president of small loans, he clashes with management. "We have many problems — this GI Bill of Rights," his unctuous supervisor informs him. The Servicemen's Readjustment Act, as the GI Bill was officially titled, passed in 1944, provided an unprecedented package of veterans' benefits, including home and business loans and college tuition. By enabling more than eight million veterans to attend college and many more to buy homes, the GI Bill spurred the growth of the middle class. Most Americans supported the bill, but conservatives worried that it represented the "thin edge of socialism."[31] Al's bank expects him to be "cautious" with the depositors' money, yet he insists on giving veterans as much assistance as possible.

Fred walks the town searching for work but finds that his years behind a Norden bombsite qualify him for no civilian employment, and he encounters some civilians who fear that returning veterans will take their jobs. A chain store has purchased the pharmacy where he worked before the war, but he reclaims his job at the lunch counter. In the film's most dramatic scene he quits after punching a customer who argues that "we fought the wrong people" in the war and were "deceived" into the conflict by "a bunch of radicals in Washington."

Sporting an American flag pin in his lapel, the customer may well have been a Silver Shirt before the war and might have joined the Fifth Columnists in *Saboteur* if given the opportunity. Homer tears the flag from the man's jacket with one of his hooks.

The incident drives home the film's prevailing theme: the bonding of veterans over experiences that people at home will never fully comprehend. In their twilight years they would be honored as the "Greatest Generation." Meanwhile, in postwar America their adjustment proved difficult, but they were expected to carry on without complaint. The expanding economy and the opportunities afforded by the GI Bill propelled them to the forefront of the increasingly suburbanized America that emerged by the 1950s. The veterans would put their commander, Dwight D. Eisenhower, into the White House and would provide the nation with much of its leadership, from Joseph McCarthy and John F. Kennedy through Richard M. Nixon and George H. W. Bush.

The Best Years of Our Lives was slated by Universal Pictures as a prestige picture and was honored by the industry, winning Oscars for Best Director, Best Picture, Best Actor (Fredric March), Best Screenplay (Robert E. Sherwood), Best Editing, and Best Music. Harold Russell became the only person in history to win two Oscars for the same role, earning Best Supporting Actor and a special award for "bringing hope and courage to his fellow veterans." Armed with his Academy Awards, Russell campaigned for the handicapped. In 1961 President Kennedy appointed him vice chairman of a presidential commission on employment for the disabled; in 1964 Lyndon Johnson elevated him to chairman, and Richard Nixon reappointed him. He seldom returned to acting but in 1989 guest starred in two episodes from a television series about the Vietnam War, *China Beach*.

TWELVE O'CLOCK HIGH (1949)

The earliest Allied air strikes against Germany were token efforts by the Royal Air Force (RAF), little more than revenge attacks staged more to benefit British morale than to unsettle the Germans. During the first two years of the war the Luftwaffe commanded the sky over Europe, thwarted only by the RAF's dogged determination in the Battle of Britain. After America entered the conflict, the pressure shifted, and Germany went on the defensive in the air. By the summer of 1942 the U.S. Eighth Bomber Command had established bases in England for a strategic bombing campaign against Nazi-occupied Europe in massive air raids intended to cripple German industry, disrupt transportation, and reduce German cities to rubble.

Americans saw impressions of this air campaign in wartime newsreels, but in the aftermath memory of the bombing raids was shaped by one enormously successful film. Based on a novel by veteran officers of that campaign, Sy Bartlett and Bernie Lay Jr., *Twelve O'Clock High* was scripted by the authors and populated by characters inspired by the officers and enlisted men with whom they served. Hollywood considered the novel a hot property; Twentieth Century Fox producer Darryl Zanuck purchased rights ahead of his rivals at Paramount but insisted on changes to the story that strengthened its impact. He shifted focus from a cast of men to their commander, Brigadier General Savage, and cast in that role an actor known for playing methodical men willing to go any distance for the cause they believed in, Gregory Peck. The U.S. Air Force, an independent service only since 1947, granted Zanuck full cooperation. The air force chief of staff, Gen. Hoyt Vandenberg, took a personal interest, supplying the production with surplus B-17s and authorizing the use of Elgin Air Force Base in Florida and Ozark Field in Alabama to stand in for the film's base in Britain. In return, Zanuck edited the screenplay to reduce references to drunkenness and soften the commanding general's nervous breakdown to nervous exhaustion at the film's climax.[32] Veterans of the Eighth Bomber Command have called *Twelve O'Clock High* the most accurate rendition of their combat experience on film for its depiction of the tension and danger they experienced on their missions.[33] A documentary feel was introduced by the inclusion of combat footage shot during the war. The exploding fighter planes, the bombers plunging to earth in tailspins, and the tiny figures of men parachuting from their doomed craft are real.

Twelve O'Clock High is framed by the postwar journey of retired

Maj. Harvey Stovall, in a performance for which Dean Jagger earned an Oscar as Best Supporting Actor. Stovall returns by train and bicycle to the fictional Archbury base once occupied by the fictional 918th Heavy Bombardment Group, a unit modeled on the 306th Group, in which the prototypes for many of the story's characters served.[34] The airfield is overgrown with weeds but resonates with memories. Stovall's nostalgia brightens the beginning and end of a story with many harrowing moments. In *Twelve O'Clock High*'s opening wartime scene the B-17s of the 918th are returning from a raid, greeted on the runway by a fire engine and an ambulance. The reception is necessary because most bombers suffered damage from German gunfire, and many limp home with one dead engine and hulls perforated by shrapnel and bullets. One of the wounded bombers is obviously in trouble and lands roughly, on its belly, crushing a tent alongside the runway and tearing up the sod before halting. The crew emerges shaken. One man vomits discreetly against the plane. Another speaks of the dismembered arm still lodged in a turret, the gunner having been bound with a tourniquet and parachuted out in the hope that he would fall into the hands of German medics. The pilot is pulled from the wreckage raving, his leg broken; we are told that part of his brain has been shot away and that his frozen blood covered the windshield.

These are wrenching details for audiences of that era, as is *Twelve O'Clock High*'s dominant theme of psychological breakdown from combat trauma, the peculiar Russian roulette stress of conducting air raids against heavily defended targets deep inside enemy territory. The details are starkly accurate, a leading mark in the trend toward greater realism in cinematic war pictures embodied by the dangerous crash landing of a B-17, manned by a Hollywood stunt pilot, in the opening scene.[35] Even so, some of the challenges faced by bomber crews are alluded to only in passing, including the extreme cold at high altitude. It was usually far below zero in the uninsulated cabins, and a gunner, especially at the open side hatches, might lose a finger if it froze to the trigger. The average tour for a bomber crew was twenty-five sorties, but in the war's worst months the average life expectancy was only fifteen missions.[36]

Frustration is added to injury when the 918's commander, Col. Keith Davenport (Gary Merrill), returns to his office after his tragic mission. He is the subject of that day's broadcast from Germany by the British turncoat Lord Haw-Haw, who recounts the 918's losses in detail and with a gently mocking tone. "You lost five bombers today, didn't you?" he says, as if consolingly. Lord Haw-Haw, one of a group of Axis propaganda broadcasters whose ranks also included Americans such as Tokyo Rose, Axis Sally, and the modernist poet Ezra Pound, continues by sympathizing with the Eighth Bomber Command's mission of daylight bombing, "an incredible idea," he calls it. The turncoat tries to stir American resentment against the RAF, whose bombers fly more safely at night. Davenport is clearly crumbling from the stress and is disgruntled by the disregard for his men's lives implicit in the orders he is forced to carry out. Tomorrow he expects to lead the fourth consecutive daylight air raid.

The question of morale is raised early. The unit's flight surgeon, Major Kaiser (Paul Stewart), reports that the men "have a bellyful" and are claiming sickness to avoid tomorrow's mission. The physician worries that he has no yardstick for measuring how much stress is too much. "Are you going to push them till they go crazy?" Davenport demands that night in a meeting with Brig. Gen. Frank Savage (Gregory Peck). "Somebody's got to give them a goal."

Savage is unimpressed with Davenport's plea. He relieves the colonel and takes command of the 918th, determined to whip the unit into shape. His arrival at Archbury is similar to George S. Patton's assumption of command in the film *Patton* twenty years later. Savage berates the MP at the gate for failing to check his ID card; he demotes a sergeant to private for being out of uniform, cancels all leaves, and orders the arrest of the 918's executive officer for drinking off base. "Stand at attention!" Savage barks at the man. "You're yellow — a traitor to yourself and this Group."

A Spartan regimen of discipline is imposed on the 918th. The crews run practice missions every day to increase proficiency. "Fear is normal but stop worrying about it," Savage instructs the men. "Consider yourselves already dead." With that thought in mind, the general believes there is nothing left to worry about except dropping the bombs on target. The entire unit applies for a transfer in protest, but the wily adjutant, Stovall, a veteran of the army's World War I air service, delays forwarding the paperwork. His ploy gives Savage time to win over the unit through appreciation of their success in driving the war home to Nazi Germany. Savage is no desk officer, and like many high-ranking army air force officers, he leads his bomber group, piloting the lead B-17, the Piccadilly Lilly. He shirks from nothing that he asks his men to do. He will push them beyond endurance until they learn to push themselves.

Twelve O'Clock High stamped the look and sound of the American air campaign against Germany in memory. The B-17 Flying Fortresses were covered on all sides by ball turret guns; the squadrons flew together in tight formations like a steel wedge cutting across the sky. In the early months of America's air war against Germany, the bombers flew without escorts. The long-range P-51 fighters were deployed in large number only by 1943. As they descended over their targets, the B-17s became vulnerable to the black bursts of flak fired in "box barrages" by German antiaircraft gunners. The shrapnel easily penetrated the bombers' thin skin, causing terrible injuries among the cramped crews. Despite flying in tight formation, they could be picked off by German fighter planes, the Focke-Wulf 190s and Messerschmitt Me 109s that streaked straight down upon them at an angle the bomber crews dubbed "twelve o'clock high." The steady chug of the B-17s propellers, the whining moan of the fighters, and the rattle of machine gun cartridges fill the air. *Twelve O'Clock High* won an Oscar for Best Sound Recording.

Allied air power, with the United States and Great Britain in the lead but accompanied by squadrons from across the British Commonwealth and exiled Czech, French, and Polish pilots, played a vital role in disrupting Germany's economy and forced the Nazis to divert enormous resources for homeland defense. The strategy behind the Combined Bomber Offensive, or Operation Pointblank, was established at the Casablanca Conference (1943) and called for "the progressive destruction of the German military, industrial, and economic system, and the undermining of the morale of the German people." The operation was divided into an American dayshift and a British nightshift. The United States claimed it conducted daylight "precision bombing," but while industrial or military sites were often targeted, high-altitude bombing was more precise in theory than in execution. The British gleefully conducted what it termed as night-time "area bombing," intended to "de-house" German civilians and grind down their will to continue the war.

The morality of indiscriminate bombing, even though it had been pioneered by the German Condor Legion at Guernica during the Spanish Civil War and practiced by the Luftwaffe at Rotterdam and Coventry, troubled even some on the British side.[37] Advocates insisted that the bombing offensive weakened German morale, supplanting the triumphalism of the early war years with fatalism over eventual defeat. Recalling the British firebombing of Hamburg (July 24–25, 1943), a German officer wrote: "A wave of terror radiated from the suffering city and spread throughout Germany . . . Psychologically the war at that moment had perhaps reached its most critical point."[38] But if psychology can be difficult to measure, economic impact is more eas-ily weighed. Under the resourceful leadership of armaments minister Albert Speer, German industrial production actually increased despite air raids, yet Germany's war economy "was driven underground or dispersed away from the cities," making "transportation routes highly vulnerable to aerial interdiction." Enormous resources, including prisoners of war and slave labor, and their guards and foremen, were required to sustain infrastructure against heavy bombardment. Ger-man artillery was diverted to air defense, whose emplacements were manned by 800,000 men and boys, including Hitler Youth during the war's final years. Much of the Luftwaffe, whose primary mission had been to support the army, was redeployed to defend the Fatherland.[39]

Advocates of airpower have often overstated the value of strategic bombing, and yet the Combined Bombing Offensive, with its air raids of up to a thousand bombers often dropping four-ton "block-buster" bombs, played a crucial role in breaking Germany. About 140,000 Allied air crewmen were killed in the offensive; at least a half-million civilians died in Germany (including foreign guest and slave workers) and another 68,000 in France, which also endured heavy Allied bombing.

Savage's fierce determination was typical of the officers who led dangerous missions over Europe. Immediately popular with movie audiences, *Twelve O'Clock High* earned four Oscar nominations, winning two. It was embraced by the military and used as a leadership training film by the U.S. Air Force and corporations such as Coca-Cola. As a television series, *Twelve O'Clock High* ran from 1964 to 1967 on ABC.[40] In 1998 the Library of Congress added *Twelve O'Clock High* to the National Film Registry for its historical significance. It was not the last movie dealing with World War II to be placed on the National Registry for contributing to the public's memory of the conflict. *Patton* was added in 2003.

PATTON (1970)

Mounting a platform beneath an American flag big enough to fill a movie screen, Gen. George S. Patton Jr. begins the movie bearing his name with the sort of speech he characteristically gave to his men. Patton (George C. Scott) is a resplendent figure in cavalry britches and polished boots, a steel helmet studded with stars and a tunic covered in ribbons and medals from many nations. Clutching a riding crop and with an ivory-handled Colt revolver at his side, Patton minces no words. "No bastard ever won a war by dying for his country," he begins. "He won it by making the other poor dumb bastard die for his country." He continues by defining the character of his countrymen. "All real Americans love the sting of battle. Americans love a winner and will not tolerate a loser . . . That's why America has never lost a war and will never lose a war."

Even at the time of this World War II speech, a composite drawn from actual remarks, a brave man could have reminded the general that the War of 1812 ended in a draw. As a student of military history, Patton might have countered that the Battle of New Orleans proved the United States was a nation that could win against an empire. In any case Patton's assertion had special significance to audiences at the time of the film's release. By 1970 victory in Vietnam had proved elusive. To some moviegoers the general in his full dress with his oversize flag embodied American hubris and imperial overreach. To others he represented the never-say-die spirit behind the nation's triumph over its enemies in World War II.

The screenplay by Francis Ford Coppola, written before he directed his epochal film *The Godfather*, never told viewers what to think about Patton but offered them much to think about. It was a Rorschach test on the military and war. Coppola regarded Patton as "obviously nuts" and added: "If they want to make a film glorifying him as a great American hero, it will be laughed at. And if I write a film that condemns him, it won't be made at all."[41]

The cinematic Patton was a courageous swashbuckler, quixotic, wildly unbalanced, and scarcely stranger than the general in real life. The Patton legend was already well established in his lifetime. An NBC broadcast during the general's occupation of Casablanca described him as "a combination of Buck Rogers, the Green Hornet, and the Man from Mars," adding, "He has enough dash and dynamite to make a Hollywood adventure-hero look like a drugstore cowboy."[42] Years later Twentieth Century Fox agreed, purchasing screen rights for Ladislas Farago's biography, *Patton: Ordeal and Triumph*, and bringing General of the Army Omar Bradley, Patton's longtime subordinate and eventual superior, onboard as "senior advisor." For once the facts were no less impressive than the Hollywood legend.

Like *Lawrence of Arabia* with T. E. Lawrence, the impression *Patton* stamped on its subject was indelible in the popular imagination. The story is more historically sound than most motion picture biographies, edited into a tragic drama by Coppola and infused with poetic grandeur in performance. "I had nothing to do with evolving the character the way George C. Scott played him," Coppola admitted.

Scott, a veteran character actor transformed into a star through the film, pored over no less than thirteen biographies on Patton in an effort to understand the man he was portraying. The film was largely shot in Spain, with the Spanish army, still equipped with World War II vintage U.S. weaponry, standing in for the GIs. The negotiations with Spain proved difficult. At first the country's military refused to cooperate; the first screenplay they were presented with, badly translated into Spanish, seemed to defame Patton and all officers. But once it was retranslated with the help of a bilingual Spanish general, the shooting was allowed to begin. Nearly half of *Patton*'s budget was spent on the Spanish army.[43]

Patton came from an old southern plantation family with a long martial tradition and displayed a proclivity as a boy for war and risk taking. He grew up with a sense of superiority, a tinge of snobbery and racism. He deliberately honed his persona with its profanity and arrogance, the aristocratic bearing, the scowl, and the ruthlessness. As a student at Virginia Military Institute and West Point, he was diligent but struggled hard to make the grade, probably because of dyslexia and attention deficit disorder, whose symptoms can include the flexibility of mind coupled with the tireless pursuit of goals he displayed throughout his military career.[44] Patton's West Point class-mates perceived him as pompous and overambitious. He was already an unembarrassed self-promoter, announcing that he would be first from the class of 1909 to make the rank of general. After graduating, he married the daughter of a Boston textile magnate and became the wealthiest officer in the U.S. Army. He saw himself as a man of destiny and welcomed any opportunity to emerge from the tedium of the peacetime army. As a cavalry lieutenant, he volunteered to serve with Brig. Gen. John J. Pershing's Punitive Expedition into Mexico against Pancho Villa's insurgents (1916), where he attacked the rebels from automobiles in the U.S. Army's first mechanized assault.[45]

A year later, when Pershing was given command of the American Expeditionary Force in France, Patton accompanied him as aide-de-camp, but the nascent field of armored warfare appealed to his sense of adventure. On the strength of being the only American who had ever led a charge from a motor vehicle, he became the first soldier in the newly established Tank Corps. There was as yet no doctrine for employing tanks, but Patton, whose previous writings on tactics concerned only cavalry sabers, eagerly developed procedures for the iron horse of the new century. He composed the U.S. Army's basic manual for tank warfare with clarity and originality, foreseeing that the tank would "assume the role of pursuit cavalry and 'ride the enemy to death.'" As commander of the First Tank Brigade in its assault on German lines, his standing order set the tone for the defiant belligerence captured so well by George C. Scott: "American tanks do not surrender."[46]

The *Patton* screenplay never alludes to the general's past or personal life; he emerges as a primal force, an ancient warrior king conjured back to life to fight a dangerous enemy as the world hangs in balance. After the dramatic speech that opens the movie, *Patton* picks up the story at a low moment in American military history, the aftermath of the Battle of Kasserine Pass (February 1943). The U.S. Army's first encounter with the Wehrmacht in the Tunisian desert had ended in defeat. The disheartening performance of American armor was blamed on lack of air cover and the poor leadership of Maj. Gen. Lloyd Fredendall, described by Patton's biographer Carlo D'Este as "one of the most inept senior officers to hold command" during the war. Ordered to take charge of the Second Corps and push the Axis out of Africa, Patton cuts a dashing figure upon arrival, riding a halftrack as if astride a charging steed. It was a theatrical entrance but not unrealistic. The real Patton loved dramatic entrances.

From Patton's perspective the troops he inherited from Fredendall are undisciplined rabble. "They don't look like soldiers. They don't act like soldiers," he says, determined to knock them in line. Mild-mannered Maj. Gen. Omar Bradley (Karl Malden), extolled in the press as the "GI's general," defends their poor performance.[47] "Some of our boys were just plain scared," he offers. Patton will have none of it. On a snap tour of the base hospital, he ejects two soldiers with self-inflicted wounds as unworthy of resting under the same roof as the courageous. "There'll be no battle fatigue in my unit," he insists. "I'm not going to subsidize cowardice."

Patton drives to the site of an earlier battlefield, an engagement in the Carthaginian wars. "Two thousand years ago, I was here," he announces. He was not merely identifying with a chapter from history. A believer in reincarnation, the real Patton imagined that he had been a great general in many previous lives.[48] As Patton gazes across the barren North African landscape, he expresses great respect for his German opponent, Gen. Erwin Rommel, and wishes he could joust with the "Desert Fox" in the Tunisian sands. Alas, he concedes, the age of knighthood had ended. "The world grew up. Hell of a shame," he says. Coppola's dialogue in these scenes catches the spirit of the man.

Although Patton would have gladly crossed sabers with Saladin during the Crusades and felt at home in the fields of the Peloponnesian War, he was a brilliant modern strategist in deploying the armaments of a mechanized age. He was a scholar of conflict. Patton second-guessed Rommel, reversing the failure at Kasserine by defeating the Afrika Korps at El Guettar (March 1943) because he took the time to read the Desert Fox's book on tank warfare.

Many incidents from the film that could strike viewers as pure Hollywood are actually drawn from reality. Prominent among them is the scene in which a scowling Patton dresses down an RAF commander in his office for failure to provide air cover, moments before the Luftwaffe arrives, dropping bombs and strafing his headquarters.[49] Coppola's artistic license is displayed as Patton races outside and fires on the overflying Focke-Wulf fighter-bombers with his Colt. Whether or not Patton tried to down the enemy aircraft like a cowboy shooting snakes, the gesture would not have been out of character.

Patton's chief departure from truth occurs in its depiction of Britain's field marshal, Bernard Law Montgomery, and the rivalry between him and his American counterpart. Monty is spoofed in *Patton* as a vainglorious cartoon of an English officer. In reality Patton liked the man who had halted the Afrika Korps at El Alamein, calling him "wonderfully conceited and the best soldier . . . I have met in this war."

There was tension between U.S. and British forces over the capture of Sicily from the Axis, yet Montgomery was happy to allow Patton to take Messina. The race to secure the strategic city was more a sporting contest and had been exaggerated by sensationalistic reporting long before Coppola. Aside from the enemy, Patton's greatest conflicts in the Sicilian campaign occurred with Omar Bradley, who complained that the general "steamed about with great convoys of cars and great squads of cameramen."[50] The scene from *Patton* in which Monty marches into Messina as a conquering hero, with bagpipes blaring, only to be greeted by a smirking Patton in the city center, never occurred.

The Allies secured Sicily after a costly struggle, but what happened in the aftermath, in August 1943, nearly ended Patton's career. Acclaimed as the hero of the first assault against Axis Europe and a likely candidate to command the anticipated invasion of France, Patton kindled a firestorm when, in separate incidents, he exploded in rage while touring evacuation hospitals, slapping soldiers across the face who complained of nervous exhaustion, calling them "yellow bellies," "shirkers," and worse, and even drawing his revolver on them. The film captures the sequence of events accurately, with allowances for the trimming and concision necessary to keep the narrative in focus.

Patton's hatred of "malingerers" was undisguised; he had no sympathy for victims of battle fatigue and sincerely believed that the only cure was self-discipline and fortitude. It has even been suggested that Patton, who unlike many generals relished being at the front line under fire, may himself have been suffering from combat stress disorder at the time of these incidents. Complaints by lower-ranking officers over Patton's conduct reached the Allied supreme commander, Gen. Dwight D. Eisenhower, who rebuked his subordinate for being out of line and ordered him to apologize. The affair caused more problems when it leaked to the press. Some members of Congress demanded Patton's dismissal, but the army's chief of staff, Gen. George Marshall, and Roosevelt's secretary of war, Henry L. Stimson, refused. In a letter to the U.S. Senate, Stimson underscored the need for Patton's "aggressive, winning leadership in the bitter battles which are to come before final victory."[51] As shown in the movie, Patton was punished by being handed a dummy command, a nonexistent Potemkin village army poised on the British coast for an amphibious assault on Calais. The Allies had no intention of undertaking such an operation, but the ploy fooled the Germans, who refused to believe that an officer of Patton's caliber could be sidelined for slapping a soldier. As a result, the Nazis diverted their strength away from the actual target of the Allied invasion, Normandy. Patton fumed at being used as a decoy, but he served his purpose well.

Patton made a final claim on destiny after he was given command of the Third Army in July 1944. His aggressive pursuit of victory helped spearhead the Allied advance through France and culminated in triumph after the bitter fighting in the snow forests of the Ardennes Mountains during the Battle of the Bulge (December 1944–January 1945). The battle was Germany's last desperate counteroffensive on the western front and cost the Americans more casualties than any other action in Europe. The ferocity of Patton's assault and his refusal to bend to caution resulted in the relief of the besieged 101st Airborne Division at Bastogne, the turning point of the battle, and is well represented in the film. After continuous combat for 281 days, Patton's Third Army captured thirty-two thousand square miles of German territory and over 650,000 German prisoners and inflicted serious casualties on the enemy. He ended the war with distinction.[52]

Patton longed for a role in the expected invasion of Japan but was appointed military governor of Bavaria instead. When his statements on retaining Nazi administrators proved impolitic, even if he was correct that trained hands were needed to keep Germany from collapse, he was relieved of command once again by Eisenhower. His contemptuous attitude toward the Soviets is accurately depicted in Coppola's screenplay. "Up until now we've been fighting the wrong people," he declares in one scene, dreaming of turning the tanks on the USSR and leading an American-German invasion of Eastern Europe. Patton foresaw an acrimonious divorce between Stalin and the West and a new conflict on the horizon, even if his preemptive solution was unpalatable at a moment when the world was tired of war.

Patton ends as the general walks into an uncertain future. In actuality Patton was posted to an insignificant command, tasked with writing the history of the war in Europe, and died after a freak automobile accident on December 21, 1945. *Patton* won seven Oscars, including Best Picture, Best Director for Franklin J. Schaffner, and Best Screenplay for Coppola and Edmund H. North, but only six statues were claimed at the 1971 Academy Awards. George C. Scott won for Best Actor but declined by telegram, the first actor to refuse to accept an Oscar. He later explained, "I have to do what is valuable to me: calling my soul my own."[53]

SCHINDLER'S LIST (1993)

More than any battle fought during World War II, perhaps more than the war itself, the Holocaust stands as a signal event of the twentieth century. The Nazi campaign to exterminate European Jewry involved military, political, and economic objectives and was prioritized by Germany's leaders above even the defeat of the nations they engaged in war. Militant anti-Semitism was the bedrock of Nazi ideology, and even as Soviet and Western armies pushed into Germany, the Nazis continued to wage war against a people without a nation of their own.

Documentary images of the death camps after their liberation in 1945 cast a shadow over the popular imagination but were slow to enter popular culture and made few appearances on film in the early postwar years. Bearing witness to the Holocaust was regarded as a sacred trust among survivors. Few took literally the injunction by cultural critic Theodor Adorno, "To write poetry after Auschwitz is barbaric,"[54] but his statement amplified the caution over the limits of representation and especially the suspicion among Old World intellectuals who continued to associate movies and popular music with peep shows and carnivals. The only significant film of the early postwar years to touch on the Holocaust was Orson Welles's *The Stranger* (1946), which included a short sequence of documentary footage from the death camps but was primarily a thriller about a prominent Nazi hiding in the United States. *The Diary of Anne Frank* (1959) was the first important dramatization of the victims. Based on the journal of an adolescent Dutch Jewish girl concealed along with her family and other Jews in the garret of an Amsterdam office building, *Anne Frank* focuses on the human stories among the confined group of Jews without depicting the machinery of genocide. A few prominent Hollywood pictures reflected on the aftermath of the Holocaust, especially *Exodus* (1960), on the role of displaced European Jews in the founding of Israel, and *Judgment at Nuremberg* (1961), on the postwar trial of secondary Nazis for crimes against humanity.

Mainstream audiences were first exposed to a full reenactment of the destruction of European Jews in the phenomenally popular, much discussed NBC miniseries *Holocaust* (1978). The four-part saga of a fictional German Jewish family popularized the previously little-heard term *Holocaust* and shaped understanding of the Holocaust in popular discourse. It also introduced Meryl Streep, who went on to win an Oscar as a Polish victim of the Nazis in *Sophie's Choice* (1982). Directed by Marvin J. Chomsky, whose previous production was the similarly influential miniseries *Roots*, *Holocaust* won four Emmys and two Golden Globes. It also exposed the contested issue of depicting the genocide on film when Holocaust survivor and Nobel Prize—winning author Elie Wiesel condemned the series as "untrue and offensive."[55]

With the success of the miniseries, the tragedy of European Jews finally had a generally accepted name (the Hebrew word for "calamity," *Shoah*, had been the preferred term among the Jewish community), but the annihilation had yet to inspire an unforgettable cinematic landmark. Fifteen years later Steven Spielberg rose to the challenge with *Schindler's List*, a film that more or less defines public memory of the Holocaust. A movie based on the same material as *Schindler's List* was proposed to MGM as early as 1963, but not enough time had passed for Hollywood to feel comfortable with a production on the topic.[56] Several European films addressed the Holocaust after 1970, but all were confined to art houses and never reached large audiences.

"In contrast, *Schindler's List* has penetrated historical consciousness on a global scale and has transformed the image of the Holocaust as perceived by millions of people all over the world," wrote Yosefa Loshitzky, communications professor at Jerusalem's Hebrew University. He added that Spielberg's film "signifies the victory of collective memory transmitted by popular culture over a memory contested and debated by professional historians."[57] *Schindler's List* won seven Oscars, including Best Picture and Best Director.

Universal Studios, whose executives saw the gripping story as a potential project for Spielberg, Hollywood's great storyteller of the 1980s, purchased the rights to *Schindler's List*, the 1982 novel by Australian author Thomas Keneally. In 1983 the director told one of the Jews who Schindler had saved that ten years would pass before he reached the maturity necessary for the project. Spielberg was wary of the responsibility for depicting the Holocaust. He urged Roman Polanski, a Holocaust survivor, to direct the movie, but many more years would pass before the Polish-born Polanski would feel comfortable with the topic. Spielberg's interest in *Schindler's List* was sustained by publicity surrounding Holocaust deniers, including the book by best-selling British author David Irving, *Hitler's War* (1977). Despite an appearance of objectivity, most Holocaust deniers were associated with neo-Nazi or far-Right circles, and it was feared that their efforts to question the magnitude of Nazi anti-Semitism might falsify public understanding at a time when old age began to claim many Holocaust survivors. For Spielberg making *Schindler's List* was an important part of his journey to reconnect with his Jewish roots.[58]

Spielberg began work on *Schindler's List* while filming his blockbuster dinosaur thriller *Jurassic Park* (1993), eventually leaving the editing room to start shooting the Holocaust story on location in Poland. Keneally's original screenplay would have resulted in a production even longer than the over-three-hour movie eventually screened in theaters. Steven Zaillian, an Armenian American who grew up with stories of the Armenian Genocide in Ottoman Turkey during World War I, wrote the final screenplay.[59]

Nearly all three hours of *Schindler's List* are filmed in black-and-white, as were war movies, newsreels, and documentary photographs from World War II. Most memories of the era are in shades of black-and-white. In the film's first wartime scene German clerks in the occupied Polish city of Kraków set up tables with typewriters on the streets and begin registering the city's Jews, typing out the first of the movie's famous lists. At the time *Schindler's List* was filmed, little scholarly work had been done on the story's real-life protagonist, Oskar Schindler. Keneally wrote that Schindler was the principal author of the roster of Jewish names, the "list of life" that saved nearly eleven hundred Jews from the SS.[60] The truth sifted from surviving paperwork and eyewitnesses affirms Schindler's primary role but is more complicated than the easy-to-follow arc of the story told by Keneally, Spielberg, and Zaillian. Schindler never actually dictated a list, but several lists associated with the survival of the German entrepreneur's Jewish workers circulated at different times. Schindler left it to his Jewish clerks, especially Marcel Goldberg, to compile the names.[61]

Spielberg cuts smoothly from the gritty Kraków streets to the expensive clutter of Schindler's bedroom. The audience never sees the face of Schindler (Liam Neeson) during the several minutes he spends dressing, selecting from among his many shirts and suits, slipping on cuff links, and knotting his silk necktie. He pockets a bundle of cash — profusions of banknotes are one of the film's visual motifs — and for a final touch fastens his Nazi Party pin to his lapel. Armed with money and symbols of status, Schindler makes a dramatic entrance at a Kraków nightclub frequented by the city's new German rulers. His mission for the night is to make friends and pacify potential enemies; his ultimate objective is to set himself up as an industrialist, plucking riches from the ruins of Poland. In life and on film Schindler represented the German analog to the American Dream, which meant heading not west but east. Although not the first German to think in those terms, Hitler encapsulated them in *Mein Kampf*, urging Germans to "turn our gaze toward the land in the east."[62] As Schindler brags in the screenplay, he came to Kraków with a single suitcase and will leave a wealthy man.

Spielberg divulges nothing of Schindler's past, allowing him to emerge as an intriguing cipher, a riddle to be solved gradually. The real Schindler was a man with a past before he arrived in Kraków. He was born in 1908 in Sudetenland, a predominately German province of the Austro-Hungarian Empire that passed to Czechoslovakia after World War I. Classmates at his technical school nicknamed him "Schindler the Crook," and his reputation as a ne'er-do-well followed him into adulthood. He spent more money than he earned, tangled with the police, and jumped from venture to venture.[63]

Most Sudeten Germans advocated secession, leaving Czechoslovakia and uniting with either Austria or Germany, and by the 1930s cast their support behind a local pro-Nazi party. Planning for the absorption of Sudetenland into the Reich, the Abwehr, German military intelligence, recruited agents in the province. In 1935 Schindler was added to their network. The Abwehr was interested not only in undermining the Czechs but also in undercutting the SS, whose SD (Security Service) branch ran its own spy ring in Sudetenland. Schindler was not, at least in his early life, a deeply philosophical man. Money and the commonplace prejudices of his upbringing explain his interest in the Abwehr, and he carried the impressions he gathered there into his wartime career. The Abwehr looked with contempt upon the SS, whose minions Schindler would bribe and outwit to save "his Jews." According to Schindler's biographer, "Oskar developed a distrust of the SD, the Gestapo, and other Nazi Party organizations" during the 1930s and as an Abwehr agent "developed the skills and contacts" that served him well in Kraków.[64]

Schindler was arrested by the Czech secret police, which called him "a spy of big caliber and an especially dangerous type"; he was released after the Munich Agreement (1938) and resumed his work for the Abwehr, gathering intelligence useful in the German invasions of Czechoslovakia and Poland. Schindler joined the Nazi Party in 1939, despite his disinterest in ideology as well as questions raised by the

Nazi examining board over his character. In a one-party state party membership can be crucial for advancement, and Schindler gambled that Germany would soon become Europe's predominant state.[65]

By the time Schindler arrived at Kraków in late 1939, the old Polish city had been transformed into the capital of a quasi-state formed from those parts of Poland not absorbed into the Reich or occupied by the Soviets, who invaded the country within weeks after the Germans began their assault. Hitler's attorney, Hans Frank, presided over Poland as governor-general from Kraków's old royal castle, but his authority was challenged on one side by the German army and on the other by the SS. The administrative ambiguity was a microcosm of the Nazi "system of half-jurisdictions" that left Hitler as supreme arbiter over squabbling subordinates with overlapping authority.[66]

Capitalizing on the administrative ambiguity of occupied Poland, Schindler carved a niche for his ambitions from a land where — more than even Germany itself — brutality was unrestrained by legal scruples, local sentiment, or outside observers. Hitler told Nazi and military officials that in Poland "the devil's work" would be done: it was the "racial laboratory" where methods for exterminating the Jews would be perfected; Poles and other "inferior races" would be reduced to slave labor; and land and other assets would be "Aryanized" on a massive scale.[67]

The nightclub scene in Spielberg's film, showing Schindler lavishing German officials with dinner and expensive wine and gaining their ear through money and charm, encapsulates the reality of Schindler's emergence. As Schindler explained after the war to émigré German director Fritz Lang, he was able to save his Jews with help from highly placed friends, especially in the Abwehr but also in the army's Armaments Inspectorate, who "partly anti-Nazi, or at least opposed to the SS and its methods."[68]

The army's inspector for armaments in Poland, Gen. Maximilian Schindler, was no relation to the much younger Oskar Schindler, but the two men got along well, and many Germans assumed they were father and son. Spielberg ignores this point, much as many other details were edited to maintain a manageably small roster of major characters, but accurately depicts how the appearance of being well connected aids Schindler in securing control over Jewish property. He was not the only carpetbagger to arrive in Kraków, and competition was fierce. Reichsmarschall Hermann Göring decreed the confiscation of all property belonging to Poland's Jews save personal possessions and the equivalent of four hundred dollars in cash. It was a bonanza for the unscrupulous.

Schindler's first coup was to lease a bankrupt Jewish-owned enamelware factory, a defense contractor with Poland's military that would now service Germany's war effort. Enjoying the game of business more than the hard work, Schindler ran his various enterprises with the help of Jewish managers. In the film Schindler has only one Jewish aide-de-camp, Itzhak Stern (Ben Kingsley). In reality three Jews assisted Schindler at various times and in different capacities. Along with Stern, Schindler worked closely with Mietek Pemper and Abraham Bankier. To shape the complicated reality into compelling drama, the screenplay transforms Stern into a composite of all Jews at the top of Schindler's organization.

Kingsley portrays Stern as initially wary of the glib German entrepreneur, but the rapidly declining circumstances of Poland's Jews leave him with few options. Schindler is seen driving hard bargains to secure Jewish "investors," leveraging their catastrophe to his advantage. Even his eagerness to hire Jewish workers begins with the profit motive. "Poles cost more. Why should I hire Poles?" he asks. The cinematic Stern proves almost as adept at manipulating the Nazi system as Schindler and stands as his employer's muted voice of conscience in the film's first half. With a forged work certificate, Stern is able to pass off a teacher as a metal polisher, providing the otherwise doomed man with sanctuary as an "essential worker" at Schindler's plant.

As for Schindler, he begins by describing his Jewish workers as having no purpose but "to make money for me" yet acknowledges Stern's importance by admitting, "I couldn't have done this without you." The one-armed machinist Lowenstein, who thanks him profusely, calling him a "good man," makes Schindler uncomfortable. His interest in the welfare of his employees is entirely proprietary and bound up with his self-invention as a man of influence not to be trifled with. When the ss arbitrarily round up his workers to shovel snow outside Kraków's Jewish ghetto, he is outraged. "I lost a day of production," he tells the ss. When Lowenstein is summarily executed, Schindler angrily responds, "I expect to be compensated!" Schindler gradually begins to echo Stern; the influence of a Jew upon whom he relies and has come to admire broadens his perspective. When Stern's name appears on a list of Jews to be deported from Kraków to the death camps farther east, Schindler storms into the station and plucks his trusted accountant from a train already inching down the tracks, terrorizing the responsible Nazi functionaries with threats to send them to the Russian front for their impertinence.

The character of the fortune-hunting Schindler who arrives in Kraków, however self-serving, is put in context by contrast with his opposite among the Germans, ss Hauptsturmfuhrer Amon Goeth (Ralph Fiennes). As commandant of the Płaszów concentration camp near Kraków, Captain Goeth is offhandedly casual in his murderousness; he shoots inmates of his camp with a rifle from the balcony of his villa for sport, with the disregard of a small boy picking off crows with an air rifle. Schindler knows he is not a good man, but he recognizes evil in Goeth and wonders about the degrees of distance separating them.

Spielberg brilliantly shows Schindler's turning point without a word of dialogue. While riding horses with his mistress on a hill overlooking the Jewish ghetto, Schindler watches with disturbed mien as Goeth's forces raid the Jewish neighborhood, dragging residents from their homes and ransacking everything. Schindler's hilltop conversion, derived from Keneally's novel, is mythic; the event never happened as scripted but alludes to an incident or series of incidents that moved Schindler's heart.[69]

The raid on the ghetto is the film's most terrifying scene; it actually occurred, but in stages, from June 1942 through spring 1943. The raids resulted from ss chief Heinrich Himmler's order to close the ghettos and deport their residents to Poland's five death camps or into slave labor. Filming with unsteady handheld cameras to heighten the grainy, documentary impression, Spielberg captures the berserker hatred of the ss against their mostly hapless victims, many of them elderly or children, and Goeth's determination, as a true believer in Nazi racial dogma, to slaughter them. He promises his men that in "liquidating" the ghetto, they will help change the direction of history, achieving Nazism's goal of a new order based on the supremacy of Aryans and the elimination of Jews. The ss troops pour from trucks, shouting and blowing whistles, their attack dogs snarling, driving out the ghetto's inhabitants with rifle butts and killing some of them at random.[70]

The meager remaining possessions of the Jews are seized. In a poignantly wordless scene the camera pans slowly across a warehouse where confiscated Jewish goods are being sorted: jewelry, children's dolls, Judaica, family photos, even gold fillings — the material remnants of individuals and an entire society lost forever. The brutality is often surreal. An ss man plays Mozart on the piano in a Jewish apartment as his companions spray a neighboring room with their submachine guns.

Spielberg has been charged with ignoring Jewish resistance and supporting the impression that all Jews filed to their death without fighting back. In fact, the depiction mirrors the reality in many cases. Armed resistance was difficult, according to historian Alfred Katz, because many Jews "were on the brink of physical and mental exhaustion" from meager rations and poor living conditions. The Kraków ghetto was home, however, to an armed Jewish group whose several hundred members, including women, were recruited from the Zionist and Communist groups. Purchasing weapons from Polish peasants and receiving some aid from the underground Communist People's Army, the group conducted raids into Kraków, including attacks on nightclubs such as those depicted in the film. Their efforts resulted in severe reprisals.[71] But even one of Spielberg's critics, after castigating him for perpetuating "the image of a weak, feminized Jew," concedes,

"The film is so focused on its purpose, one of its primary strengths, that we are forced to comprehend the intense obsession of the Nazis . . . to destroy all of the Jews."[72] Spielberg could have alluded to armed Jewish resistance with a quick visual, but the cinematic dramatization of that aspect of the Holocaust was left to Polanski, who won an Oscar for his depiction of the Warsaw ghetto uprising in the film *The Pianist* (2002).

Shocked by the destruction of the Kraków ghetto and the Nazis' relentless push toward a "Final Solution of the Jewish Question," Schindler is quietly convinced of the righteousness of providing Jews with sanctuary in his factory but is forced to couch his protection in the language of ownership and profit. "They are mine!" he reminds the SS and distributes bundles of cash to ameliorate their qualms over looking the other way. Goeth may be a convinced ideologue, but like many Nazis in Poland, he is not above exploiting his power of life and death for personal gain.

Some of the most unforgettable images from *Schindler's List* concern the transportation of Jews to death camps in crowded, suffocating cattle cars, the undisguised horror of mass graves, the ashes of burned bodies falling like snowflakes from the chimneys of death camp crematoriums, and the terror of Schindler's female employees sent to Auschwitz by bureaucratic accident. Meanwhile, Schindler and Stern furiously type out their list of essential Jewish workers, saving over eleven hundred lives.

The number looks small alongside the six million victims of the Holocaust, but as the Talmud insists, "He who saves the life of one man saves the world." Yad Vashem, Israel's Holocaust Martyrs and Heroes Remembrance Authority, honored Schindler as a Righteous among the Nations, as shown in the coda of Spielberg's film. Schindler died in 1974. Stern, prominent in the campaign to name Schindler as a Righteous Gentile, died in 1969. Goeth was arrested in the fall of 1944 by the German Criminal Police and charged with corruption and abuse of prisoners. SS regulations prescribed an austere adherence to murder in the name of ideology and sanctioned sadism and self-serving actions. "Individuals who have offended against this principle," Himmler warned, "will be punished according to an order which I issued at the beginning and which threatens: He who takes so much as one mark shall die."[73] Schindler was also arrested in connection with Goeth but was released with the assistance of friends in high places. Goeth survived the Third Reich but not for long. He was convicted of war crimes by a Polish court and hung at Płaszów in 1946.

Schindler's List earned seven Academy Awards, including Best Picture and Best Director.

FLAGS OF OUR FATHERS (2006) AND LETTERS FROM IWO JIMA (2006)

An aged U.S. veteran of Iwo Jima awakens from a battlefield nightmare at the start of *Flags of Our Fathers* as a young author tries to piece together the story of the men who served in that long-ago battle. Iwo Jima was the second-to-last stepping-stone on America's "island hopping" campaign in the Pacific. When it fell, only Okinawa stood between U.S. forces and Japan. Iwo Jima is only five miles long and four and ahalf miles wide, but it is 750 miles from Tokyo and is considered Japanese soil. Six thousand eight hundred Americans from the Third, Fourth, and Fifth Marine divisions gave their lives to take the island during Operation Detachment, as the invasion was code-named; over 18,000 defenders were determined to die holding the eight-square-mile piece of their homeland. Only 216 Japanese were taken prisoner.[74]

Iwo Jima entered American mythology for the iconic photograph of five marines and a navy corpsman raising the Stars and Stripes on a rocky summit. As *Flags of Our Fathers* shows, the photograph circulated above the fold on hundreds of front pages across the United States as the thirty-five-day battle (February — March 1945) continued to rage, becoming a symbol of valor in the face of great adversity. The photo became a postage stamp and was cast in bronze as the U.S. Marine Corps Memorial in Washington DC. The legend of Iwo Jima proved helpful in thwarting postwar proposals to abolish the corps and fold its responsibilities into the U.S. Army.[75]

The public was allowed to believe that the marines in the picture raised the flag under enemy fire, but director Clint Eastwood told the more complicated full story. "Every jackass thinks he knows what war is, especially if he's never been in one," a veteran tells the author whose narrative provides the framework for *Flags of Our Fathers*. "They like things simple — heroes and villains . . . Most times they are not who we think they are." *Flags of Our Fathers* presents a more nuanced picture than John Wayne's *Sands of Iwo Jima* (1949), Hollywood's previous depiction of the battle.

For Eastwood, the embodiment of cool under fire as the star of *Dirty Harry* and *Magnum Force*, *hero* is a word much abused, and public memory is often an oversimplification born of duplicity and wishful thinking. The principal protagonists of *Flags of Our Fathers*, Pfc. Ira Hayes, Pfc. Rene Gagnon, and Pharmacist's Mate John "Doc" Bradley, reject the honor of being called heroes. They were just men under fire doing their job, bonded to each other through training and combat, like millions of other men in uniform. As for the public memory of the flag raising at Iwo Jima, it conflicts with the personal memories of the men in that famous photograph.

Flush from the success of his World War II movie *Saving Private Ryan* (1998), Steven Spielberg purchased film rights for *Flags of Our Fathers*, a best-selling nonfiction book by James Bradley and Ron Powers about the men who raised the flag over Iwo Jima, and eventually brought in Eastwood to direct. Although *Saving Private Ryan* presents a relatively straightforward narrative of heroism, Spielberg chose a director with different ideas for *Flags of Our Fathers*. In Eastwood's hands the story leapfrogs in time. The present is depicted as the final opportunity for the Greatest Generation finally to speak out on the unspeakable things they saw; the Battle of Iwo Jima is juxtaposed with its often unsatisfying consequences in the lives of Hayes (Adam Beach), Gagnon (Jess Bradford), and Bradley (Ryan Phillippe). Dubbed as heroes for dubious reasons and paraded as if in a patriotic circus, the trio is unable to articulate the cold sweat and determination in the midst of horror that was the true measure of their courage. In the case of Hayes, an American Indian, his heroic status was no shield against bigotry.

The marines' ascent up Suribachi, the mountain whose gun emplacements command the volcanic island, is the movie's focal point. On February 23, five days into the battle, a platoon reaches the top, mounts the Stars and Stripes from a hastily rigged metal pole, and fights off Japanese stragglers. Secretary of the Navy James Forrestal, descending from a landing craft after the beach is secure, orders the flag brought to him. An outraged marine commander at the foot of Suribachi decides to keep it for himself and his men, sending a squad up the mountain to raise a second flag for Forrestal, the one captured by combat photographer Joe Rosenthal and distributed to the news media. "I took a lot of other pictures that day — none of them made a difference," an elderly Rosenthal recalls in the movie. "The cruelty [of battle] is unbelievable, but somehow we need to make sense of it. To do that, we need an easy way to understand truth . . . And if you can get a picture? The right picture can win or lose a war."

The United States would have captured Iwo Jima and defeated Japan without that picture, and yet its contribution to morale impressed most observers at the time. The photo was an important symbol for Americans anxious for the war to end in the Pacific even as it was ending in Europe. Germany was crumbling under incessant Allied air raids and in the vise grip of Soviet and Anglo-American armies. Soldiers and civilians feared, and not without reason, that the conquest of Japan would be more difficult and claim even greater casualties. Japanese soldiers had already fought tenaciously over outlying islands, taking a heavy toll on the United States for every inch of ground. Attacks by kamikaze pilots in rickety planes with barely enough fuel for a one-way flight were indicators of Japanese desperation and the destruction of its military-industrial capacity but were also signs of a willingness to charge into death rather than surrender. The photograph of the flag at Iwo Jima steeled American morale and, as the film shows, helped raise money for the war effort in the final war bond drive. Hayes, Gagnon, and Bradley are sent on fund-raising tours, reenacting their ascent of Suribachi on papier-mâché mountains in sports stadiums as fireworks explode, crowds cheer, and brass bands play. The men are troubled; they know they were not the first to reach the mountaintop and arrived only after the summit had been secured; some of their buddies have died since that day on Suribachi; sometimes they even seem uncertain of who exactly was in that picture shouldering the flagpole.

With its combination of live action, computer imaging, and a willingness to show the gore concealed from previous generations of moviegoers, *Saving Private Ryan* set a high bar for battlefield reenactments. Eastwood met the challenge in his memorable re-creation of the landing at Iwo Jima. The air is dominated by U.S. Navy and Marine Corps fighter-bombers spraying the island with rockets. The surrounding sea is covered with hundreds of ships, including fat troop carriers and great battleships with their giant guns lobbing shell after shell onto Suribachi and a swarm of landing craft nosing onto the sand before disgorging platoons of troops.

The marines walk up the gently rising shore into the eerie silence of a desolate, sulfurous, and smoking landscape, wondering about the lack of response from the enemy. "Maybe they're all dead?" one of them offers. Soon enough, the slits open on the hidden pillboxes, and machine gun barrels emerge from their dark interiors to rake the slopes. The big guns dug into the hillsides begin shelling the Americans. In no time bursting fireballs, spent cartridges, and body parts are everywhere.

Flags of Our Fathers is a sophisticated presentation of the psychology of frontline soldiers, the fraught relations between reality and popular memory, and even the power of apparently random events to change or end life. More satisfying as a war movie, in the traditional sense of men and honor tested under fire, is the companion piece Eastwood filmed alongside *Flags of Our Fathers*, *Letters from Iwo Jima*. *Letters* presents the Battle of Iwo Jima from the opposite side, the Japanese perspective, and many of its battle scenes snap into place with those of *Flags of Our Fathers* like pieces of a puzzle.

Eastwood became fascinated with the island's defenders, who fought with the realization that "they weren't coming back," while researching *Flags of Our Fathers*. "I didn't want to tell two stories in the same movie — it's very difficult to do successfully," he said of his decision to direct two films from the material he had gathered.[76] Eastwood was probably alluding to the unsuccessful *Tora! Tora! Tora!* (1970). The Japanese-American coproduction, which presented the attack on Pearl Harbor from both sides, was described by critic Roger Ebert as "one of the deadest, dullest blockbusters ever made."[77]

The Japanese half of *Tora! Tora! Tora!* was not the only foreign-language film from the Axis perspective on World War II to achieve a wide international audience. German writer-director Wolfgang Petersen's *Das Boot* (1981) is dramatic fiction set aboard *U-96*, a submarine prowling the Atlantic in search of Allied shipping. The real-life commander of *U-96*, Heinrich Lehmann-Willenbrock, served as a consultant and heightened the sweaty realism and technical accuracy in the cramped quarters of the wartime submarine. As shown in the movie, the real *U-96* was sunk at berth by Allied bombers near the war's end. The popularity and reputation of *Das Boot* may have inspired Eastwood to explore the enemy in human terms.

Eastwood was especially interested in Iwo Jima's Japanese commander, Lt. Gen. Tadamichi Kuribayashi, and sketched out his character from a slender book of letters the general had written years before he was assigned to his final command. Eastwood's longtime screenwriter, Paul Haggis, in collaboration with a Japanese American writer, Iris Yamashita, wrote the script. It was then translated into Japanese with great care for reproducing the spoken language of the period. "We wanted to show that there were many perspectives," Haggis said, explaining the range of sympathetic and unsympathetic Japanese characters, including real officers as well as their fictionalized subordinates. Haggis and Yamasita pored over Japanese battlefield accounts, while the costume and set designers recreated Iwo Jima's village from a single prewar photograph and Japanese uniforms from period photos, official handbooks, and the memorabilia of military collectors.[78]

Letters from Iwo Jima is built around two sets of characters, the highborn and the low, Kuribayashi (Ken Watanabe) and Baron Nishi

(Tsuyoshi Ihara), and a pair of enlisted men, privates Saigo (Kazunari Ninomiya) and Kashiwara (Takashi Yamaguchi). "Damn this island, the Americans can have it," Saigo says to his friend while digging trenches near the beach. A martinet captain overhears that remark and beats them for their lack of patriotism until the newly arrived Kuribayashi intervenes. The general dresses down the captain and orders the ditch digging to cease. There is interservice rivalry as well as conflict between old dogmas and new tactics. The naval officers and the marines they command assume that a stand will be made on the beach. Kuribayashi has a better idea. He will lure the invaders inland and ambush them in crossfire, raining destruction onto their crowded beachhead from artillery emplacements hidden in the hillsides.

Kuribayashi and Nishi are more traveled and worldly than their subordinates and have little patience with mindless stereotyping of the alleged weakness and lack of will of Americans. Kuribayashi's ivory-handled Colt, similar to the one carried by Patton, was a gift from U.S. Army officers during his stint as deputy military attaché in Washington DC (1928–31). Although of samurai descent, the real-life Kuribayashi, as implied in the film, had opposed Japan's war policies and told his wife in a letter, "The United States is the last country in the world Japan should fight."[79] Kuribayashi earned the respect of the American commander assigned to capture Iwo Jima, marine general Holland Smith, who said, "Of all our adversaries in the Pacific, Kuribayashi was the most redoubtable."[80]

Nishi was a champion equestrian, winning the gold medal for show jumping at the 1932 Olympic Games in Los Angeles. In *Letters from Iwo Jima* Nishi brings his champion horse, Uranus, to the island, only to see the animal killed in an American air raid. Actually, Uranus remained in his home stable and survived his master by one week. The film minimizes true disagreements between Kuribayashi and Nishi but also depicts the synergy and sympathy between them. In a remarkable scene the baron is compassionate to a captured marine. The encounter cannot be confirmed but reflects a legendary incident.

Kuribayashi and Nishi are depicted as fatalists in *Letters*, persisting despite the hopelessness of their mission. "Do you know how many cars the Americans can produce in one year?" Kuribayashi asks, reflecting his respect for America's vast military-industrial potential. Cavalry officers imbued with an aristocratic spirit, they realize their era is ending. In the film Nishi brings Kuribayashi the fatal news that the Combined Fleet, Japan's principal naval strike force, lay at the bottom of the Pacific. Air support at Iwo Jima was also lacking. Most aircraft had been withdrawn to protect the home islands from American air raids already engulfing Japan's cities in firestorms. After Iwo Jima fell, the island would become the forward launch point for American B-17 and B-29 bombers. Kuribayashi and Nishi are honor bound to mount the fiercest, most intelligently conceived resistance possible.

Even before the U.S. armada surrounded Iwo Jima, the Japanese lacked the resources to provision the island's garrison fully. Saigo complains to Kashiwara about yet another supper of weed soup. "We'll be dead before the Americans get here," he says as their comrades grumble over the backbreaking work in intense heat. The troops were busy digging Kuribayashi's twelve-mile honeycomb of tunnels, linking deeply dug bunkers that would withstand the punishing U.S. bombardment and had to be taken foot by foot. Once the attack is under way, the Japanese begin to exhaust their bullets and shells. There is conflict, and contradictory orders, between Kuribayashi and his subordinates. The general wants to conserve the lives of his men in well-coordinated defensive operations, while some of his officers insist on suicide attacks according to their narrow interpretation of bushido, the samurai warrior's code, which had been distorted by Japan's militarists.[81] Regardless of tactics, the battle was lost before it began; Kuribayashi's goal was to inflict maximum casualties on the invaders and to hold out as long as possible, a delaying action to gain time for Japan to prepare its defense of the home islands.[82]

Kuribayashi's body was never identified, and his fate is impossible to determine. Many believe he died after leading a final assault, as depicted in *Letters from Iwo Jima*. "Be proud to die for your country," Kuribayashi tells his men in the film, unsheathing his samurai sword.

Iwo Jima was the rehearsal for an even deadlier amphibious assault in the thrust toward Japan, the Battle of Okinawa, which claimed 12,500 American lives and 250,000 Japanese dead, more than half of them civilians. The anticipated final attack on Japan was aborted after a new weapon, the atom bomb, was dropped on Hiroshima and Nagasaki. The destruction of these cities, triggering Japan's surrender and occupation under Gen. Douglas MacArthur, spared the country even greater deaths, but the devastating new weapon cast an ominous shadow over humanity. Anxiety over the prospect of atomic warfare dominated the conflict to come, the Cold War.

CHAPTER THREE

The Cold War (1947–1991), including the Korean War (1950–1953) and the Vietnam War (1955–1975)

The Cold War can be defined in three ways. First, it was a period of anxiety over the expected conflagration between the United States and the USSR, the aborted nuclear Armageddon between the superpowers. Second, it was a war conducted by other means, a campaign by the capitalist West and the Communist East to sway the minds and win the hearts of the world. It has been described as "a *prestige race*" as the superpowers competed for cultural and scientific as well as military and economic achievements.[1] Finally, it was a web of local conflicts subsumed into the American-Soviet rivalry for global supremacy, along with a pair of major wars, in Korea and Vietnam, in which the United States fought nations allied with and aided by the Soviet Union.

The roots of the Cold War were ideological. Vladimir Lenin did not conceive his seizure of power as merely a coup within Russia but imagined his Communist Party was the vanguard of world historical forces moving against the capitalist economic order. Lenin had not even secured control over Russia before his agents encouraged Communist revolts in Hungary and Germany, where short-lived regimes were proclaimed. The capitalist West held the Soviet Union at bay,

even as anxiety over communism spurred the rise of fascism in Italy
and Nazism in Germany. World War II gave Lenin's successor, Joseph
Stalin, the opportunity to advance the cause. Communism rode into
the Baltic States, Poland, Czechoslovakia, Hungary, Bulgaria, Romania, and East Germany on Soviet tanks. Neighboring Yugoslavia and
Albania fell to local Communists without the aid of Soviet troops.
Other European nations, especially Greece and Italy, were expected
to follow. When Mao Zedong's Communists secured control over
Mainland China in 1949, America's wartime ally President Chiang
Kai-shek and his Nationalist Party fled to the island of Taiwan while
claiming to be the legitimate government for all of China. Without
a common enemy the wartime alliance between the West and the
Soviets disintegrated. An era of uncertainty commenced.

While the Marshall Plan, announced by Secretary of State George
Marshall in 1947, helped rebuild the shattered economies of Western
Europe, President Harry S. Truman adopted the policy of contain-
ment, fencing Communist states behind a hedge of allies spanning
much of the globe. In a speech before the U.S. Congress the president
promised "to support free people who are resisting attempted subjuga-
tion by armed minorities or by outside pressures." Diplomat George
Kennan, who proposed meeting force with counterforce should the
Soviets try to expand beyond their existing ring of client states, helped
shape the Truman Doctrine, which became the cornerstone of U.S.
foreign policy during the Cold War.[2] Tension mounted as the Soviets
blockaded Allied-occupied West Berlin in 1948 and exploded an atom
bomb in 1949. Truman supplied Berlin by air, breaking the blockade,
but was unable to prevent the spread of nuclear weapons. The Berlin Airlift (1948–49) inspired the formation of the North Atlantic
Treaty Organization (NATO), joining the United States, Canada, and
most of Western Europe in a military alliance. The Soviets responded
by establishing the Warsaw Pact, a counter-alliance of Communist
Eastern European nations.

The United States was drawn into war in 1950 when Communist North Korea under Kim Il Sung, grandfather of the country's

current leader Kim Jong Un, invaded South Korea after receiving arms and encouragement from Stalin. With the South Korean army in retreat, the United States persuaded the United Nations (UN) Security Council to authorize an international task force to defend South Korea. The Security Council resolution passed only because the Soviet ambassador was absent from the meeting, in protest of the exclusion of Communist China from the UN, and unable to wield his country's veto.

Although contingents arrived from Great Britain and the Commonwealth, most NATO members, and other nations, Gen. Douglas MacArthur was named UN supreme commander, and the bulk of his forces were American. After a daring amphibious landing at Inchon (1950), MacArthur drove the North Korean army back to the Chinese border, almost reuniting the Korean peninsula, until China rushed over a million "volunteers" into the peninsula. The surprised, outnumbered Americans were pushed back to the 38th parallel, roughly where the war began. The conflict became a political firestorm in the United States after Truman fired MacArthur for disobeying orders and publicly contradicting the president's policy by advocating bombing China and deploying nuclear weapons. Truman's successor, Dwight D. Eisenhower, used the nuclear threat to bring the war to an inconclusive end with an armistice in 1953.

Although the United States lost 23,300 service members before combat ended, Korea has been dubbed America's "Forgotten War."[3] The conflict is overshadowed in public memory by World War II and Vietnam and by anxiety over the atom bomb and Communist subversion during the early Cold War years. It was an unpopular intervention. Surprisingly, given the feverous temperature of anti-Communist sentiment, 56 percent of Americans called it a "useless war" in an October 1951 Gallup Poll.[4]

Regarded without favor during a time when the level of dissent seen during the Vietnam War was impossible, the Korean War never became the subject of a movie that kindled the popular imagination. Director Samuel Fuller's 1951 Korean combat films, *The Steel Helmet* and *Fixed Bayonets*, are much admired by cineastes but little seen by the public. The characteristic film from the war's aftermath, *The Bridges at Toko-Ri* (1954), is a major production starring William Holden, Grace Kelly, Fredric March, and Mickey Rooney. Impressive as is the thrilling aerial photography and the realism of its rough sea deck landings by jet fighter planes on aircraft carriers, the picture's screenplay adheres to the era's standard Hollywood playbook and holds little interest nowadays, and its theme of combat pilots confronting fear is better handled in *Twelve O'Clock High*. Few movies were made about Korea in later years. In director Robert Altman's satirical *M.A.S.H.* (1970) Korea was generally understood as a stand-in for Vietnam, and the film was soon eclipsed in memory by the long-running TV comedy it inspired (1972–83), which was more focused on likable characters than the war. *Inchon!* (1981), a titanic box office disaster, was dismissed as propaganda for its connection with Korean religious leader Sun Myung Moon, who financed the project.

The Cold War conflict at home, often subsumed under the heading of "McCarthyism," after the anti-Communist crusade of Senator Joseph McCarthy, dominated public attention during the 1950s and has received more attention than the Korean War in scholarship as well as popular culture. After Soviet archives were opened to scholars in the early 1990s, including records of the Soviet Committee for State Security, the KGB, and its predecessor agencies as well as the American Communist Party, whose archives were deposited in Moscow, there could be little doubt that American Communist leaders willingly conducted espionage on behalf of the USSR. Communists acting as Soviet agents gave valuable intelligence on U.S. diplomacy and technology, including the atom bomb, and spied on Trotskyites and Russian émigrés.[5]

Several celebrated cases of espionage dominated news and public opinion. One of the most notorious among them concerned State Department official Alger Hiss, accused by former Communist journalist Whittaker Chambers of passing diplomatic secrets to the Soviets. A contemporary columnist called the case, with no exaggeration, "a controversy which has shaken a generation."[6] Hiss resolutely maintained his innocence, even after a perjury conviction stemming from his testimony before the House Un-American Activities Committee (HUAC). A patrician Democratic Party insider, Hiss was turned into a symbol of "pink" and treasonous liberalism by the Right. Yet partisan motives did not mean that Hiss was innocent; his guilt was finally established with the opening of Soviet archives after the end of the Cold War.[7] His conviction in 1950 was secured by the introduction of circumstantial evidence by Congressman Richard M. Nixon and became a springboard for Nixon's rise in American politics.

More serious were the charges leveled against Ethel and Julius Rosenberg. The married couple was convicted of passing atomic secrets to the USSR on the testimony of a coconspirator, Ethel's brother David Greenglass. They were executed in 1953. Although the Communist-led Left proclaimed their innocence and impugned their conviction as a miscarriage of justice, liberal columnist Max Lerner spoke for the national mood at the time when he declared, "The sentence is drastic, yet it is scarcely possible to challenge its justice."[8] Most Americans believed that possession of the atomic bomb by the Soviets made nuclear war more likely and that the Rosenbergs had exposed their fellow citizens to the threat of annihilation.[9]

The apprehension over Communist influence in the United States put a chill on some aspects of American culture. In 1947 HUAC held highly publicized hearings into allegations of Communist influence in Hollywood. Congressional investigators eager for headlines cited a decade of political activism among movie stars to justify the inquest. The victory of the Screen Writers Guild as a bargaining unit in Hollywood was interpreted as a victory for the Left. In World War II Hollywood made a few pro-Soviet movies, such as *Mission to Moscow* (1943) and *Song of Russia* (1944), which were viewed with suspicion once the Cold War began. In the war years stars such as Danny Kaye and Myrna Loy joined the Hollywood Democratic Committee and spoke out for the New Deal and the United Nations as well as defeating the Axis. The FBI began an extensive surveillance program of Hollywood actors, directors, and writers suspected of ties to the Communist Party or the Soviet Union, despite the wartime alliance. Long before the HUAC hearings, "the Hollywood right accused movie industry activists of associating with Communists and insisted that their political ideas posed a threat to national security." Liberals and leftists scoffed at such claims, especially the outspoken Edward G. Robinson, whose refusal to denounce the Communists led one fan to castigate him for associating with "large numbers of commies."[10]

HUAC issued subpoenas for dozens of people working in the movie industry; most of them testified, whether gladly or with reluctance. Invoking First and Fifth Amendment protections for freedom of association and against self-incrimination, a group of screenwriters, directors, and producers, dubbed the "Hollywood Ten," refused to answer questions about their Communist affiliations. They were fined, imprisoned, and barred from working in Hollywood. The Hollywood Ten were only the most prominent names on a blacklist of several hundred figures in the movie and cultural industries, including Stella Adler, Charles Chaplin, Howard DaSilva, John Garfield, Dashiell Hammett, Lillian Hellman, Burl Ives, Arthur Miller, and Zero Mostel. Some were Communists, but many were simply associated with progressive causes. "As damaging to the American cinema as the loss of individual talent was the pervasive mood of fear, distrust, and self-loathing that settled over Hollywood in the wake of the hearings," wrote film historian David Cook.[11]

The FBI's extensive monitoring of Hollywood never found evidence that anyone in the industry had engaged in espionage, yet the agency worried that Communists in the industry would use movies to spread subversive ideas. FBI director J. Edgar Hoover was wary of HUAC, regarding the committee as a panel of grandstanders likely to undermine his own counterintelligence programs, but he supplied HUAC with dossiers identifying Communists in the movie industry.[12]

The most notorious witness in HUAC's investigation of communism in American culture, Elia Kazan, had won an Oscar for *Gentleman's Agreement* (1947) and acclaim for the Broadway premiere of *Death of a Salesman* (1949) and for transposing *A Streetcar Named Desire* from stage to screen (1951). In 1952 Kazan admitted to having been a member of the Communist Party from 1934 through 1936 and named the other members of his cadre in New York's seminal Group Theatre, including playwright Clifford Odets and acting teacher Lee Strasberg. He was vilified as a turncoat by the American Left until his death; some celebrities refused to applaud when he received a lifetime achievement Oscar at the 1999 Academy Awards. As biographer Richard Schickel explained, "He became the celebrated informer — the namer of names nearly everyone could name, the great symbolic stooge, rat fink of the era."[13]

In the aftermath Kazan directed a cinematic landmark, *On the Waterfront* (1954), with screenwriter Budd Schulberg. After his past Communist Party membership had been exposed in HUAC hearings, Schulberg felt compelled to name other Communists in order to continue working in the movie industry. Widely interpreted as a justification for informants, *On the Waterfront* starred Marlon Brando as a longshoreman who finally agrees to crack the silence and testify against the mobsters controlling his union.[14]

Despite or perhaps because of the pressure of McCarthyism, the 1950s were culturally fertile years. In Hollywood, Cold War anxiety often played out in the crime dramas of film noir.[15] The canon of American fiction was enriched by the publication of J. D. Salinger's *The Catcher in the Rye* (1951), Ralph Ellison's *Invisible Man* (1952), and Vladimir Nabokov's *Lolita* (1955) as well as the emergence of Saul Bellow, Norman Mailer, and Flannery O'Connor. Poet Allen Ginsberg and novelist Jack Kerouac were the most prominent figures in the Beat movement, which took an oppositional stand against the postwar drift of American society; like the folk music revival that began with such blacklisted figures as Pete Seeger and Burl Ives, it became a milieu for leftist politics. By the early Cold War years the center of gravity in visual art had shifted from Paris to New York, where the abstract expressionism of Jackson Pollock and Marc Rothko challenged assumptions about art. With the ascent of Elvis Presley, rock and roll music emerged by 1956 as the soundtrack of young America, the first loud stirrings of the Baby Boom.

The science fiction dream of space exploration became a reality in the 1950s with missiles developed from the Nazi German rocket program. The USSR beat the United States into space with the launch of *Sputnik 1* (1957). The satellite had no military value, but the advent of missiles capable of placing *Sputnik* in orbit signaled that no city in America was safe from atomic warheads launched on intercontinental ballistic missiles. *Sputnik 1* triggered a "space race" between the superpowers, which vied to launch communication and spy satellites, interplanetary probes, manned space missions, and a moon landing. Eisenhower determined that a new civilian agency, the National Aeronautics and Space Administration (NASA), would take the lead in space, and John F. Kennedy promised to put Americans on the moon by 1970, a pledge fulfilled by *Apollo 11* (1969).

To maintain surveillance over Soviet nuclear and military capabilities, the United States violated the USSR's airspace with overflights by U-2 spy planes, which flew above the reach of surface-to-air missiles. In 1960, however, a U-2 piloted by Francis Gary Powers descended from engine trouble and was shot down. When the Soviets announced the downing of the jet on the eve of a summit meeting between Eisenhower and Premier Nikita Khrushchev, the United States, assuming that Powers had died and his plane had disintegrated, claimed that the aircraft was a weather plane that had strayed off course. Khrushchev then revealed that Powers had been captured, catching Washington in a lie and jeopardizing the summit. Eisenhower did not apologize but promised to end the U-2 flights. Although the summit took place, no progress was made toward a hoped-for agreement to limit the nuclear arms race.

The Cold War never erupted into a military contest in Europe, where NATO and the Warsaw Pact maintained a balance of power. Symbolizing military and political stalemate on the Continent, the Berlin Wall was erected in 1961 by the Communist East Germans to halt the exodus of its citizens to the West. From 1961 until the Wall fell in 1989, East German soldiers and police killed six hundred people who attempted to escape across or under the wall. U.S. troops watched from their border post facing the wall, "Checkpoint Charlie," the site of a near-confrontation between American and Soviet tanks in 1961.

Elsewhere in the world, the U.S. Central Intelligence Agency (CIA) was active in overthrowing suspected pro-Soviet leaders and supporting friendly regimes through covert operations in Iran, Laos, the Philippines, Guatemala, and Congo. In the Middle East the Soviets armed and supported Syria, Egypt, and Palestinian militants, while the United States aided Israel and pro-Western states such as Saudi Arabia and Jordan. After the Yom Kippur War with Israel (1973), Egypt expelled its Soviet advisors and became a U.S. ally.

Only once did the Cold War edge toward a nuclear showdown, in the Cuban Missile Crisis (1962), and only once after Korea did the United States engage in a full-scale war against a Soviet ally, in Vietnam. Cuba became a flashpoint after Fidel Castro's guerrillas overthrew the country's pro-American dictatorship, established a Communist regime, and began expropriating property owned by American businesses. The Kennedy administration favored the overthrow of Castro but was uncertain over the extent of U.S. involvement. A force of fourteen hundred anti-Communist Cuban exiles trained and armed by the United States landed at the Bay of Pigs (1961), hoping to topple Castro. The United States did not provide the expected sea and air support for the operation, and the Cuban military quickly thwarted the invasion in what became a major embarrassment for Kennedy. Despite dwindling American support, Cuban exile groups continued a campaign of commando raids against Castro for many years.

In October 1962 Khrushchev took the biggest gamble of the Cold War by installing ballistic missiles in Cuba, capable of striking most cities in the continental United States within minutes of launch. The Soviet bases, photographed by a U-2 reconnaissance mission, were regarded as a provocative threat. After weighing options, such as invading Cuba or launching air strikes, Kennedy announced a blockade of the island. Nuclear war seemed imminent, the superpowers were on a collision course, and Americans stockpiled canned goods and prepared to retreat to the nearest fallout shelter. The crisis abated when Soviet ships, bearing more missiles for Cuba, turned back before crossing the U.S. Navy's picket line. Eventually, the USSR removed the missiles it had already based in Cuba in return for America's promise not to invade the island. The Kennedy administration's response to the Cuban Missile Crisis waited for depiction in Hollywood until the made-for-TV *Missiles of October* (1974), based on Attorney General Robert Kennedy's memoir *Thirteen Days* (1969), and the Kevin Costner film *Thirteen Days* (2000), drawn from a book containing newly declassified information, Ernest May and Philip Zelikow's *The Kennedy Tapes: Inside the White House during the Cuban Missile Crisis* (1997).

American involvement in Vietnam began during World War II, when the Office of Strategic Services (OSS), the forerunner of the CIA, armed and trained Communist leader Ho Chi Minh's Vietminh guerrillas to raid Japanese outposts in Indochina. The United States stepped aside when France reoccupied the colony after the war. Mobilizing nationalism and anticolonial resentment, the charismatic yet enigmatic Ho led a fierce rebellion against the French and a bloody civil war against rival Vietnamese factions from the dense marshes and impenetrable jungles of his country.[16]

The United States provided assistance to the French from 1950 but declined requests for military intervention. Ho fought on against the French and their local allies, gambling that a long struggle would wear down the patience of the French public. He repeated the strategy in the following decade. "Americans do not like long, inconclusive wars — and this is going to be a long, inconclusive war," North Vietnam's premier Pham Van Dong warned even before U.S. combat troops entered the fray.[17] After their stronghold at Dienbienphu fell to the Vietminh in 1954, the French withdrew from Indochina. In 1954 Vietnam was partitioned at the Geneva Conference into a Communist North, headquartered in Hanoi, and a pro-Western South, with Saigon as its capital, in a deal brokered by Chinese premier Zhou Enlai.[18]

The Truman administration already accepted the "Domino Principle," which assumed that Southeast Asia would follow if Vietnam fell to communism.[19] As part of the Cold War policy of containing communism, Eisenhower declared South Vietnam as essential to U.S. security. Pledging to "support any friend, oppose any foe," Kennedy stepped up assistance. By 1962 twenty-five thousand U.S. advisors were in the country, and they were inevitably drawn into combat with South Vietnam's Communist guerrillas, the National Liberation Front, or Vietcong, armed and led by Hanoi. At first the Kennedy administration supported South Vietnam's autocratic president, Ngo Dinh Diem, calling him "the cornerstone of the Free World in Southeast Asia, the keystone to the arch, the finger in the dike." Kennedy soon became disillusioned by Diem's corruption and failure to impose security despite waves of repression. Journalist Stanley Karnow, reporting from Vietnam, recalled that "the villages, open to Diem's troops by day, were run by the Vietcong at night," a situation that persisted through the various administrations governing South Vietnam.[20] Kennedy acquiesced to a military coup that resulted in Diem's murder in November 1963, three weeks before Kennedy's assassination in Dallas.

The new U.S. president, Lyndon B. Johnson, took a tougher stand against North Vietnam, which sent supplies and reinforcements to the Vietcong down the Ho Chi Minh Trail, a fifteen hundred – mile network of jungle paths. In 1964 Johnson expanded the war after U.S. destroyers were allegedly attacked by North Vietnamese torpedo boats near its coast in the Gulf of Tonkin. Authorized by Congress through the Gulf of Tonkin Resolution, Johnson ordered air raids on North Vietnamese supply depots. He assumed Ho could be cowed by a show of force, but the Communist regime pursued its agenda of unifying Vietnam with single-minded determination. Generously supplied by the Soviet Union, the Vietnam People's Army was reckoned as one of the best combat infantry forces in the world and proved more than a match for South Vietnam's military.

After the Vietcong struck at U.S. airbases, 2,500 marines landed at Da Nang and waded ashore for the cameras, to evoke memories of successful amphibious operations in World War II. The strength of U.S. combat forces in Vietnam, commanded by Gen. William

Westmoreland, grew rapidly to 184,000 by 1966 and 500,000 in 1968. Despite the massive deployment, the Johnson administration regarded Vietnam as a "limited war" fought with conventional arms and avoiding direct confrontation with the USSR and China, which by then had broken with the Soviet bloc and was engaged in armed clashes with its former ally along the Sino-Soviet border in the 1960s.

Escalation was the term used by U.S. politicians and pundits to describe the sharp upward spiral of America's commitment. Meanwhile, North Vietnam embarked on a total war with a complete mobilization of its resources. The United States launched the most concentrated air attacks in history on the Ho Chi Minh Trail but failed to cut North Vietnamese infiltration. When not engaged in combat, U.S. troops lived in a lavishly stocked re-creation of American life, complete with a television station whose weather forecasts — not of Vietnam but from across the United States — were delivered by attractive "weather girls." The Robin Williams comedy *Good Morning, Vietnam* (1987) focuses on the Armed Forces Radio Service, whose American-style broadcasts reproduced a sense of home for the troops.

The battle for the countryside, where the majority of Vietnamese lived, was brutal. The Vietcong and the South Vietnamese executed tens of thousands of villagers, and the U.S. pacification program included torture of suspects and the destruction of communities suspected of harboring guerrillas. In the most notorious incident U.S. infantry killed nearly three hundred villagers, including women, children, and the elderly, at My Lai, a village suspected of harboring the Vietcong (1968). The troops involved were convinced that villagers knew where the Vietcong had planted mines and booby traps but refused to warn them.[21] United States "search and destroy" patrols were conducted in a frustrating and deadly routine; the enemy was usually unseen, sniping from the jungle with Russian-made AK-47 assault rifles, a durable and easy-to-use weapon.

South Vietnam depended on America for survival, yet the alliance was thorny. The United States deemed the country's military as largely unreliable, and relations with South Vietnam's principal leaders, President Nguyen Van Thieu and Prime Minister Nguyen Cao Ky, were sometimes testy. "The Vietnamese Communists always treat us as a puppet of America," Ky complained in a television interview. "But the American people also consider us a puppet of America."[22]

Domestic opposition to the Vietnam War became the prevailing issue in U.S. politics and a determining factor in the war's outcome. The 1960s were already a time of social and cultural upheaval; the civil rights movement galvanized many young people with a sense of purpose, and the new music pouring from transistor radios and phonographs, with the Beatles and Bob Dylan in the lead, endowed the generation coming of age with a sense of identity. A counterculture took shape, and politics shifted toward radicalism in light of the draft. Peacetime conscription, which continued after the Korean War in order to support the nation's global network of bases and alliances, had been viewed as an inconvenience at worst by young Americans, until the buildup for Vietnam resulted in much larger call-ups of draft-age men. As casualties mounted, the prospect of military service in a far-away war sent tens of thousands into the streets in protest and became the issue around which the New Left could mobilize. In October 1967 fifty thousand demonstrators marched on the Pentagon calling for an end to the war in an event documented by Norman Mailer's 1968 nonfiction novel *Armies of the Night*. North Vietnamese diplomat Ha Van Lao likened the American streets to "a front in the war."[23]

The war continued to escalate. In November 1967 Johnson ordered air attacks within five miles of Hanoi, and the press began reporting on the "Credibility Gap." The Johnson administration and the Pentagon claimed the war was going well, but there was much skepticism over official reports on the progress of battle and the casualties inflicted on an enemy that seldom left bodies behind. Defense Secretary Robert McNamara, considered the architect of American strategy, grew reluctant to continue the fighting and resigned in 1968. Many years later he pondered his experience with documentary filmmaker Errol Morris in the Oscar-winning *Fog of War* (2003). "What is morally appropriate in a wartime environment? How much evil must we do in order to do good?" McNamara asked. "Recognize that at times you will have to engage in evil, but minimize it. People did not understand at that time there were recommendations and pressures that would carry the risk of war with China and carry the risk of nuclear war. And he [Johnson] was determined to prevent it."

American hopes for victory dimmed after a series of coordinated attacks in January 1968 coinciding with Tet, the Vietnamese lunar New Year. The Tet Offensive was conceived by Gen. Vo Nguyen Giap, the Vietnamese Communist commander who had defeated the French at Dienbienphu, and involved simultaneous assaults on a hundred towns and cities in the country's South by North Vietnamese regulars and Vietcong guerrillas. The U.S. embassy in Saigon was seized and occupied for several hours. Network television flashed images of pain and doubt on the faces of GIs into American living rooms. Vietnam was the first televised war, and unlike future conflicts — from Grenada through the Persian Gulf, Iraq, and Afghanistan — the news was uncensored. Some commentators wondered how American morale would have fared in World War II had television cameras accompanied the landings at Anzio or Iwo Jima. In the aftermath of Tet, Walter Cronkite, the avuncular anchor of *CBS Evening News* and America's most trusted newscaster, declared, "The bloody experience of Vietnam is to end in a stalemate."

The impact of Tet was real but has often been oversimplified. With increasing casualties, public enthusiasm for the war had slipped since the escalation began. Although the Gallup Poll graphed this declining support, it also registered that many Americans were not antiwar as such but against the war as it was being fought and favored an all-out assault on North Vietnam. The United States had no way of knowing that Tet was also disheartening to the Vietnamese Communists. Years after achieving victory, Gen. Tran Do complained of heavy casualties and added: "In all honesty, we didn't achieve our main objective, which was to spur uprisings throughout the south. As for making an impact in the United States, it had not been our intention — but it turned out to be a fortunate result."[24]

Attacked from all sides, Johnson announced he would not seek another term as president. The eventual nominees of the major parties, Democratic vice president Hubert Humphrey and his Republican challenger, Richard M. Nixon, both promised an end to America's combat role in Vietnam. Lt. Gen. Curtis LeMay, running with Governor George Wallace on the American Independent Party ticket, was a hard-liner widely quoted for promising to bomb North Vietnam "back to the Stone Age."

Determined to achieve "peace with honor," President Nixon pursued a program of "Vietnamization," even though the phasing out of U.S. combat troops in favor of South Vietnamese forces led to rapid advances by North Vietnam in the spring of 1972. He also adapted LeMay's proposed tactics, deploying massive airpower, including B-52s dropping heavy payloads, to break the spring offensive and as the strategy for ending the war with a stepped-up air offensive against North Vietnam's cities in December 1972. American losses were heavy. North Vietnam shot down fifteen B-52s and eleven other aircraft in December, but the bombing broke the deadlock at the long-stalled Paris peace conference. North Vietnamese negotiator Le Duc Tho reached agreement with Secretary of State Henry Kissinger and signed an accord on January 27, 1973. The rapid release of American POWs was a negotiating point. Since 1961 nearly nine thousand U.S. aircraft had been lost over Indochina, and nearly six hundred crewmen had been captured. Many of them were treated as "war criminals" by their captors and tortured at the "Hanoi Hilton" and other camps.[25]

Nixon believed he had given Thieu a chance to survive and had obtained an honorable peace. More realistically, Kissinger negotiated to provide a "decent interval" between America's withdrawal and North Vietnam's inevitable conquest of the South. Kissinger was proven correct. Saigon fell to the North on April 30, 1975, with unforgettable televised images of anti-Communist Vietnamese clinging to the U.S. helicopters evacuating the embassy.

Some 58,000 Americans died during the Vietnam War, and another 300,000 were wounded. Vietnamese civilian and military deaths may have topped 2 million. The conflict was viewed as a debacle, a scar on America's self-image, and resulted in at least a decade of caution in foreign policy and military intervention.

Nixon hoped to make his impression on history through foreign policy, and although he will always be remembered for the domestic Watergate scandal, his foreign policy initiatives were significant. Sensing an opportunity to exploit the bitter rift between the USSR and China, Nixon pursued a policy of détente with the Soviets to ease tensions while opening relations with the Chinese, over opposition from the fervent anti-Communist wing of the Republican Party, at a time when the United States still recognized the exiled Nationalist regime on Taiwan as the legitimate government of China. Kissinger flew secretly to Beijing in 1971 through the good offices of Pakistan's military, which enjoyed close ties with Communist China and the United States, for discussions with Zhou Enlai. The following year Nixon startled the world by flying to Beijing for a summit with Communist leader Mao Zedong. Their meeting was the turning point leading to Mainland China's admission to the UN and the end to the country's diplomatic and economic isolation.[26]

The aftermath of Nixon's resignation in 1974, following the Watergate scandal, brought many reasons to believe that communism was on the march across the world. Marxists took power in the newly independent African nations of Angola and Mozambique, armed by the Soviets and supported by Cuban troops battling United States-supplied rebels backed by South Africa. In Southeast Asia the fall of Laos and Cambodia to local Communist insurgents after North Vietnam's victory seemed to validate the Domino Principle, but discord among the Communist nations of Asia soon became apparent. In 1979 Vietnam defeated the Chinese behemoth in a border war and invaded Cambodia, toppling the murderous, Chinese-supported Khmer Rouge regime.

At the end of 1979 the Cold War heated up when the USSR sent troops into Afghanistan to depose an idiosyncratic Communist regime and install a Communist faction more to the Kremlin's liking. Gen.

Ivan Pavlovsky commanded the Soviet forces; his military record included crushing the "Prague Spring" in 1968 by forcibly removing Czechoslovakia's Communist reformer Alexander Dubček. This time Pavlovsky operated with even less concern for the pretense of appearances. The deposed Afghan Communist leader was murdered by his Soviet bodyguards and replaced by a compliant Party boss who "invited" the Soviet army to restore order. A rural insurgency of Muslim jihadists, the mujahideen, was already under way, and the sudden presence of foreign troops only inflamed the uprising. The various mujahideen groups found support in Saudi Arabia, Iran, and across the Muslim world. The United States responded to the Soviet invasion by sending arms and money to the mujahideen, funneling aid through Pakistan's military intelligence agency, the InterServices Intelligence (ISI). Before long Afghanistan became the Soviet Vietnam.[27]

Angered by the Soviet move into Afghanistan, President Jimmy Carter withdrew the SALT II arms control treaty from Senate consideration, declared an embargo on grain sales to the USSR, and ordered the U.S. boycott of the 1980 Moscow Summer Olympic Games. Military spending increased, and although the draft was not restored, young men were once again required to register for Selective Service. Cruise missiles and stealth warplanes, which soon became key components in the American arsenal, were developed during the Carter administration.

Defense spending swelled under Carter's successor, Ronald Reagan, a president determined to restore American prestige after Vietnam and take a tougher, oppositional stand against the Soviet bloc. Reagan was not content to contain communism or maintain a fragile peace. His objective was to win the Cold War.

The coming decade brought many surprises and was rife with paradox. Reagan, an anti-Communist activist and Cold Warrior since the 1940s, became a peacemaker determined to defeat the "Evil Empire." Reagan fought the Soviets with economic pressure and denial of technology to squeeze the beleaguered Communist economies. Previous presidents viewed trade as an avenue for cooperation; Reagan deployed trade policy as war by other means. He opposed the Soviet-Cuban allied Sandinista regime in Nicaragua by arming the Contra rebels, and aided right-wing dictators in El Salvador and Guatemala against leftist insurgents. Reagan stationed nuclear weapons in Western Europe, angering the local populations but unsettling the Soviets.

Sapped by Afghanistan and challenges in Eastern Europe from Poland's Solidarity movement under Lech Walesa and the installation of Polish Catholic prelate Karol Wojtyła as Pope John Paul II, the USSR continued to stumble after the death of Communist Party leader Leonid Brezhnev in 1982. Replaced in quick succession by two elderly Party bosses who died soon after assuming office, the country's leadership remained uncertain until the ascent of Mikhail Gorbachev as president of the USSR in 1985. Gorbachev inherited a stagnant economy and a society that had lost faith in the Marxist principles on which it was founded. Gorbachev realized that internal reforms and amicable relations with the West were essential for the survival of the Communist system. He established a surprisingly cordial rapport with Reagan and Britain's Conservative prime minister, Margaret Thatcher, during a series of summit meetings.

Reagan's belligerent peacemaking, including his demand during a speech at the Berlin Wall for Gorbachev to "tear down this wall!" had results. Treaties were signed to reduce nuclear weapons, and the Soviets reduced troop levels in Eastern Europe and withdrew from Afghanistan. In reforming his own society through twin campaigns of perestroika (reorganization) and glasnost (openness), Gorbachev unleashed forces he could not control. The effort to turn the Soviet economy from guns to butter unleashed desire for the more lavish consumer lifestyles glimpsed in Western broadcasts and advertising, and the process of making the Communist system freer only increased demands for greater freedom. By the end of 1989 the Berlin Wall was demolished by East German citizens, the Communist regimes of Eastern Europe were swept from power, and Germany was on its way to reunification. In China a pro-democracy movement was crushed by troops at Beijing's Tiananmen Square; the country's Communist rulers maintained political control while opening their economy to state-guided capitalism.

Gorbachev survived a military coup by Communist hard-liners in the summer of 1991, but his grip on authority could never be regained. The coup marked the ascent of Russian president Boris Yeltsin, whose bold opposition to the attempted military marked him as the first significant post-Soviet leader in the region. The pent-up nationalism of captive ethnic groups led to ethnic violence and anti-Soviet rioting in many areas as the Soviet Union broke apart during 1991 into twelve independent republics. Border conflicts and secessionist movements continue to trouble the region in the twenty-first century.

As 1991 ended, Gorbachev handed over the Soviet nuclear codes to Yeltsin as Russia became the legal successor state to the USSR. The Soviet Union was formally dissolved on December 26, 1991, as the red flag was lowered from the Kremlin for the last time. The Cold War was over, a conflict concluded not by military victory but through the defeat of a failed idea, but history did not end with the triumph of Western democracy and capitalism. The world was confronted by a series of crises, including civil war in the former Yugoslavia, the Rwandan Genocide, and the rise of Islamist terrorist groups bent on overturning Western hegemony.

THE MANCHURIAN CANDIDATE (1962)

The Manchurian Candidate opens in Korea, 1952, but the film's only combat scene concludes swiftly as a Soviet airborne unit ambushes an American night patrol led to the front by a treacherous Korean guide. The GIs are clubbed with rifle butts, rushed into waiting helicopters, and flown to Manchuria, where they are programmed by a team of Chinese and Russian psychologists from the Pavlov Institute. The Cold War is the conflict named in the screenplay, and in the film the Communist bloc expects to win through subversion rather than invasion.

Directed by John Frankenheimer and written by George Axelrod from the best-selling novel by Richard Condon, an author who used the thriller genre as social critique, the plot of *Manchurian Candidate* was inspired by reports that "brainwashing" had been used to coerce several thousand U.S. P O W s into signing anti-American "petitions" or "confessing" to war crimes while in Chinese captivity. The word *brainwash*, first used in 1950 by the *Miami News*'s Edward Hunter, a journalist in the pay of the C I A, was applied to the mistaken belief that Chinese or Soviet science had developed groundbreaking techniques for mind control. As the C I A later discovered in a study commissioned from neurologist Harold Wolff and Cornell University's Lawrence Hinkle, the Communists achieved their confessions only through the brutal application of methods long known to police interrogators. Condon had contacts within the intelligence establishment and was apparently aware of C I A mind control experiments in the early 1950s involving the hallucinogenic drug L S D and hypnosis. He may also have derived the title for his novel from a C I A report about P O W s repatriated through the Soviet Union who "apparently had a blank period of disorientation while passing through a special zone in Manchuria."[28] The alleged brainwashing of P O W s, a topic of public anxiety in the 1950s, is largely remembered today through its depiction in *The Manchurian Candidate*.

In the book and screenplay the subconscious mind of one of the P O W s taken by the Soviets, S. Sgt. Raymond Shaw (Laurence Harvey), was subverted through a combination of drugs and psychological pressure. Returning home as an unknowing, unwitting assassin, Shaw is programmed to respond to seemingly innocuous commands given over the telephone by an unseen caller.

The Manchurian Candidate affirms American anxiety over the enemy within while satirizing the anti-Communist excesses of McCarthyism. By the time Condon's book was published in 1959, and more so before the film's release, McCarthyism had ebbed from its high-water mark, and Senator Joe McCarthy died in 1957, after having been censored by the U.S. Senate. It is not true that McCarthy was able to stifle all overt manifestations of dissent against his program during the height of his power (1950–54). The term *McCarthyism* was coined in a 1950 column by *New York Post* commentator Max Lerner, who lashed out against the senator's "smell of moral decay," "verbal hooliganism," and "unscrupulous shifting of ground."[29] In 1953 cartoonist Al Kapp satirized McCarthy in his popular daily comic strip, *Pogo*, introducing a short-lived, conniving character called Simple J. Malarkey against the objections of some newspapers, which threatened to cut *Pogo* from their pages.[30] And yet as historian Stephen J. Whitfield recently put it, because of McCarthyism "the spectrum of reputable opinion narrowed, shriveling the framework within which realistic political changes were entertained."[31] The American Communist Party was neither a specter nor a democratic institution but a tightly knit organization whose agenda was determined by Soviet policy. The anti-Communist crusade associated with McCarthyism, however, dampened free expression, endangered constitutional rights, and became an excuse for the Right to reverse the New Deal and for segregationists to condemn the rising civil rights movement as being Communist inspired. In the end the excesses of McCarthyism undermined the anti-Communist movement.

In the film Raymond Shaw's stepfather, Senator Johnny Iselin (James Gregory), is an easy-to-spot stand-in for McCarthy. Bumptious and often drunk, Iselin hurls scurrilous attacks against public figures and maintains that he has a list with the names of Communists holding sensitive government jobs, but the exact number of names changes each time he raises the charge. Iselin is a dangerous fool controlled by his wife, Eleanor Shaw Iselin (Angela Lansbury), a twentieth-century Lady Macbeth.

The Manchurian Candidate hurls the ultimate insult at McCarthyism by accusing the Iselins of being Soviet agents, their fanatical patriotism a blind for treason. As film critic Pauline Kael observed in a seminal essay, the film played with an idea many Americans already harbored. "Why, if Joe McCarthy were working for the Communists, he couldn't be doing them more good!"[32] The twist was that the Iselins did not know that their son, the sullen and resentful Raymond, had been turned into a key player in their own game while in Communist captivity. Raymond and his parents believe the story constructed at the Pavlov Institute and implanted in the minds of the men from the captured night patrol that he single-handedly saved his unit from a superior enemy force.

Raymond returns home covered in unwarranted glory, awarded the Medal of Honor upon the recommendation of his commander and fellow captive, Capt. Bennett Marco (Frank Sinatra). Marco, who has no idea he has been brainwashed, suffers from the recurring nightmare whose depiction endows *The Manchurian Candidate* with scenes of surreal drama. The nightmare, representing a garbled memory of his captivity, involves a line of drowsy, sleep-deprived U.S. POWs seated onstage facing a lecture hall filled with Russian, Chinese, and North Korean auditors. The smiling lecturer, Dr. Yen Lo (Khigh Dheigh), injects a dose of levity into his discussion of how "our American visitors" have been "conditioned" over the course of several days. Like an academic delivering a conference paper, Dr. Yen cites a raft of scholarly articles to support his contention that the moral conscience of a subject can be suspended under hypnosis. As proof, he calmly asks Raymond, an unpopular sergeant, to kill the soldier in his unit he least dislikes. Raymond follows his instructions without question and shoots the man, splattering his blood across a huge photograph of Stalin overlooking the stage. Marco wakes up screaming each night. With a little investigating, he learns that the unit's other survivors suffer from variations of the same bad dream.

A troubled young man before enlisting in the army to escape his hated stepfather and incestuous mother (a point made clear in the novel and suggested by a prolonged frontal kiss on screen), Raymond pads through the film like a sleepwalker. When he answers a phone call from his Communist handler, he hears a voice saying, "Raymond, why don't you pass the time playing a little solitaire?" The command triggers a responsive state in which Raymond is receptive to any command, including assassinating the Republican presidential candidate at the party's national convention with a sniper's rifle from a window commanding the hall. If successful, the plot would place the nomination — and possibly the nation — in the hands of the dead man's running mate, Raymond's stepfather, Senator Iselin.

The film's suspense builds as Marco eventually convinces his superiors that something is amiss with Raymond Shaw, and it mounts as Marco's FBI-CIA-army intelligence task force scrambles to identify the Communist plot involving Raymond. The special challenge is that even Raymond has no idea that he is the tool of a conspiracy.

Released during the height of the Cuban Missile Crisis and one year before the assassination of John F. Kennedy by a lone gunman with ties to the Communist world, *The Manchurian Candidate* made little impression at the time of its release. A myth grew up around the film that Sinatra had withdrawn it from circulation immediately following the Kennedy assassination, though it was in fact shown on television in the mid-1960s. But *The Manchurian Candidate* did disappear from view for many years before resurfacing in the 1980s, after home video had reshaped movie watching and the public's perception of cinema history.[33] After surfacing on VHS and DVD, *The Manchurian Candidate* was acknowledged as a classic of Cold War cinema and as the most memorable fictionalized dramatization of Joe McCarthy.

A powerful documentary, *Point of Order* (1964), offers a glimpse of the real man. *Point of Order* covers one of the first political media events to unfold live in America's living rooms, the 1954 hearing before McCarthy's Senate Permanent Subcommittee on Investigations. McCarthy used the committee as a sounding board for his allegations of Communist infiltration of agencies such as the Voice of America and eventually the U.S. Army. His challenge to the army — and by implication the retired general of the army, President Dwight D. Eisenhower — proved his undoing. Outraged by the drafting of his committee's chief consultant, G. David Schine, McCarthy launched hearings, charging the army with drafting Schine to forestall his investigation into Communist infiltration of the military. The army was prepared to hit back.

The enormous public attention McCarthy had accrued brought an unprecedented audience to the afternoon television broadcast. According to the Gallup Poll, 89 percent of adult Americans followed the hearings and as many as twenty million watched the broadcasts.

Poll numbers also showed that few Americans regarded McCarthy's conduct or accusations as credible.[34]

Named for McCarthy's frequent interjection on parliamentary procedure throughout the committee's sessions, *Point of Order* was assembled by New York writer Daniel Talbot. "I was totally apolitical but this was a fascinating piece of Americana," he later said. "I read McCarthy as a kind of W. C. Fields character selling snake oil."[35] Most Americans agreed about the snake oil but found the salesman far less endearing than the star of the 1941 comedy *Never Give a Sucker an Even Break*. McCarthy's overheated belligerence, mirthless humor, and five-o'clock shadow proved entirely unsuited to the new medium of television. Marshall McLuhan might have appreciated the more telegenic calm of the senator's opponent, the army's counsel Joseph Nye Welch, later described by Roy Cohn, McCarthy's chief aide, as "a courtly gentleman, a deft, sly wit" with "an unerring sense for the jugular" as he deflected attacks and exposed McCarthy's witnesses to deflating cross-examination.[36] "Have you no decency, sir?" Welch demanded after McCarthy revealed that Welch's law partner was a former member of the Left-leaning National Lawyers Guild. "At long last, have you left no sense of decency?" Welch possessed such presence that director Otto Preminger cast him as the judge in his courtroom drama, *Anatomy of a Murder* (1959).[37]

Within weeks of the hearing McCarthy became the butt of jokes by television comedians Steve Allen and Milton Burle. On December 2, 1954, the Senate voted 67–22 to reprimand him. Afterward McCarthy faded into twilight, ignored by the news media and most of his colleagues, but he continued to rail against the Reds. A biographer described him as the "pale ghost of his former self."[38]

McCarthy was memorably satirized in *The Manchurian Candidate*, but it was television that brought him down. As *Village Voice* film critic J. Hoberman wrote, "*Point of Order* demonstrates the way that television inevitably recasts news as entertainment, subsumes politics in personality, elevates anecdote to history, and in the final analysis, substitutes its own flickering image for collective memory."[39]

FROM RUSSIA WITH LOVE (1963)

The most famous fictional spy to emerge from the Cold War never directly confronted the Soviets, at least not on the big screen. James Bond, the creation of British writer and intelligence operative Ian Fleming, squared off against Communist agents in several books and on television in *Casino Royale* (1954), a little-seen and less-remembered episode in the CBS Climax Mystery Theater. In *Casino Royale* Bond, played by American actor Barry Nelson, confronted a Russian agent called Le Chiffre (Peter Lorre). The Yankee perspective was an experiment that failed. Bond would be British, as were most of the characteristic Cold War masters of espionage in movies and television.

The settings for Cold War spy fiction were usually exotic and often featured agents of America's most dependable ally, Great Britain. In one notable exception, director Samuel Fuller's *Pickup on South Street* (1952), espionage played out in a gritty urban milieu where traitors passed off stolen microfilm at seedy rendezvous. Despite Fuller's resolute anticommunism, J. Edgar Hoover objected strongly to the film, claiming to detect an unpatriotic subtext. Twentieth Century Fox producer Darryl F. Zanuck refused to censor the film (some scenes had already been cut for their violent content by the Motion Picture Production Code Office) but deleted references to the FBI in the movie's advertising campaign.[40] Thelma Ritter received an Oscar nomination for her role in *Pickup on South Street*, and Roger Ebert honored the film in hindsight as a classic, yet *Pickup* had few imitators. The jet-setting James Bond became the most popular archetype for Cold War espionage.

Ian Fleming's biographer John Pearson repeatedly noted "distinct resemblances" between the author and his character. Leaving Britain's Sandhurst military academy without graduating, Fleming, like Bond, chaffed against authority while willing to be part of the establishment. A scion of wealth, Fleming enjoyed fast cars, expensive clothes, disposable bed partners, and hideaways in distant places. Bond's cruel face mirrored his creator.[41]

A man of Fleming's class and temperament had little difficulty finding employment with British intelligence. In 1939, before the outbreak of World War II, Fleming accompanied a trade mission to Moscow, ostensibly as a *Times* of London correspondent but actually as a spy for the Foreign Office. "The sliding steel doors, the heavily-armed guards, the armor-plated walls, and the bomb-proof devices with which Stalin's court surrounded itself appealed profoundly to his imagination," Pearson wrote. When war came, he received a commission and was assigned to the Naval Intelligence Division, which had, with the defeat of Germany in 1918, set covert operating standards envied by governments the world over. According to Pearson, "Fleming had a finger in virtually everything, and before the war had lasted many months this reserve lieutenant knew more secrets and had more real power than most of the senior officers in all three services."[42]

Along with working inside the Admiralty's secretive Room 39, the inspiration for Bond's home office, the London headquarters of Britain's MI6 foreign intelligence service, Fleming organized the 30 Assault Unit, an "intelligence commando" whose objective was to seize the enemy's secrets rather than destroy its installations. The 30 Assault took part in the Allied landing in North Africa, where it secured German and Italian codebooks. During the D-Day assault in Normandy, the unit was tasked with capturing a German radar system intact. Fleming was dispatched to Washington DC, where he conferred with Maj. Gen. William J. "Wild Bill" Donovan, the chief of the newly created OSS. Fleming schooled the green Americans, inexperienced in the ways of foreign intrigue, in the methods of British intelligence. He conducted covert actions inside the United States against Japanese consular officials, British traitors, and American pro-German or isolationist groups. As Agent 17F, Fleming helped run a major British intelligence operation out of Rockefeller Center. He even carried a fountain pen that squirted tear gas.[43]

In 1952 Fleming wrote the first of a dozen James Bond thrillers at Goldeneye, his beach house in Jamaica. From the start the author was interested in selling his novels as screenplays. Aside from the failed *Casino Royale*, his efforts led nowhere, yet his influence was felt even before the release of the first successful Bond movie. In 1961 CBS began airing a British-produced series, *Danger Man*, starring Patrick McGoohan as John Drake, a NATO special agent. Many elements of *Danger Man*, including the fabulous gadgets, were borrowed from Fleming's novels. The short-lived *Danger Man* continued to morph throughout the 1960s. Next it became the more popular series *Secret Agent* (1964–66), with Drake now working for Britain's MI9, which in reality was a military intelligence agency that had been disbanded after World War II. Finally, in *The Prisoner* (1967–68) McGoohan's character angrily tries to resign, only to be confined to a surreal resort where material comfort is guaranteed but freedom denied.

Fleming was not content to be the source of ideas for competing spy heroes and continued to promote his work for film. Bond finally attracted the attention of Canadian producer Harry Saltzman and his partner, Albert R. Broccoli. Saltzman, reportedly an intelligence officer during World War II, negotiated the six-picture deal with United Artists that inaugurated the longest-running franchise in Hollywood.[44] The release of the first Bond movie, *Dr. No* (1962), coincided with the rising popularity of the Bond novels in the United States, spurred by an article in *Life* magazine that numbered *From Russia with Love* among John F. Kennedy's favorite books.[45] "Bond's place in American culture was set by an endorsement from Kennedy," wrote cultural historian Jeffrey S. Miller, who added that Kennedy's assassination "brought to the fore the conspiratorial dangers of the world in which Bond worked."[46] There was talk of casting Richard Burton, James Mason, Patrick McGoohan, or David Niven as Bond, but Saltzman decided to craft the spy's cinematic image around an unknown actor. Sean Connery, a working-class Scot and Royal Navy veteran with an unremarkable career in British movies, was made-to-order. Sexy and unflinching, he was an angry young man who looked good in an evening jacket. Connery set the bar for all future Bonds as a resourceful killer with Hugh Hefner appetites, a fantasy drawn from Fleming's estimation of his own character and accomplishments.

The sinister Oriental villain of *Dr. No* was derived from Sax Rohmer's Fu Manchu stories, which Fleming had devoured as a boy at Eton.[47] In the novel Dr. No works for the Soviets; his private Caribbean island is a secret base with sophisticated electronic systems to scramble the guidance systems of American missiles. In transposing the book to film, screenwriter Richard Maibaum made several important changes. Most significantly, all references to the Soviets were removed. This change was probably made at the behest of Saltzman, whose capitalistic concern for markets in countries with flourishing Communist parties, such as France and Italy, resulted in a shift from the historic to the mythic. In the movie Dr. No's paymasters are a sinister international organization that would surface repeatedly in the Bond franchise, SPECTRE. At the time of *Dr. No*'s release in the United States, shortly after the Cuban Missile Crisis, few viewers noticed the distinction between the Soviets and the more mysterious villains of the screenplay. The *Saturday Evening Post* even credited Fleming with the gift of prophecy. "We know that the Russians *do* build missile bases in nearby Caribbean islands (*Dr. No*). They *do* plot carefully to get beautiful girls into the beds of Allied agents (*From Russia with Love*). Fleming said it first."[48]

Maibaum introduced another significant change with his tone of self-aware levity. The Bond books were humorless, while the movies had many tongue-in-cheek moments. "Unintentionally, a formula developed in the writing," one critic observed. After a cliff-hanging suspense scene, "Bond would throw away a funny play on words to make the audience laugh." Some elements remained from the books, including the unsettling association of sex with sadism and Bond's inevitable encounters with sexually willing sidekicks. In *Dr. No* Ursula Andress played the first cinematic Bond Girl, Honey Ryder, whose seam-bursting, skintight pants required continual mending on set.[49] The film's CIA agent, Felix Leiter (Jack Lord), has a relatively minor part. Brittania still rules in the Bond universe.

Doubling the box office sales of *Dr. No*, *From Russia with Love* pushed Bond to the center ring of pop culture.[50] Along with the Beatles and the Rolling Stones, Bond became one of Britain's most familiar contributions to the global culture of the "Swinging Sixties."

From Russia with Love works as a tightly paced Cold War spy adventure, the final Bond movie for many years in which the human factor outweighs the spectacle of gadgetry. Agent 007 must rely on physical prowess, courage, and knowledge of spy craft to triumph over impossible situations. Entering his Istanbul hotel room, Bond's first steps involve checking the backs of the framed pictures for hidden microphones. Yet he possesses devices considered futuristic at the time, including a pager and a car phone. MI6's research and development chief, Q, his cipher name alluding to the real-life penchant of British operatives to conceal themselves behind initials, provides Bond with a secret agent's attaché case. The contents, including a folding sniper's rifle with an infrared scope and a tear gas canister disguised as a tin of talcum powder, are indeed realistic.

The novel *From Russia with Love* focuses on the larger-than-life Soviet agents Grant, Klebb, and Kronsteen. Once again, in his screenplay Maibaum, under Saltzman's direction, eliminated the Soviets as the story's heavies. SPECTRE returns in the film version and plays the Soviets against the British in a deadly conspiracy. The villainous trio become SPECTRE agents: relative newcomer Robert Shaw plays Grant; Klebb is played by Lotte Lenya, widow of composer Kurt Weill and a cabaret and film star in Weimar Germany; and the little-known Polish-born Vladek Sheybal becomes Kronsteen. As in *Dr. No*, the British stand more or less alone in the covert war against evildoers. The CIA is briefly alluded to as a friendly rival to MI6.

The Istanbul setting, retained from the novel, is put to good use for realism as well as exotic local color. Crowds of thousands press against the scenes being shot on city streets, and real fire and police units respond to the indoor explosions staged inside a building standing in for the Soviet consulate.[51] The film kept core plot elements concerning a seductress, Tatiana Romanova (Daniela Bianchi), and a top secret Soviet coding machine, Lektor, used as bait to trap Bond. The fictional Lektor was based on Enigma, the typewriter-sized encryption machine used by the British to decipher coded German messages during World War II. As part of the covert operations center at Bletchley Park that spurred the development of computer technology, the Enigma project contributed to shortening the war against Germany. Britain kept the project's existence secret until the 1970s. At the time *From Russia with Love* was released to theaters, few people understood that it provided a glimpse into a hidden world of technological breakthroughs.

The Bond movies played into a conspiratorial view of world events inspired by the reality of covert operations and official secrets; 007's milieu was a funhouse magnification of the vast hidden bureaucracies influencing the direction of politics from the Manhattan Project through the CIA and its foreign counterparts. "Spying is a dirty trade," Fleming told an interviewer, but he was determined to turn his trade into entertainment.[52] Bond's success encouraged a plethora of television spies on American networks during the 1960s. Best remembered is *The Man from U.N.C.L.E.* (1964–68), whose fictitious international agency owed something to the lessening of tension between the United States and the USSR following the Cuban Missile Crisis. The show featured the American Agent Solo (Robert Vaughn) partnered with the Russian Illya Kuryakin (David McCallum) but reporting to an Englishman, Alexander Waverly (Leo G. Carroll). *The Man from U.N.C.L.E.*, according to Jeffrey Miller, maintained the "iconic 'British' superiority in matters of international spying that Fleming's novels and the Bond films had already established."[53]

The blunt-edged heroism of Fleming's stories may have become a prevailing theme in popular culture, but a strong, contrary wind blew from another British spy-turned-author, David John Moore Cornwell, better known by his pen name, John le Carré. During the 1940s he served with British army intelligence and debriefed refugees fleeing the Soviet bloc. After graduating from Oxford, he worked for MI5, Britain's internal security bureau, and MI6, its foreign espionage agency. The principal protagonist in many of le Carré's novels, George Smiley, is a world-weary agent acutely aware of the moral ambiguity of his profession. In dark moments he wonders whether his Soviet counterparts are any worse than his own colleagues or his American allies, and yet he soldiers on.

Le Carré has been described as an "amused ironist" recounting "in careful detail the mundanities and inefficiencies of the secret world."[54] His novels are more psychological than physical, sex is more dutiful than pleasurable, and people matter more than gadgets. The first film based on his work, *The Spy Who Came in from the Cold* (1965), starred Richard Burton in a starkly realistic story of duplicity and intrigue in East Germany. The moral twilight of le Carré's world has often provided an intriguing source for cinema and television. Among the best-known Cold War — themed productions from his work are *The Deadly Affair* (1966), directed by Sidney Lumet and starring James Mason; *The Russian House* (1990), with Sean Connery; the BBC series *Tinker, Tailor, Soldier, Spy* (1979), with Alec Guinness as Smiley searching for a Soviet mole in a case inspired by the real-life treason of Kim Philby; and the 2011 film remake of *Tinker, Tailor* with Gary Oldman as Smiley.

According to le Carré, there is "solace" for the audience in his fictional conspiracies of double agents and intrigue, not the solace of escapism that has always been an obvious charge against Fleming. "They know that it's around them," he said of conspiracies in a 1986 interview. "They know they live in an increasingly secretive society in many ways where they're cut off from the decisions of power." His fiction at least provides each conspiracy with a "sense of resolution."[55] The spy movies of the Cold War era provided audiences with the comforting idea that the forces with the power to destroy the earth had human faces and that the worst of their plans might yet be foiled.

DR. STRANGELOVE, OR: HOW I LEARNED TO STOP WORRYING AND LOVE THE BOMB (1964) AND FAIL-SAFE (1964)

Scientists in all the warring nations of World War II were aware of the possibility of atomic weapons. Fearful of being beaten in the race by Nazi Germany, the United States invested enormous sums on a vast military-scientific-industrial undertaking, the Manhattan Project. The operation was concealed so completely that the vice president, Harry S. Truman, only learned of it after Franklin D. Roosevelt's death. After the first bomb was tested at Los Alamos, New Mexico, on July 16, 1945,

Truman ordered the new weapon deployed against a pair of Japanese cities, Hiroshima and Nagasaki. The Japanese government surrendered after witnessing the devastation caused by the new weapon.

The destruction of Hiroshima on August 6, 1945, was greeted in the United States with gleeful headlines and a genuine sense of relief that the war would end without recourse to an invasion of Japan, an operation whose casualties might have been incalculable. Yet even in the first days after Hiroshima was leveled, the media registered anxiety over the Promethean release of atomic energy. NBC commentator H. V. Kaltenborn, the dean of broadcast journalism, wondered whether "Anglo-Saxon science" had "created a Frankenstein." The *New York Times* declared that the bomb had caused "an explosion in men's minds as shattering as the obliteration of Hiroshima," an idea echoed decades later by historian Paul Boyer, who wrote of Hiroshima's "terrifying suddenness," which changed "the fundamental ground of culture and consciousness."[56]

A shadow fell over the war's end by the awesome realization that humanity had obtained the power to destroy itself and the shadows cast by the photographs of billowing mushroom clouds in *Life* magazine's August 20, 1945, issue. Tensions rose dramatically after the Soviet Union tested its first atom bomb in August 1949. Stalin believed that the USSR could survive a nuclear attack because of the country's size but was determined to build an atomic arsenal to intimidate the West. Soviet science would eventually have unlocked the bomb's secrets, but its weapons program, directed by the feared chief of the People's Commissariat of Internal Affairs (NKVD) secret police, Lavrentii Beria, was hastened with the help of a network of spies.[57]

With America's nuclear monopoly broken, the prospect of a world-ending World War III seemed likely unless steps were taken. Some policy makers argued that the development of even more powerful weapons would restore America's advantage, yet after the United States tested the hydrogen bomb in 1952, the Soviets followed suit three years later. Some thought to contain the danger through nonproliferation, but by the 1960s Britain, France, and China had joined the nuclear club, and other nations would gain admission in the coming decades. Others pinned their hopes on arms control agreements, a topic discussed at summit meetings between U.S. and Soviet leaders through the conclusion of the Cold War, yet arms control was always more a gesture of goodwill than a concrete solution, given that both nations soon possessed more than enough warheads to destroy the earth several times over.

In the aftermath of the successful Soviet atomic test, the U.S. government tried to reassure its citizens that nuclear war would be a survivable interruption of life's routine, not the end of life. *Duck and Cover* (1951), a civil defense film whose cartoon of a bow tie — wearing turtle menaced by a dynamite-wielding monkey represented the official line. In the event of nuclear war civilians should withdraw into their shells, meaning fallout shelters, and wait out the radiation. If caught outside or in school, children should lie down and cover their faces. "Be ready everyday and do the right thing if the atomic bomb explodes," the narrator cautions.[58] The atomic age was under way, and some people tried to reassure themselves that harnessing the elemental power of the universe was simply another step in the progress of modern life. "Atomic Cocktails" were served in lounges, a French fashion designer dubbed his daring new bathing suit the bikini after America's 1946 nuclear test at Bikini Atoll in the Pacific, and the 1947 Manhattan telephone directory listed over forty businesses with *atomic* in their name, including the Atomic Underwear Company.[59]

Hollywood first approached the bomb with *The Beginning or the End* (1947), a melodrama based on the Manhattan Project and the destruction of Hiroshima. The movie portrayed President Truman agonizing over the decision to drop the bomb; in reality Truman said he "never had any doubt that it should be used."[60] Albert Einstein took MGM producer Louis B. Mayer to task for the film's distortions, and the *Bulletin of Atomic Scientists* condemned it as a "horrible falsification."[61]

Boyer pointed out that while the response of mainstream literature to the atom bomb was "tentative and muted," the science fiction subculture had no difficulty absorbing and magnifying the news from Hiroshima. Atomic energy and weapons had cropped up persistently in this genre. In 1944 the astonishing accuracy of a story on an atom bomb in *Astounding Science Fiction* drew the attention of the War Department. The authorities questioned the magazine's editor, John W. Campbell Jr.[62] Once the bomb fell, science fiction was endowed with a prophetic role and began its ascent toward respectability.

Nevertheless, Hollywood studios still deemed science fiction as B movie material. The low-budget productions often opened up fascinating, funhouse glimpses into the actual preoccupations of people rather than socially sanctioned themes of the "quality pictures." Anxiety over the environmental effects of atomic bombs inspired a Ray Bradbury story that found its way to the screen as *The Beast from 20,000 Fathoms* (1953). The tale of a prehistoric creature come to life from exposure to radiation opened the door to the Japanese cult favorite *Godzilla* (1954). Two prominent genre films addressed nuclear issues directly. In director Robert Wise's *The Day the Earth Stood Still* (1951) an alien emissary warns world leaders that their nuclear folly will not be tolerated in the galactic order. Robert Aldrich's morally complex thriller *Kiss Me Deadly* (1955) involves a plot to smuggle a suitcase-sized doomsday device to an unnamed foreign power.

Stanley Kramer's *On the Beach* (1959) was Hollywood's first A-list feature on World War III. A melancholy odyssey set in a world half-destroyed, the protagonist is a U.S. submarine commander (Gregory Peck) sailing across the South Pacific for home, hoping that some of America survived the nuclear holocaust that obliterated much of the Northern Hemisphere. *On the Beach* was set in 1964, a token of the era's pessimism over the prospects of atomic war.

In a remarkable synchronicity two complementary yet contrasting films released in 1964 stared into the abyss of nuclear war, Stanley Kubrick's *Dr. Strangelove* and Sidney Lumet's *Fail-Safe*. In both movies the catastrophe was triggered by events outside the control of the U.S. president and Soviet premier, leading to a nuclear attack on the USSR by American bombers. The leaders of the superpowers confer by phone as the planes penetrate Soviet airspace, but their conversations fail to avert disaster. Both stories involve unhinged military officers obsessed with Communist duplicity, albeit the problem is isolated in *Fail-Safe* but systemic in *Strangelove*. Ironically, the can-do spirit of the American pilots ensures Armageddon in both films. In *Fail-Safe* and *Dr. Strangelove* sinister professors work out the calculus of nuclear holocaust without blinking.

Despite many similarities, the tone of the two movies is as unalike as the character of their directors. Lumet's film is earnest and straight-faced, the work of a liberal reformer who tries to measure the good in every character and believes the world might yet be saved. Kubrick's is sardonic and profoundly pessimistic, his characters caricatures of crazy or ineffectual men; in the end the world disintegrates in blinding flashes of thermonuclear heat. And yet their messages on the madness of the arms race and the danger of disaster are essentially the same. *Dr. Strangelove* and *Fail-Safe* were released when memories of the Cuban Missile Crisis and the pent-up atomic anxiety of the previous decade remained sharp. The audience of 1964 was acutely aware that the world had narrowly averted World War III; the sociopolitical environment had loosened enough by then to permit the sober reflection of *Fail-Safe* as well as the dark hilarity of *Strangelove*.

Kubrick's film had a greater impact. "A new generation enjoyed seeing the world as insane; they *literally* learned to stop worrying and love the bomb," wrote film critic Pauline Kael, fretting that the film denied any possibility of solving the arms race.[63] But Kael was missing the redemptive dimension of *Dr. Strangelove* — that the film's broad appeal was not so much in the story but in its attitude of rejection, its discrediting of the idea that supposedly rational actors had their fingers on the doomsday button. *Dr. Strangelove* has endured as a classic because its humor is still provocative. *Fail-Safe* is more a period piece but one whose morality play remains compelling. In 2000 George Clooney produced and starred in a made-for-TV remake.

The Strategic Air Command (SAC), the arm of the U.S. Air Force responsible for nuclear-armed bombers and intercontinental ballistic missiles, is the locus of both films. As part of its mission, SAC maintained combat-ready bombers in the air at all times, prepared to retaliate in the event of a Soviet attack. In *Fail-Safe* most SAC officers are conscientious in carrying out the painfully difficult orders of the president, played by Henry Fonda. They must aid the Soviets in shooting down the SAC bombers to forestall nuclear retaliation. In *Dr. Strangelove* Brig. Gen. Jack D. Ripper (Sterling Hayden) is a lunatic who orders an attack against the USSR.

With a trademark cigar glued to his mouth, Ripper resembles SAC's real commander at the time *Dr. Strangelove* was shot, Curtis LeMay, an officer known for his fierce pronouncements on America's enemies and for assuming control over SAC's operational strategy. Not unlike the blustering Ripper, LeMay was reluctant to submit his plans for review by his superiors.[64] "War is too important to be left to politicians," Ripper tells his adjutant, an RAF exchange officer, Group Captain Mandrake (Peter Sellers). "I can no longer sit back and allow Communist infiltration." Ripper rambles on about a conspiracy to "sap and impurify all of our precious bodily fluids" through fluoridation, a reference to the fringe Right's belief that fluoridated water was a Communist plot to undermine public health.[65] SAC's motto, "Peace Is Our Profession," was shown to ironic effect several times in the film.

A popular comedian in Great Britain, Sellers had appeared in Kubrick's previous film, *Lolita* (1962). Along with his role as Mandrake, Sellers played two other characters in *Dr. Strangelove*, President Merkin Muffley and the president's advisor, the German professor who gives the film its name. Sellers's three characters occupy distinct positions along the moral spectrum.

The fussbudget Mandrake is the closest to a hero in the story. Although summoning physical courage only gradually, Mandrake opposes Ripper but is unable to stop him; when paratroops seize the mutinous SAC base after a firefight, Mandrake faces down their idiotic commander, Col. Bat Guano, and manages to get word of Ripper's scheme to the White House from a pay phone, despite lack of proper change for a long-distance call. Mandrake is endowed with a sense of right and wrong but is incapable of halting the vast machinery of madness.

Modeled after Democratic presidential contender Adlai Stevenson, Muffley is a reasonable but ineffectual figure yoked to a system he cannot control.[66] K. Strangelove is unapologetically evil, an unreconstructed Nazi, and an angel of death whose gleeful proposals for surviving the impending atomic Armageddon are eagerly embraced by the boorish Soviet ambassador as well as the none-too-bright U.S. Air Force commander, Gen. Buck Turgidson (George C. Scott). In Strangelove's scheme a computer would chose 100,000 Americans, based on fertility and a cross-section of skills, to live in deep mineshaft fallout shelters, joined by top military and political leaders. With a few turns of his slide wheel, Strangelove determines that the earth's surface will be habitable in a hundred years. Merkin wonders whether the survivors might "envy the dead," but Turgidson is already setting the stage for a postapocalyptic contest between the remnant of the United States and the USSR. We must not allow "a mineshaft gap" he sputters, parodying official concerns in the 1960s over a supposed "missile gap" favoring the Soviets over the Americans.

The public came to believe that Strangelove was satirizing Henry Kissinger, then a Harvard professor and advisor to the National Security Council who rose to prominence in political circles with his book *Nuclear Weapons and Foreign Policy* (1957). Kissinger actually advised placing less emphasis on nuclear deterrent, arguing against "the secret dream of American military thought: that there exists a final answer to our military problem, that it is possible to defeat the enemy utterly, and that war has its own rationale independent of policy."[67] Instead, Kissinger proposed that the United States prepare for "limited wars" against Soviet-backed proxies, a policy Johnson adopted in Vietnam. Kubrick never spoke of Kissinger. In preparing for cowriting the screenplay with the anarchic humorist Terry Southern, Kubrick read everything available from the era's nuclear war theorists, citing Herman Kahn and Edwin Teller as well as military and technical journals. Kubrick regarded the dialogue as reflective of the ideas actually governing America's policy of nuclear deterrence. Cooperation with the U.S. military was out of the question, given its satirical treatment in the screenplay, but Kubrick, working with declassified descriptions, recreated the interior of the B-52 bomber at the story's heart with remarkable fidelity, down to the toggle switches on the instrument panels.[68]

Kubrick intended Sellers to play a fourth character, Maj. T. J. "King" Kong, the gung ho B-52 pilot who stops at nothing to deliver his twenty-megaton payload to its target. "This is it," Kong tells his crew when he receives the attack code. "Nuclear combat toe-to-toe with the Russkies." The snare drums of "When Johnny Comes Marching Home Again" are heard on the soundtrack as he encourages his men, "The folks back home is a-countin' on you." Sellers claimed difficulty mastering Kong's Texas accent and was replaced by a character actor familiar to fans of western movies, Slim Pickens. The actor arrived on set at London's Shepperton Studio wearing a ten-gallon hat, a sheepherder's jacket, and high-heeled alligator cowboy boots. Kubrick counseled him to just be himself in the role.[69] In the climactic scene Kong straddles one of the aircraft's bombs (marked "Nuclear Warhead Handle with Care") and releases it, riding the bomb to its target whooping and waving his cowboy hat. Pickens had begun his career as a bronco rider.

Dr. Strangelove concludes on yet another ironic note as the world explodes to the tune of Vera Lynn's "We'll Meet Again," a morale-boosting number on the hit parade during World War II. In World War III there will be no homecomings for anyone.

Remarkably, the screenplay for *Strangelove* was given the seal of approval by the Motion Picture Association of America (MPAA), which allowed it to be screened at commercial cinemas. Kubrick assured MPAA president Geoffrey Shurlock that the bikini worn by Turgidson's mistress-secretary would not be of the "extreme type" and promised to reduce the number of *hell*s and *damn*s in the dialogue. Kubrick's "nightmare comedy," as he called it, was unlike anything audiences had seen and remains startling even today. Laughing at the unthinkable was a bracing experience for many moviegoers in 1964.

Dr. Strangelove captivated two young men who would become important filmmakers, Steven Spielberg and Oliver Stone. Elvis Presley was so amused by the film that he watched it several times in one evening.[70]

Dr. Strangelove was inspired by a novel more serious in tone, *Red Alert* by Peter George, an RAF officer and British intelligence agent. *Fail-Safe* was based on the best seller by Harvey Wheeler and Eugene Burdick, the author of the 1958 novel *The Ugly American*. Kubrick and Lumet were unaware of each other's films as they began their productions. After learning of *Fail-Safe*, Kubrick initiated a lawsuit on behalf of George, charging plagiarism. Lumet claimed he first heard of *Dr. Strangelove* when Kubrick sued.[71] The action was dropped when Kubrick's studio, Columbia Pictures, acquired distribution of *Fail-Safe*, holding its release until after *Dr. Strangelove*'s premiere.

The black comedy of *Dr. Strangelove* eclipsed the Greek tragedy of *Fail-Safe*, whose U.S. president finds himself in a situation he cannot control but one that controls him. The striking scene of the president preparing to use the hotline to Moscow is shot from an angle in which the bulky phone dwarfs the anxious man steeling himself to make the most difficult call of his life. In *Fail-Safe*, unlike *Dr. Strangelove*, moral agency still exists. Henry Fonda's president is unable to stop a disaster but at least can limit its extent. The film's end, in which New York is destroyed in compensation for the leveling of Moscow, is an ironic nod to the theories of *Fail-Safe*'s Strangelove, Professor Groeteschele (Walter Mathau), a Pentagon advisor who speaks coldly of confining the casualties of nuclear war to only sixty million.

The Strategic Air Command was disbanded in 1992 with the dissolution of the Soviet Union and the end of the Cold War. The B-52s of SAC never delivered a hydrogen bomb to an enemy target but became the workhorses of heavy bombardment from Vietnam through the 2001 invasion of Afghanistan. Although Kubrick regarded SAC's motto, "Peace Is Our Profession," with scorn, the strategy of deterrence may have served its purpose. While the Cold War erupted into costly wars in Korea and Vietnam, it never became a head-on clash between NATO and the Warsaw Pact or a nuclear exchange between the United States and the USSR. If the Cold War had turned into World War III, the result might have resembled the closing scene from *Dr. Strangelove*, which leaves a vivid memory of a catastrophe that never occurred.

APOCALYPSE NOW (1979)

Hollywood did not respond to the war in Vietnam the way it had to World War I, World War II, or even the Korean War. There was no rush to valorize America's role in Vietnam, no sense of patriotic urgency. The first significant Hollywood movie on the war was released almost grudgingly in response to the prodding of one of America's most familiar stars, John Wayne. After returning from a 1966 tour of South Vietnam, where he met the troops and signed autographs, the "Duke" became a stalwart defender of the war's aims and was determined to present the case for America's involvement. "I owe it to them," he said of the soldiers he met in the field. He added, "I honestly believe there's as much need for us to help the Vietnamese as there was to help the Jews in Germany."[72]

Wayne secured the rights to Robin Moore's 1965 novel *The Green Berets*. Along with S. Sgt. Barry Sadler's number one hit "Ballad of the Green Berets" (1966), the novel represented pop culture's fascination with the elite U.S. Special Forces established after World War II to engage in covert and unconventional warfare. Paramount Pictures said no to Wayne's offer to make the movie, feeling the war had become too controversial. Universal Studios said yes but quickly reversed itself, citing the war's growing unpopularity. Finally, Warner Brothers–Seven Arts signed on, investing money in exchange for a lower-than-normal fee for Wayne's services as actor and director. Wayne quarreled with the studio and with the U.S. Army, which allowed him to film at Fort Benning, Georgia, and to use planes, helicopters, motor vehicles, and soldiers as extras. When an early frost colored the green woods of Fort Benning, standing in for the jungles of Vietnam, in autumnal colors, the production was completed in Hollywood on hastily constructed sets.[73]

After its release in 1968, *The Green Berets* was blasted by critics; demonstrators waving Vietcong flags protested outside New York theaters, and Congressman Benjamin Rosenthal, a Democrat from New York, condemned the Defense Department for spending taxpayers' money on a "glorified portrayal of the Vietnam War," a movie made "for propaganda purposes." Nevertheless, *The Green Berets* found an audience, grossing seven million dollars in the first three months of release, but Wayne's attempt to show Vietnam through the lens of his earlier World War II and Indian Wars movies struck a false note. The drift of public opinion against Vietnam left *The Green Berets* behind.[74]

Antiwar sentiment was prevalent among the younger generation of Hollywood stars. Jane Fonda drew applause from the Left and rancor from elsewhere along the political spectrum for visiting Hanoi in 1972. She was photographed wearing a helmet, seated at an antiaircraft gun, as if ready to shoot down incoming American planes, and broadcast appeals on Radio Hanoi calling on U.S. pilots to be aware that their missions included civilian targets. She shot footage in North Vietnam showing bomb damage to dikes and dams, stirring international outrage and causing Richard Nixon to pause the air campaign. Fonda later apologized for posing with the antiaircraft battery. "That two-minute lapse of sanity will haunt me until I die," she wrote in her 2005 memoir.[75]

Fonda's celebrity status drew attention to her work on behalf of the antiwar movement, but her cinematic image as the star of the science fiction soft-core porn flick *Barbarella: Queen of the Galaxy* (1968) undercut her credibility in many eyes. As journalist Ronald Brownstein quipped, John Wayne "had an easier time pushing his views because he had played war heroes for so long that many Americans confused him with the genuine article."[76] Fonda later won an Oscar for *Coming Home* (1978), playing the wife of a U.S. Marine Corps officer in Vietnam who falls in love with a paralyzed Vietnam veteran.

Vietnam was universally regarded as a stigma on America's reputation, both by detractors, who felt it should never have been fought, and supporters, who believed that victory was stolen by a lack of political will. As the *Washington Post* declared in 1974 after U.S. combat troops had departed, it was "the war everyone wants to forget." The *Chicago Tribune* described scenes from the refugee-choked collapse of South Vietnam in the spring of 1975 as "almost Goyaesque in their horror." Mirroring the unforgettable televised images of helicopters desperately lifting off from the roof of the U.S. embassy, leaving many pleading South Vietnamese behind, a *Chicago Daily News* reporter wrote, "My last view of Saigon was through the tail door of a helicopter." He added, "Then the door closed — closed on the most humiliating chapter in American history."[77]

Amid that climate several years passed before even Hollywood mavericks ventured into the subject of Vietnam. Director Michael Cimino, who had been a medic attached to a Green Beret training camp, was first with *The Deer Hunter* (1978). The movie begins with a leisurely immersion in the lives of its working-class protagonists (Robert De Niro, John Savage, and Christopher Walken, who won a Best Supporting Actor Oscar for his role), following them through blue-collar bars, a wedding celebration, and a hunting trip. *The Deer Hunter* focuses on the character of working-class American men before they report for duty and the damage the war inflicted on their psyches.

They were eager to fight. The taciturn Green Beret at the wedding reception shrugs in response to their gung ho attitude, which seems drawn from the dialogue of old John Wayne movies from World War II. "I hope they send us where the bullets are flying and the fighting's the worst," one of them says. Their wish is granted.

The Deer Hunter troubled critics of various political persuasions but connected with audiences hungry to see the war on the big screen. It defeated *Coming Home* at the Academy Awards for Best Picture and earned Cimino the trophy for Best Director. British film critic David Thomson recently called it "one of the great American films" and "one of the few American films that work like a novel" in the complexity of its allusions, symbolism, and foreshadows.[78]

Towering over all Vietnam movies, Francis Ford Coppola's *Apocalypse Now* (1979) defined the war as morally ambiguous and doomed;

its endurance as a classic is a result of the haunting power of its visual imagery as well as its refusal to make a definitive political statement. The wealth of mutually contradictory interpretations comes in part from the conflicting views of the two men most responsible for shaping the story. Coppola was opposed to the war, while screenwriter John Milius supported it.

Apocalypse Now began in 1968 during discussions between Milius and a fellow University of Southern California film student, George Lucas. Milius was already collecting stories from Vietnam veterans that would appear in the finished film, including GIs surfing after a firefight and the Vietcong hacking off the arms of children inoculated with the polio vaccine as part of the U.S. campaign to win hearts and minds. "As a matter of fact, I wanted to go to Vietnam, but I had asthma, couldn't get in anything," Milius said. "George and I would talk about the battles all the time and what a great movie it would make." Milius already had *Apocalypse Now* in mind for the title; Lucas spoke of shooting it in 16 mm and mixing in broadcast news footage to imbue the project with harsh realism.[79]

Lucas found it easier to find backing for the nostalgic *American Graffiti* (1973), set at the eve of U.S. combat in Vietnam. By 1974, when his friend Coppola obtained rights to Milius's screenplay, Lucas was already at work on *Star Wars*. Coppola asked Milius to direct *Apocalypse Now*, but their differences of opinion over the war precluded further collaboration. Yet Coppola denied any intention of making a message movie, telling *Playboy* that *Apocalypse Now* was "about war and the human soul." Decades later Coppola continued to insist that he "never thought *Apocalypse Now* is particularly an anti-war film."[80]

From the onset Milius was inspired by Joseph Conrad's 1899 novella on the psychological toll of imperialism, *Heart of Darkness*. Drawn from Conrad's experiences in the Congo Free State, whose savage administration belied Western claims to cultural superiority over colonized peoples, the story concerned the chief of an inland trading station, Colonel Kurtz, a man around whom fantastic rumors had grown. The protagonist, a company agent called Marlow, travels by steamer to meet Kurtz up a river "resembling an immense snake uncoiled . . . with its tail lost in the depths of the land." Native unrest is in the air. Marlow passes a warship "firing into a continent" at unseen foes. "There was a touch of insanity in the proceedings." In Marlow's account "going up that river was like travelling back to the earliest beginnings of the world, when vegetation rioted on the earth and the big trees were kings." In *Apocalypse Now* Marlow is transformed into Capt. Benjamin Willard, but much of the backdrop imagery is retained.

According to Milius, his screenplay focused on "man's inherent bestiality" and was a "no holds barred" immersion in the reality of war. Coppola began excising what he called the "offensive paramilitary stuff." As with *Casablanca*, the final screenplay of *Apocalypse Now* was written with the production well under way. Coppola recalled making "a million notes and marks" in his paperback copy of *Heart of Darkness* as he shot *Apocalypse Now*, cross-referencing Conrad with Milius to compose "a journey into issues related to morality in modern times," when technology can "amplify our evil instincts." But while *Casablanca* was filmed with rapid efficiency in the comfort of Warner Brothers' Hollywood studio, *Apocalypse Now* was mired in the jungles of the Philippines. It was, as Coppola admitted, "a project in jeopardy."[81]

Finding a location and logistical support was only the beginning of Coppola's problems. In 1975 the director provided the Pentagon with a copy of Milius's script, explaining that it was a work in progress subject to revision. Coppola sought advice as well as access to military bases and hardware. The military was split over the screenplay. Some Department of Defense officials advised working with Coppola, arguing that because he seemed determined to make the movie with or without official support, the military's input might mollify the film's more objectionable aspects. But the army refused to cooperated "in view of the sick humor or satirical philosophy of the film," objecting to the surfing scene, the depiction of drug use, and the idea that a renegade commander would be "terminated with extreme prejudice" rather than brought home for a court-martial. Coppola approached

Australia, which had sent sixty thousand troops and lost over five hundred men in Vietnam. Perhaps mindful of the controversy the war had stirred, the government turned Coppola down, insisting that the Royal Australian Army was "not a film-extra agency." Only a few years later its army would happily participate as extras in *Gallipoli*. Coppola finally found a willing helper in Filipino president Ferdinand Marco, who found a suitable stand-in for Vietnam on the island of Luzon and provided cheap labor, along with military personnel and helicopters with the same armaments used by the United States in Vietnam.[82]

The Philippines was an ideal setting but no paradise. The production was plagued by oppressive heat and dampness, poisonous snakes and venomous insects, and finally, by a typhoon that destroyed the sets. Casting was problematic. Harvey Keitel was originally set to play Captain Willard, but Coppola fired him after shooting a few scenes, feeling he was not right for the part; instead, Martin Sheen was chosen for the starring role. Marlon Brando, tapped to play Colonel Kurtz, agreed to be on set for only one month. Expenses mounted, and Coppola was forced to put himself at financial risk to complete the project.[83]

Apocalypse Now begins with the thrum-thrum of helicopters, the jungle erupting in plumes of orange napalm, and the monotonous whir of the overhead ceiling fan as Willard lies awake in his Saigon hotel room. Clearly unhinged and suffering from combat stress, he lashes out at his own image by smashing a mirror. Sheen was emotionally fragile throughout the production, finding the heat and humidity of the Philippines disagreeable. Coppola played up his discomfort, making it a marker of Willard's emotional unease, but the actor and director were playing with disaster. Sheen suffered a heart attack and struggled to find medical attention before the production was completed.[84] The smashing of the mirror was a spontaneous gesture, and Sheen insisted on continuing the shoot despite the blood flowing from his hand and the worsening pain.

"I wanted a mission," Willard declares in the first of his hard-boiled, film noir–style voiceovers. "I was going to the worst place in the world and I didn't even know it yet." The voiceovers, a narrative device running throughout *Apocalypse Now*, were added in postproduction. They bestowed a stronger presence on Willard, who often acts like a passive witness to events rather than a participant. The voiceovers were written by war correspondent Michael Herr, author of *Dispatches* (1977), a best-selling account of his experience in Vietnam.

Willard is brought to a U.S. headquarters, an air-conditioned outpost of American suburbia well stocked with the comforts of home. Among the officers on hand is a staffer played by Harrison Ford, fresh from the set of *Star Wars*. Willard is presented with a dossier containing a photograph of Colonel Kurtz in Green Beret uniform. The general presiding uncomfortably over the meeting is troubled by a taped broadcast from Kurtz's jungle lair on the Cambodian border that seems to call out the hypocrisy of the war. "What do you call it when the assassins accuse the assassins?" Kurtz demands in his broadcast. Kurtz, the general begins hesitantly, was a brilliant, outstanding officer, but "his methods became," he pauses to chose the right word, "unsound." Like his namesake in *Heart of Darkness*, Kurtz is playing the part of the white demigod among the natives. He is "beyond the pale" and must be "terminated." Willard's mission is classified. "How many people had I already killed?" Willard asks himself in a voiceover, adding: "But this time it was an American — and an officer. It wasn't supposed to make any difference to me, but it did."

Colonel Kurtz's covert war against the Vietcong, and his private army of indigenous Montagnard tribesmen from the Vietnamese highlands, drew inspiration from several real-life sources: the Montagnard units recruited to fight alongside U.S. Special Forces; the Phoenix Program, a CIA-led counterterrorism operation that interrogated and killed Vietcong suspects and sympathizers; and the "Secret Army" recruited by CIA among the Hmong people of Laos to combat Communist insurgents.

The dossier Willard receives on Kurtz prompts him to muse: "The war was being run by a bunch of four-star clowns who'll give the whole circus away. Kurtz kept winning it his way," even if this meant assassinating South Vietnamese officials suspected by being North Vietnamese agents. By all evidence Kurtz had identified them correctly and saved American lives through his actions. The Vietcong are scared of him. "I am beyond their timid, lying morality," Kurtz told his son in a Nietzschean letter photocopied in the dossier. The colonel's resume is impressive: a graduate of West Point and Harvard who had written a dire assessment of conditions in Vietnam in a secret report that upset Washington. The dossier provides Willard with reading material for the long, uneasy ride upriver, which begins in earnest after he witnesses units of the First Cavalry Division in action against a Vietcong-governed village. In 2013 *Entertainment Weekly* called that assault "the single most riveting sequence in any war film."[85]

Other than for ceremonial purposes, the U.S. Army has had no horse units since 1943, but its cavalry regiments continued in various capacities and during the Vietnam era were mounted in helicopters. Bell UH-1 Huey and AH-1 Cobra helicopter gunships provided mobile firepower and carried the cavalry's airmobile units to their targets, but their mechanized steeds were vulnerable to ground fire. By the end of the war a total of five thousand U.S. helicopters were lost, many to Soviet-made heat-seeking missiles. As shown in *Apocalypse Now*, the cavalry maintained much of its old esprit de corps. Its commander, Lt. Col. Kilgore (Robert Duvall), sports the traditional hat and yellow kerchief of the cavalry. By some accounts he was based on Lt. Col. George S. Patton IV, son of the World War II general, who commanded armored units in Vietnam.[86] A bugler blows "charge" as the helicopters, crossed sabers painted on their noses, take off for their attack. Seemingly impervious to enemy gunfire, Kilgore speaks and moves with the swagger and bluster of George C. Scott's Patton. As Wagner's "Ride of the Valkyries" blares from loudspeakers, Kilgore's gunships swoop upon the tranquil Vietcong village with rockets and multibarreled machine guns. The army's psychological operations units conceived the use of music to demoralize the enemy; other small details, including the air cavalrymen sitting on their helmets to protect private parts from ground fire, are also drawn from reality.

Coppola spoke of finding beauty in "fantastically grotesque and destructive things," especially his "ballet of the helicopters." The battle sequences are often surreal through their strange juxtapositions of burning grass huts and flaming cars, a helicopter lifting off with a cow dangling below from straps, and a TV news crew (a cameo performance by Coppola) hollering instructions at GIs. The war flashes by like a hallucination; many of the troops are high on marijuana and LSD. The air cavalry scenes were shot aloft with real helicopters, lending a palpable edge of danger to the cinematic dance of death. Filming was often delayed when the Philippine air force pulled out its units to fight nearby insurgents. Sound editor Walter Murch won an Oscar for replicating the sonic dimension of battle and the machinery of war. Coppola wanted Vietnam veterans watching *Apocalypse Now* to hear the war as it really sounded. A Vietnam veteran, helicopter pilot Dick White, oversaw the copter scenes.[87]

The heart of the film is the long journey in the river patrol boat (PBR) ferrying Willard to Kurtz's lair. The fiberglass-hulled PBR was part of the U.S. Navy's "brown water" fleet; boats of this class often conveyed Special Forces on raids into enemy territory because of their shallow draft, maneuverability, and quiet engines.[88] The crew of Willard's PBR is not the American microcosm typical of the squads featured in many World War II movies but a plausible Vietnam-era ensemble. Half are African American, including Chief (Albert Hall), a serious and career-minded junior officer; and Mr. Clean (a fourteen-year-old Laurence Fishburne), very young and eager for harmless adventure. Chef (Frederic Forrest) is a working-class white man from New Orleans who may have volunteered to escape the army draft. The presence of champion surfer Lance Johnson (Sam Bottoms) is unexplained; he may have signed up out of patriotism.

As they proceed along the river, Willard and the sailors are "going back in time," according to Coppola.[89] They are shedding their ties to civilization. The PBR stops at a U.S. base for recreation provided by a trio of dancing Playboy Playmates (and introduced by the real-life concert promoter Bill Graham). The pent-up sexual energy of the men in the audience is released as a riot, from which the Playmates barely escape. When the PBR inspects a sampan hauling produce to market, misunderstanding escalates into massacre by a crew anxious over the presence of unseen enemies. The last U.S. base along the river is meant to guard a bridge, a structure destroyed every night by the Vietcong, who ruled the darkness in much of rural Vietnam, but rebuilt each day by the Americans in an exercise in futility. The tails of downed U.S. bombers rise from the river like the bones of prehistoric monsters. A sniper kills Mr. Clean. Indigenous tribesmen attack with darts and spears, impaling Chief. The perimeter of Kurtz's realm is ringed with skulls mounted in an archaic gesture of warning and doom.

Kurtz's palm-shrouded sanctum rises on terraced steps from the river's edge, a stony edifice constructed by production designer Dean Tavoularis with Angkor Wat in mind. It is a temple fit for an ancient king with claims to divinity, the role Kurtz arrogated for himself. Along with Conrad, Kurtz's character shares roots with H. Rider Haggard and other nineteenth-century authors who wrote of white adventurers, beyond the fringe of empire, regarded by the natives as gods. Milius's conception hewed closely to such models. "Do you know what it is to be a white man who can summon fire from the sky?" Kurtz demands in an unfilmed passage from Milius's script. Coppola was determined to fashion a more sophisticated, ambiguous character but found his inspiration ebbing by the time he reached the film's climax. The Kurtz seen in *Apocalypse Now* resulted in large part from the contributions of Marlon Brando, with assistance from story editor Dennis Jakob. Jakob placed James George Frazer's classic *The Golden Bough* on Kurtz's nightstand, suggested that the colonel recite verses from T. S. Eliot's "The Wasteland," and saw the character as representing the archetype of the Fisher King.[90]

Brando, who arrived in the Philippines alarmingly unprepared and overweight for his role, stamped the character of Kurtz in his own image. He brought the colonel to life in ways the screenplay never suggested. "What I'd really wanted from the beginning was to find a way to make my part smaller so that I wouldn't have to work as hard," he explained.[91] Brando put Kurtz in black Vietnamese pajamas to hide his own bulk. After twisting his ankle the first day on set, Brando's Kurtz reclined on an oriental daybed, enhancing the aura of menace. The darkness of Kurtz's lair concealed Brando's obesity but deepened the mystery.[92]

A tribe dwelling nearby the production, the Ifugao, stood in for the Montagnard. They were paid for their performance in food and medicine and given a water buffalo. Coppola cut between the sacrifice of the buffalo and Willard's sacrificial killing of Kurtz, linking the climax to primeval rites of death and renewal described in *The Golden Bough*. Willard's mission is accomplished. One rogue American officer is dead, as if the scapegoat for the war's failure, but the conflict would continue. "The way we made it was very much like the way the Americans were in Vietnam," Coppola explained. "We were in the jungle, there were too many of us, we had access to too much money, too much equipment, and little by little we went insane."[93]

Two years passed between the end of the shooting in the Philippines and *Apocalypse Now*'s debut at the Cannes film festival, where it shared the Palme d'Or with Volker Schlöndorff's bitterly satirical World War II film, *The Tin Drum*. Over a million and a half feet of exposed negatives sat in the editing room as Coppola pieced together his sprawling epic. The famous opening scene was assembled from "fills," taken as the cameras rolled between scenes, after Coppola decided that the footage offered entrée into the mind of Willard. Finally, the doom-laden tones of "The End" struck the director as an appropriate beginning for *Apocalypse Now*. He had known the recording artists, the Doors, from his days at the film school at the University of California, Los Angeles.[94] Forty-nine minutes of footage omitted from the movie's original release were included in Coppola's reedited version, *Apocalypse Now Redux* (2001).

"The guess here is that the general public is not interested in another Vietnam film," critic Gene Siskell wrote upon the release of *Apocalypse Now*.[95] His guess was proved wrong by the film's enormous and rapid success at the box office and, more important, its enduring role in shaping popular perception of the war as a surreal nightmare. As Siskell's colleague Roger Ebert put it on the twentieth anniversary of the film's release, "*Apocalypse Now* is the best Vietnam film, one of the greatest of all films, because it pushes beyond the others, into the dark places of the soul." It won two Academy Awards.[96]

Apocalypse Now would not be the last Vietnam movie to find a wide audience. Director Oliver Stone served two terms of duty in Vietnam and returned repeatedly to the war for inspiration. The conflict "provided him with both an avenue for personal exploration and a tool for understanding larger historical questions" about the nature of war and American society.[97] Fascinated by Joseph Conrad and fleeing an unhappy life, Stone taught English in Saigon and eventually joined the U.S. Army as an infantryman, turning down the opportunity for Officer Candidate School. Although personal motivations determined many of his choices, Stone believed in the war's objective of containing communism and protecting the boundaries of the "Free World."

Stationed near the Cambodian border, his opinions and ideals crumbled under the pressure of reality. Corruption was rank, with quartermasters selling supplies on the black market, and the danger of night patrols in the jungle was intensified by the invisibility of the Vietcong. Stone was wounded, and many of his buddies were killed. Drug use was prevalent. Stone would later speak of his decision to join the army as "a terrible mistake" and the war as a game in which the poorer classes of Americans and Vietnamese were expendable pawns.[98] And yet Stone wanted to be in the heart of the action, volunteering for a First Cavalry Division reconnaissance platoon, where he met the men who inspired the characters in *Platoon* (1986).

At the time Stone began writing his screenplay for *Platoon*, Hollywood remained gun shy over Vietnam. With the success of *Coming Home* and *The Deer Hunter*, Stone was commissioned to write a screenplay based on a memoir by paralyzed Vietnam veteran Ron Kovic, *Born on the Fourth of July*, but the studios became wary of producing too many Vietnam pictures. The impact of *Apocalypse Now* cleared the way. Stone eventually got around to directing *Born on the Fourth of July* (1989), but *Platoon* stands as his most memorable depiction of the war.

Winning Oscars for Best Picture, Director, Sound, and Editing, *Platoon* is the story of a unit of GIs on patrol in a place Stone knew from wartime experience, the remote jungle near the Cambodian border. The film excelled in its depiction of the tension of waiting for an enemy that could be everywhere and nowhere. Its battles are usually inconclusive, fought not for ideals but for survival. *Platoon* is notable as the breakout film for Martin Sheen's son, Charlie, who played the middle-class novice among the unit's lower-class survivors.

The experiences of another Vietnam veteran, Gustav Hasford, became the basis for perhaps the final great film on the war, *Full Metal Jacket* (1987). Stanley Kubrick adapted Hasford's novel *The Short-Timers* (1979) with assistance from *Dispatches* author Michael Herr. The director praised Hasford's novel for its economy and for omitting "the scene where the guy talks about his father, who's an alcoholic, his girlfriend — all that stuff that bogs down and seems so arbitrarily inserted into every war story."[99] Following a U.S. Marine Corps recruit, Joker (Matthew Modine), through basic training, his stint as a reporter for the military's *Stars and Stripes* newspaper, and his moments of decision during the Tet Offensive, *Full Metal Jacket* is a sardonic examination of the dehumanization that can occur in military service and wartime. Unwilling to travel from his adopted British home, Kubrick re-created Hue amid the partially demolished Beckton Gas Works, whose architecture resembled the French colonial neighborhoods of the Vietnamese city, and replicated the jungle with a mixture of rubber plants and palm trees imported from Spain.[100] The inscriptions on Joker's helmet exemplified the marine's ambiguous emotions: "Born to Kill" shared space with a peace symbol.

Vietnam was part of a regional struggle between Communists and anti-Communists in the former French Indochina. While Laos seldom emerged from the back pages, Cambodia was headline news even before becoming the site of the most infamous experiment by Marxist-Leninists in forcibly reconstructing society. Mao Zedong's

Great Leap Forward may have resulted in the death of thirty-six million in history's greatest famine, but contemporary news reports were scant, and no movie about it has ever been made.[101] Cambodia's tragedy is remembered by *The Killing Fields* (1984).

U.S. intervention in Cambodia — including air raids on the Ho Chi Minh Trail, the 1970 incursion to destroy North Vietnamese hideouts, and the coup that brought the pro-American regime of Gen. Lon Nol to power in 1970 — created the conditions for the ascent of the country's formerly insignificant Communist Party, the Khmer Rouge. It "would not have won power without U.S. economic and military destabilization," according to Yale University's Ben Kiernan.[102] "I witnessed the Americans' imperviousness to the realities of Cambodia," recalled François Bizot, a French scholar imprisoned by the Khmer Rouge. "Yet today I do not know what I reproach them for more, their intervention or their withdrawal."[103]

As Saigon fell to the North Vietnamese in April 1975, the Khmer Rouge under Pol Pot topped Nol and seized control of Cambodia. Once in power, they began a forced program of evacuating the population of cities and towns into the countryside and imposing a collectivized agricultural economy. Anywhere from one to three million Cambodians died during the three and a half years of Pol Pot's regime, amounting to a quarter of the country's population.[104] Pol Pot was driven into hiding along the jungles of the Thai border after Vietnam, angered by border clashes and ideological arguments, invaded Cambodia at the end of 1978 and installed a pro-Vietnamese government.

Although pushed to the margins, the Khmer Rouge, armed by China, continued to fight for control of Cambodia when *The Killing Fields* was released. The film by British director Roland Joffé put a human face on the country's tragedy by dramatizing the true story of Dith Pran, a Cambodian journalist and translator for the *New York Times*. Based on the account of Pran's colleague, *Times* Pulitzer-winning foreign correspondent Sydney Schanberg, *The Killing Fields* depicts Pran as he feigned ignorance to avoid execution. The Khmer Rouge were especially eager to kill the country's intellectuals and educated professionals. Despite winning a scholarship to a technical school in Paris, Pol Pot had been a poor student, sat for no exams, and returned home without a degree.[105]

The Killing Fields earned three Oscars, including Best Supporting Actor for the role of Pran, played by Haing S. Ngor, a physician imprisoned by the Khmer Rouge who found his way to the United States after escaping from a labor camp. In the aftermath of the Vietnamese invasion, Pol Pot had already become synonymous with genocide, but *The Killing Fields* brought the story to the general public. The film introduced a new meaning to *killing field*, previously a military term for the field in front of the line of fire. *Killing field* has since entered the world's vocabulary to describe past horrors such as the Holocaust as well as new campaigns of mass murder in Rwanda, Bosnia, and the Congo.

CHARLIE WILSON'S WAR (2007)

Although no one noticed at the time, the course of world events began to change one night in April 1980, when Charles Wilson, a wily Democratic congressman from Texas, looked up from his hot tub in the Fantasy Suite of Caesar's Palace in Las Vegas, where he was surrounded by the pleasant company of strippers, Playboy bunnies, and cocaine, and saw Dan Rather on TV wearing a turban and a beard.

The unfamiliar appearance of this familiar newsman aroused his interest. While on trek across Afghanistan for *60 Minutes*, Rather made the case that Afghans fighting against Soviet occupiers deserved American aid. As Wilson gazed at the grainy CBS footage, he began to glimpse the outline of his own future as well as the future of the world. He would provide weapons for the mujahideen, the Muslim "holy warriors" of distant Afghanistan. He, Charlie Wilson, would turn the Afghan hills into another Vietnam, this time with the Communists in the quagmire.

Directed by Mike Nichols, a veteran of theater and film who in 1998 had helmed the Bill Clinton election drama *Primary Colors*, and written by Aaron Sorkin, best known for the popular NBC White House

series *The West Wing*, *Charlie Wilson's War* (2007) would be farcical
had it not been so close to the truth. *Charlie Wilson's War* archly
transforms the news reporting of its source, the best-selling account
by award-winning journalist (and *60 Minutes* producer) George Crile,
into a ripping good, essentially true story. Sorkin fashions Crile's
book into a memorable tale of American power politics filled with
larger-than-life characters that hew close to their real-life sources. Tom
Hanks stars in the title role, spreading the charm like sweet barbeque
sauce at an Independence Day cookout, and glamorous Julia Roberts
plays Wilson's crusading millionaire accomplice, Joanne Herring.
Wilson and Herring are from Texas, where everything is bigger than
elsewhere, starting with the sky overhead and the star on the state flag.

Many of the film's most fantastic scenes conform closely to the
book, and some of the dialogue is lifted straight from Crile's account.
Entranced by Rather's coverage of the brave but poorly armed Afghan
insurgents, Wilson really did ask a staffer on the House Defense
Appropriations Subcommittee how much money had been budgeted
for the CIA's operations in support of the mujahideen. "Five million,"
answered the staffer. "Double it," Wilson said.[106]

Charlie Wilson's War depicts the congressman as a hard drinking,
womanizing, ne'er-do-well who finally had a cause to believe in. Sitting
on key committees, Wilson manipulated the secret and virtually bot-
tomless budget for the CIA through horse trading and glad-handing.
Between Herring's contacts in Pakistan and his friendship with Jewish
American groups, Wilson helped forge a covert alliance involving
Egypt, Israel, Pakistan, and Saudi Arabia in common cause against
the Soviet Union, a hollow behemoth that nonetheless appeared to
be rolling forward in its bid for global influence. Wilson's coalition
helped the Afghans fight back and eventually drive out the invader.
Wilson had been deeply involved in American foreign policy, something the film barely hints at but the book elucidates. The congressman
may have mixed pleasure with politics at every opportunity, but he
was also a hawk on defense, closely aligned with the Israel lobby and
concerned about Communist advances on the world stage.

The backdrop to *Charlie Wilson's War* was the Soviet Union's ill-conceived attempt to dragoon Afghanistan into the Eastern bloc. The remote mountainous nation had been strategically important in the nineteenth-century imperial rivalry between Britain and Russia. Rudyard Kipling had addressed Britain's "Great Game" beyond the Khyber Pass in stories and poetry, and Sherlock Holmes's confidant, Dr. Watson, was a veteran of one of England's ill-fated Afghan campaigns. But Afghanistan had receded from the attention of generals and statesmen in the twentieth century. Neutral Afghanistan became a popular tourist route for adventurous travelers in the 1960s and remained so even after the peaceful overthrow of King Zahir Shah by his cousin Mohammed Daoud Khan in 1973. Daoud's republic came to power with the aid of Communists but repressed leftists and Islamists alike while trying to extend the central government's always tenuous control over the countryside. Unrest simmered against his regime, and small cadres of Islamic militants operated against him from Pakistan. The Communist People's Democratic Party infiltrated the police and plotted from within its bridgehead in the military. Afghan officers had received training in the USSR as far back as the 1950s, and Soviet advisors were installed at the battalion level.

In April 1978 Daoud was killed in a Communist coup and replaced by Noor Mohammad Taraki, with Hafizullah Amin as his deputy. Unstable from the onset, the new administration was split by conflict between rival factions within the People's Democratic Party, the Khalq and the Parcham, whose cadres "fought occasional Wild West–style gun battles." The militant Khalq dominated and, with the more pro-Soviet Parcham in retreat, imposed an ambitious program on a reluctant nation. The Khalq mandated universal literacy and equality for women but implemented land reforms that exacerbated rural poverty. Communist planning disrupted a delicate system of obligations that had sustained village life over the centuries.[107]

Emblematic of the country's growing disorder was the kidnapping of U.S. ambassador Adolph Dubs on February 14, 1979, supposedly by Maoist rebels demanding the release of imprisoned comrades.

After Dubs and his captors were killed in a police raid, the United States closed its embassy in Kabul, the Afghan capital. The following month Russian advisors were killed during a military uprising in Herat encouraged by Maoists and mullahs. The Soviets retaliated by bombing the city, leveling many neighborhoods. Although the death toll may have reached twenty-five thousand, the carnage did not discourage rebellions in Shia-populated districts fanned by Iran's new revolutionary government.[108]

The insurgency spread despite lack of central leadership, flaring up across tribal, ethnic, and religious lines. As the Soviet military buildup continued, the Kremlin encouraged Taraki to eliminate the acrimonious and incompetent Amin, but getting wind of the plot, Amin struck first, making himself president in September 1979. Unhappy with the coup, the Soviets debated their next move. The KGB, the army, and the diplomatic service opposed the idea of invading Afghanistan; however, wrote Sorbonne political science professor Gilles Dorronsoro, "it appears the responsibility for the decision rested on the alcoholic and depressive Brezhnev."[109] On December 27, 1979, Soviet troops seized Kabul and other strategic points and installed the pro-Moscow leader of the Parcham faction, Babrak Karmal, as president. Amin was summarily executed.

The goodwill the USSR enjoyed among leftist and liberal parties in the West had been leaking away since Nikita Khrushchev's 1956 exposure of Stalinism and suffered additional losses after Soviet tanks crushed the Prague Spring in 1968. Aleksandr Solzhenitsyn's best-selling account of the Soviet police state, *The Gulag Archipelago* (1973), further diminished the Kremlin's moral authority, even as détente with the United States reinforced the USSR's international standing. "We are seeing a shift from the cold war to normal relations, to ever wider implementation of the principles of peaceful coexistence of states with different social systems," a Soviet academician insisted.[110] With the decision to invade Afghanistan came the final plunge in Soviet prestige. For Western European Communist parties in nations such as France and Italy, which had long played prominent roles in parliamentary politics, the invasion was an "acute embarrassment" resulting in loss of electoral support.[111]

The invasion of Afghanistan was also a diplomatic failure marking the end of détente with the United States. In his January 23, 1980, State of the Union Address, President Carter called the invasion "the most serious threat to the peace since the Second World War." Under Carter the United States boycotted the 1980 Moscow Summer Olympic Games, imposed a grain embargo, installed cruise missiles in Western Europe, and began the massive military buildup that gained momentum under his successor, Ronald Reagan. Secretly, Carter authorized the CIA to begin actions against the Soviets in Afghanistan, reversing the post-Watergate reforms implemented only a few years earlier, which curtailed the agency's Clandestine Service and outraged one of the pivotal real-life characters from *Charlie Wilson's War*, Greek American CIA agent Gust Avrakotos, played by Philip Seymour Hoffman in the film. In an effort to harmonize American foreign policy with professed American values, Carter had cut off aid to Pakistan, citing human rights abuses by President Mohammed Zia ul-Haq's administration. In *Charlie Wilson's War* it appears as if Wilson and Herring were the only players in the deal with Zia to supply Afghan rebels, and they were crucial, yet the initial contact came from the White House. Within days of the invasion the CIA began transferring stockpiled Soviet weapons to Pakistan's military intelligence agency, the ISI, for distribution in Afghanistan.[112] Wilson's role was to inflate a sideshow insurgency into a proxy war between the superpowers.

The movie's sexiest parts concern the late-night sessions between Wilson and Herring, a right-wing socialite straight out of *Dallas* who claims George Washington in her family tree and serves as an honorary consul in Pakistan's foreign service. She is a lioness of Texas society, the hostess of lavish political fund-raisers where deals can be struck. The man who makes their scheme work, however, is the irascible Avrakotos. Sparring with white Anglo-Saxon Protestant superiors in the agency who sniff that he is "barely American," Avrakotos is blunt spoken and clear-eyed while dropping Zen aphorisms into his reports on which missiles are best for downing Soviet helicopter gunships or piercing the armor of their tanks.

All of this was true. A working-class immigrant's son, Avrakotos harbored resentment against the "cake eaters," as he called the WASPs. Only in 1960 did the CIA begin opening its doors to the "new Americans," and Avrakotos was among the first to enter the Clandestine Service whose heritage was not confined to northern Europe. His contempt for the cake eaters was exceeded only by his visceral hatred of Communists, intensified during his tenure as CIA liaison with the Greek military junta in the 1960s. With a "brutal instinct for the jugular," Avrakotos became Wilson's advisor on Afghan strategy, which included neutralizing Soviet air superiority after the first delivery in 1986 of U.S.-made Stinger shoulder-fired missiles. The Stingers were credited by many sources with turning the tide of the war, and their arrival is shown in the film as a turning point.[113] As the United States learned in Vietnam, small teams of guerrillas with advanced weapons can thwart the mightiest war machine. The mountain passes from Pakistan into Afghanistan became America's Ho Chi Minh Trail, a lifeline for the rebels carried on the backs of mules. *Charlie Wilson's War* compresses time as if the triumph of the mujahideen was a matter of only a few years. In reality it took nine years to drive out the Soviets, and victory was uncertain for much of the time.

Until Dan Rather's *60 Minutes* segment, the broadcast seen by Wilson from his hot tub, most Americans were not imaginatively engaged in the Afghan conflict. In the era of three main commercial networks, a single episode of a prominent news program could have enormous influence. On film and in reality Wilson advocated the position soon adopted by the Reagan administration that the Cold War must end not in perpetual stalemate but in American victory, and the battlefield would not be Europe but Afghanistan. Aside from losing twenty-eight thousand dead during their occupation, Soviet forces suffered a breakdown in morale comparable to that of the United States in Vietnam, spurred by alcohol and drug abuse and the anxiety of fighting an often-unseen enemy. The Soviet situation was complicated by the Kremlin's denial that Afghanistan was anything more than a police action against bandits, despite the many veterans returning home without limbs and the transport planes laden with coffins. Russian director Alexey Balabanov depicted the unraveling of the USSR under the strain of Afghanistan in a hauntingly bizarre film released the same year as *Charlie Wilson's War*, *Cargo 200* (2007).

Afghanistan was not the sole cause of the Soviet Union's demise. The arms race with the United States had always sapped resources from an inefficient economy, and the buildup that began under Carter and intensified under Reagan, while costly to the United States, was devastating to the USSR. Leonid Brezhnev spoke of unresolved "nationality questions" at the 1981 Party Congress, an oblique reference to the rapid increase in the Muslim population of the Soviet republics of Central Asia and the Caucasus. A victory in Afghanistan might have quelled dreams of independence in Chechnya, Tajikistan, and Uzbekistan; the defeat almost certainly inflamed the desire to break away from Moscow.[114] No one, however, has been able to fashion the economic and demographic crises of the late Soviet Union into a compelling, widely seen movie. The Afghan war and Washington backstage politics are better suited for Hollywood.

On February 15, 1989, the last Soviet unit withdrew from Afghanistan across the ironically named Friendship Bridge with television news cameras bearing witness. *Charlie Wilson's War* accurately captures the U.S. reaction when the Soviets finally pulled out. Avrakotos worried that without a massive reconstruction program Afghanistan would fall into the hands of "the crazies." Wilson proposed a billion-dollar aid package to rebuild schools and infrastructure, but with the Cold War ending his entreaties went unheard amid the celebration. Congratulating itself on the trouble it had caused for the USSR, the U.S. government refused to think about unintended consequences. Schooling would now take place in fundamentalist Islamic madrasas, and the country was left in ruins. What the film failed to add was that many Afghan fighters had no idea where their weapons actually came from and credited Pakistan with enabling their victory. The conclusion of *Charlie Wilson's War* possesses the benefit of hindsight. By quietly bankrupting the Soviet Union by increasing the cost of its Afghan adventure, the United States helped end the Cold War but laid the foundation for 9/11.

CHAPTER FOUR

The War on Terror (2001–)

On the night of September 11, 2001, following the attacks on the
World Trade Center in New York and at the Pentagon, President
George W. Bush addressed a shocked nation with resolution and
moral clarity. "We will make no distinction between the terrorists who
committed these acts and those who harbor them," he promised. On
September 14, speaking at the National Cathedral in Washington D C,
he added, "Our responsibility to history is already clear: to answer
these attacks and rid the world of evil." Six days later he introduced
the term *war on terror*, but the phrase had roots. The Reagan administration had referred to a "war against terrorism" in the aftermath of
the bombing of the U.S. Marine barracks in Beirut (1983), and on the
evening of September 11 N B C anchorman Tom Brokaw expressed the
thought that "terrorists have declared war on America."

In the weeks following 9/11 many assumed that the war on terror's
objectives would be fulfilled with Operation Enduring Freedom, the
assault that began on October 7 against al-Qaeda, the perpetrators
of 9/11, and the Taliban, the Afghan regime that harbored them.
Yet the success of Enduring Freedom in expelling the Taliban from

Afghanistan's cities and installing Hamid Karzai as the country's president represented only phase 1 of Bush's war on terror. In his State of the Union address on January 29, 2002, Bush presented his vision for the war with a memorable phrase, the *Axis of Evil*, directed against Iraq, Iran, and North Korea. Bush was elected president on a primarily domestic agenda, but 9/11 allowed his more ambitious foreign policy advisors to rise to the fore. In his address Bush insisted: "I will not wait on events . . . I will not permit the world's most dangerous regimes to threaten us with the world's most dangerous weapons." The war on terror was no longer a response to acts of terrorism but promised the elimination of the threat of terror from a set of nations that stood outside the emerging world order.

Although the Bush administration was able to cobble together a "Coalition of the Willing" for its occupation of Iraq, the invasion of that country aroused hostility around the world and eroded the enormous goodwill the United States enjoyed after 9/11. Officially called the "Multi-National Force — Iraq," the separate units were given their own distinctive arm patch and badge, but the coalition was hobbled by token contingents from dozens of nations, most sending fewer than one hundred troops in an effort to curry favor for trade and arms agreements with the United States. The token coalition units were confined to base for fear of incurring casualties. Only Britain and Australia supported the U.S. occupation with significant forces.[1]

The domestic unity Bush earned in the days following 9/11 dissolved after the United States found winning the peace in Iraq to be more difficult than winning the war. Bush's successor, President Barack Obama, was determined to wind down America's military involvement in Afghanistan and Iraq, but even as U.S. combat operations in both nations ceased, the legacy of American intervention was unclear. Karzai's regime remained mired in guerrilla war with the undefeated Taliban, while Iraq, whose Shiite majority government was aligned diplomatically with Iran, was wracked with instability. As for the other components of the Axis of Evil, Iran and North Korea have maintained their nuclear arms programs and continued to contribute to global anxiety.

Obama finally achieved the goal that had eluded his predecessor, the death of 9/11 mastermind Osama bin Laden (2011), yet unrest continued in the Middle East, including attacks on the U.S. consulate in Benghazi, Libya, on September 11, 2013, that took the lives of the ambassador and three other Americans. Early in his second term Obama declared that al-Qaeda was "on the path to defeat" and the United States must refocus its counterterrorism efforts to peacetime levels. "Our systematic effort to dismantle terrorist organizations must continue," he told the National Defense University. "But this war, like all wars, must end. That's what history advises. It's what our democracy demands." Obama's remarks were controversial, with congressional Republicans complaining that victory had been declared prematurely, and the ramifications for American policy were left unclear.[2]

Security and military concerns stemming from the same complex of issues that led to 9/11 continued in the months after Obama's announcement that the war on terror was over, with the bombing of the Boston Marathon by Chechen American terrorists (April 15, 2013) and the prospect of U.S. intervention in a Syrian civil war pitting a secular dictatorship against a rebel coalition increasingly dominated by Jihadist groups aligned with al-Qaeda.

The role of cinema in memorializing the events of the war on terror was diminished by the rapidly changing media landscape. How could any filmmaker compete with the role newscasts played in shaping public consciousness of 9/11? How could the cumbersome machinery of Hollywood keep pace with the relentless 24/7 news cycle, driven in large measure by cable channels with vigorously mapped-out target demographics that increasingly isolated viewers within their own partisan worlds? In a digital age the word *film* became an anachronism, albeit one that will likely cling to the pop culture vocabulary from long habit. "Moviegoing does not quite exist anymore as a consuming public preoccupation," film critic David Thomson confessed in 2012. "The technologies are carrying us forward so rapidly we become giddy with change," he added, speaking of the proliferation of images on smartphones and new delivery systems such as YouTube and Netflix.

Thomson worried that so many small screens are diminishing the quality of seeing and meaning.[3]

Even as television news reduced the importance of films in memorializing recent events and even as websites and social media chipped away at the already fragmented audience for TV news, television drama entered a new golden age enabled by increasingly sophisticated home recording technology that allows viewers to watch shows on their own time and as often they like, rather than according to the set schedules that had always characterized broadcasting. Many of the most discussed TV programs of the twenty-first century resembled the serialized novels of the nineteenth century, with plotlines and characters developing over many years. Many of the most significant of these programs originated on cable, where content was less regulated, and involved morally ambiguous antiheroes. Prominent TV series were more often the topics of ongoing discussions than movies.[4]

The signal television show of the war on terror, 24, was already in production on 9/11 and debuted on the Fox Channel on November 6, 2001. The action of each episode occurs in "real time" with a race against the digital clock to foil a terrorist plot. The protagonist is a U.S. counterterrorism agent, Jack Bauer (Kiefer Sutherland), willing to use any means to safeguard the homeland. The program was wildly popular and won many awards, including an Emmy for Outstanding Drama Series, but it became a lightning rod for criticism of American policies in the war on terror. In 2007 Brig. Gen. Patrick Finnegan, dean of West Point, reportedly met with 24's producers to criticize the program's favorable depiction of torture as a useful interrogation method, saying that the series encouraged misdeeds among troops in the field and harmed the reputation of the United States.[5]

Depicting Bauer as an insubordinate rebel within the federal government, 24 draws from a strain in American pop culture distrustful of the agendas and capabilities of the nation's institutions. Bauer has been compared to Mulder and Scully, the renegade FBI agents of the paranormal drama *The X-Files*. According to Max Lerner, "Both *The X-Files* and 24 suggest that the government is completely dependent on mavericks among its agents in order to protect America against its enemies."[6]

Despite the shrinking share of attention movies hold for popular audiences, three films, each dealing with a particular aspect of the war on terror, have made indelible impressions. The first, *United 93*, concerns events on September 11. The second, *The Hurt Locker*, portrays U.S. military service in Iraq. Finally, *Zero Dark Thirty* focuses on the long hunt for bin Laden. Notably, one filmmaker, Kathryn Bigelow, directed two of the three.

UNITED 93 (2006)

With a frightening mix of delusion and calculation, nineteen young men, all but four from Saudi Arabia, commandeered four airliners on the morning of September 11, 2001, in a carefully planned suicide mission intended to harm and humble the United States of America. One liner struck the Pentagon; a second fell on a field outside Pittsburgh after passengers overpowered the hijackers; and the other two crashed into the World Trade Center and toppled the Twin Towers, the world's tallest structures when they were completed in 1973. Some five thousand people died in the attacks, more than had been killed at Pearl Harbor.

September 11 was a sky-blue day in New York and through much of the United States, and for many Americans the attack came as if from out of the blue. America woke up on that morning accustomed to invulnerability, distance from the problems of the outside world, and forgetfulness. For historian Alan Brinkley, commenting within days of the attack, 9/11 was a reminder that "the terrible things that have happened to people and nations elsewhere throughout history can in fact happen to us, too."[7]

Terrorism at home surprised most Americans, despite many precedents. In 1919 a wave of letter bombs were mailed by anarchists to prominent business and political leaders; one explosion damaged the home of U.S. Attorney General Alexander Mitchell Palmer. The world's first car bomb, actually a horse-drawn cart, exploded only a short distance from the site of the World Trade Center in New York's Financial District on September 16, 1920, killing 38 and maiming many more. Although no one claimed responsibility, the bombing was blamed on anarchists.[8] The Puerto Rican terrorist group the Fuerzas Armadas de Liberación Nacional (FALN) committed nearly 150 bombings and attacks in the United States from 1974 through 1983, often on purely civilian targets, killing and injuring dozens. The group was responsible for a 1977 bomb scare at the World Trade Center.[9] In 1995 antigovernment activists demolished the Alfred P. Murrah Federal Building in Oklahoma City with a truck bomb, killing 168 and injuring over 600 victims. Foreshadowing future events, 6 were killed and more than 1,000 wounded when Islamist extremists detonated a bomb in a World Trade Center parking garage in 1993. Six terrorists were convicted and sentenced to life.

The issues behind 9/11 are traceable to the post–World War I peace settlement in the Middle East, especially Britain's contradictory promises over the future of Palestine. The establishment of the State of Israel in the face of Arab opposition (1948) turned the region into a powder keg with a perennially burning fuse. After the Six Day War (1967) Muslim holy places in Jerusalem and restive Arab populations fell into Israeli hands. Uprisings by Palestinians and an influx of Jewish settlers into the occupied territories aggravated tensions, along with the rise of a revolutionary Shiite theocracy in Iran.

Through the decades of conflict, the United States was seen by Arabs to favor Israeli over Palestinian interests. America allied itself with authoritarian Arab regimes in the interest of economically crucial oil and Cold War rivalries. Ironically, America's most loyal Arab ally, Saudi Arabia, spent a percentage of oil revenue promoting its state religion, Wahhabism, a fundamentalist creed inimical to many Western values. The Saudis built mosques across the Muslim world and financed Wahhabi preachers, often with intolerant and inflammatory messages. The Wahhabis advanced alongside the Muslim Brotherhood, a movement born in the post—World War I anticolonial struggles that sought to transform Arab societies according to a religious model.

From such currents came the ideology of Islamism, positing rigid, selective interpretations of Sharia law as the basis for social order. Its leading intellectual figure, the Egyptian writer Sayyid Qutb, condemned secular Arab politics along with American materialism and its influence on the Arab world. His writings called for Jihad, a holy war against the West and its allies that justified the use of violence by a "righteous vanguard" leading the world to salvation. Qutb was influential in empowering militant Jihadist groups, including al-Qaeda, the perpetrators of 9/11.[10]

The immediate causes of 9/11 were embedded in Afghanistan, where defeat of the Soviet occupation became the rallying cry for Jihadists in the 1980s. Many Islamist groups fighting the Soviets were avowedly anti-American, albeit willing to deal with one devil to defeat another. With some justification Islamist rebels claimed credit for the eventual collapse of the Soviet "Evil Empire." Emboldened, they dreamed of taking down the world's remaining superpower.

Civil war continued in Afghanistan following the USSR's pullout, with much of the country falling to the Taliban by 1996. The Taliban (Arabic for "students") grew out of the fundamentalist religious schools of Pakistan encouraged by the spread of Wahhabism. Once in power, they imposed one of the most extreme and dogmatic Islamic regimes in history. Under their rule Afghanistan became a sanctuary for al-Qaeda, an organization founded in 1988 by Saudi multimillionaire Osama bin Laden.

Although bin Laden probably accepted American aid in the fight against the Soviets in Afghanistan, he turned on the United States, incensed by the stationing of American troops in Saudi Arabia during the 1990 preparation for the Persian Gulf War against Iraq. For bin Laden the arrival of U.S. forces in the land of Mecca and Medina, Islam's holiest cities, was a prelude to an occupation linked to Israel's seizure of Islam's third holy city, Jerusalem. He spoke of a "Crusader-Jewish" conspiracy bent on the destruction of the Muslim faith, and his paranoia found an audience among Muslims dismayed by the course of recent history. In a 1998 pronouncement bin Laden declared the killing of Americans and their allies as the "individual duty of every Muslim."[11]

Bin Laden's wealth enabled al-Qaeda to become the nexus of an international Jihadist network and organize a series of attacks against U.S. interests from tribal lands in Yemen and Somalia and under the eyes of friendly regimes in Sudan and Afghanistan. By 1993 al-Qaeda was already on the watch lists of Western intelligence agencies. In 1994 the group bombed Western compounds in the Saudi capital of Riyadh, killing five Americans. Four years later al-Qaeda blew up the U.S. embassies in Kenya and Tanzania, killing over two hundred. The Clinton administration responded by cruise missile strikes against suspected al-Qaeda sites in Sudan and Afghanistan but with little effect. In 2000 the USS *Cole* was attacked by suicide bombers at port in Yemen with a loss of seventeen sailors.

Early in 2000 a congressional committee under senators Gary Hart and Warren Rudman warned that a "direct, catastrophic attack against American citizens on American soil is likely." By the summer of 2001 the CIA, which had been tracking bin Laden for over a half-decade, began testing armed drones in the Nevada desert against a mock-up of the al-Qaeda leader's villa in Kandahar.[12]

In the aftermath of 9/11 questions were raised over the Bush administration's apparent lack of preparedness or even awareness, especially given that the CIA had thwarted several al-Qaeda operations in the past, including plots against the Lincoln and Holland tunnels in New York (1993) and U.S. airliners in Asia (1995). CIA director George Tenet spoke of al-Qaeda as "a tremendous threat" in the summer of 2001 and was "nearly frantic" over the prospect of an attack. During that time an FBI agent reported suspicious activities by Arab students at American flight schools.[13] Legal guidelines dating from the post-Watergate era precluded the CIA and the FBI from sharing information. The bipartisan 9/11 Commission, impaneled to investigate the attack, found "four kinds of failures: in imagination, policy, capabilities, and management." Responsibility for the failure was spread across many agencies.[14]

The shock of 9/11 was worldwide, as was the observation that the attack resembled a Hollywood action thriller. Columnist Andrei Codrescu recalled: "The whole world gathered around televisions to watch the horror visited upon us. My friend Zoana wrote from Romania that she had been watching with her son. She sent her heartfelt condolences and said, 'We keep waiting for Bruce Willis to show up and for the movie to end.'"[15] Writing on the tenth anniversary of the attack, film critic Roger Ebert recalled watching the first reports of 9/11 played over and over on television and thinking, "How often have we seen such sights in fantasy? How many imagined disasters, natural and man-made, have destroyed the cities of the earth?" He added, "Certainly, it seemed that no work of fiction could encompass the horror."[16]

The pillars of smoke rising from the World Trade Center became the disaster's iconic image, and at first it seemed almost sacrilegious to display those buildings in any context but 9/11. The Twin Towers were digitally removed from the New York skyline of films in production in the fall of 2001. Ebert grappled with the difficulty filmmakers confronted in approaching an event whose perverse inspiration appeared to be cinema itself. He proclaimed a short subject by a Mexican filmmaker from a little-seen collection of segments by eleven directors, *September 11* (2003), as the best 9/11 film. Alejandro Gonzalez Inarritu's short contribution to the project "has greatness, because it fully respects the horror" by consisting of a black screen, occasionally interrupted by split-second flashes of bodies falling from the Twin Towers.[17] Inarritu's short film magnifies rather than dramatizes impressions left by the incessant news coverage.

Unlike the unforgettable surprise attack that defined a previous generation, Pearl Harbor, the subject or backdrop of many popular movies, 9/11 has proven more difficult to capture. News of Japan's assault flashed to the nation by radio, an entirely different reception than on 9/11, when many Americans witnessed the fall of the second tower live on television. The images of the crumbling World Trade Center were repeated virtually without end for many days. Television cameras rushed to the scene and recorded much of the destruction as it unfolded. The continual repetition of images from real life accompanied by updates from news anchors virtually erased the opportunity for imaginative distance between the events and the perception of the events. As a result, conventional cinematic narration seemed entirely inadequate. The major Hollywood motion picture on 9/11, Oliver Stone's fact-based drama about first responders, *World Trade Center* (2006), failed to stir the popular imagination, just as an array of smaller films focused on stories of everyday lives cut short failed to measure up to the weight of televised interviews with survivors and their families.

Only one film has influenced the public memory of 9/11, and it concerns an incident from which there were no visual images but only the anguished and defiant messages of passengers on their cell phones. British writer-director Paul Greengrass's Oscar-nominated *United 93* (2006) re-created events aboard United Airlines Flight 93, hijacked after takeoff from Newark on the morning of September 11 and eventually brought down in Pennsylvania by passengers who stormed the cockpit before the plane could strike its target in Washington DC. No one survived the crash.

United 93 succeeds in telling a plausible version of the events, with facts carefully assembled from the 9/11 Commission Report, transmissions from cockpit to control tower, and anguished calls from the passengers. Greengrass had recently directed a Hollywood action movie, *The Bourne Supremacy* (2004), but had earned his stripes for making *United 93* from an earlier docudrama, *Bloody Sunday* (2002), about an infamous melee in Ulster between British troops and Roman Catholic protestors during Northern Ireland's "Troubles" of the 1970s. The sensitivity surrounding the depiction of the 9/11 events dissuaded many filmmakers from touching the subject. Greengrass was careful to involve the families of Flight 93 victims, as did the actors playing the passengers. "It wouldn't be right to do with without meeting the family members," said cast member Daniel Sauli.[18]

Like *Bloody Sunday*, *United 93* jump-cuts between the interlocked scenes of a historical catastrophe, thrusting its cameras into the heart of chaos but artfully editing the images, choreographing the confusion into an emotionally riveting account. In both films no one, not even the perpetrators and agitators, is entirely in charge of the rapidly unfolding scenario. Wisely, in *United 93* Greenglass worked with a cast of unknown actors as terrorists and victims, air traffic controllers and air force personnel. As a result, the characters never remind us of stars but of people in a real-life drama. The four terrorists are grim and tightly knotted young men, not monsters but people performing monstrous deeds, desperately papering over their empty souls with pious invocations that only brought shame to their faith. Until the hijacking begins, the pilots engage in the usual banter. One of them almost missed the flight due to bad weather the previous night. The flight attendants gossip. As they wait in the terminal, the passengers are glued to their cell phones and newspapers. Except for the terrorists, locked in their stubborn conviction, everyone aboard Flight 93 absent-mindedly observes the routine — buckling seat belts, stowing away carry-ons, waiting in claustrophobic boredom for a landing they will never see.

United 93 spends much time in New York's control tower, whose staff watch uncomprehendingly as a plume of smoke rises from the World Trade Center, and in the headquarters of the North American Aerospace Defense command, which gathers most of its information the way most Americans did on that day, by watching CNN. The good guys at those ends of the drama are the ones who keep their heads as the pattern of ordinary expectations dissolves. No one working in civil aviation anticipated a hijacking, and those old enough to remember such events from the Nixon years imagined a standoff on the tarmac, not suicide and mass murder. The military had no plans for countering aerial terrorism, no rules of engagement, and it did not have enough fighter planes ready on the runways. Everything had to be improvised, and some of the decisions were good ones.

There is no single hero in *United 93*, no John Wayne or Humphrey Bogart to save the day. Talking together in hushed voices, the passengers and crew form a community of crisis and come to the conclusion that the hijackers plan to crash their plane into a landmark. They can wait to die as individuals, or they can fight back collectively. Together they find the courage to act. "Let's roll," passenger Todd Beamer says before charging the cockpit.

Those words, like much of *United 93*'s dialogue, were real, overheard on cell phone transmissions from the doomed plane. Two months after the attacks Neil Young released his song "Let's Roll" in a grim tribute to the heroism of the passengers. George W. Bush used the phrase several times in speeches during the coming months. It became the watchword for America's response to 9/11.

THE HURT LOCKER (2008) AND ZERO DARK THIRTY (2012)

The Hurt Locker opens with scratchy video transmitted from a camera mounted on a "bot," a tiny tank-treaded remote control vehicle sent ahead of the human bomb disposal squad. The setting is Baghdad 2004, one year into the U.S. occupation of Iraq, and although American forces suffer from sniping, most casualties result from improvised explosive devices (IEDs), roadside bombs often rigged from artillery shells, hidden amid the abundant debris of a city falling to pieces and touched off by cell phone signals. The film concerns an explosive ordnance disposal unit, three men with the world's most dangerous job. One team member, Staff Sergeant Thompson (Guy Pearce), dies during the opening scene, engulfed in a slow-motion plume of smoke and rubble, when an Iraqi, from a crowd of onlookers, triggers the bomb from his mobile phone. Thompson's effects are sent home in a metal locker. His replacement, Sergeant James (Jeremy Renner), is strangely unconcerned by the imminence of death.

Directed by Kathryn Bigelow, who had enjoyed an eclectic career with independent cult films such as *Near Dark* (1987), the bleak millennial drama *Strange Days* (1995), and the Cold War thriller *K19: The Widowmaker* (2002), *The Hurt Locker* is a soldier's story free of overt political allusions. The screenplay by Mark Boal, a journalist embedded with an ordnance disposal detail in Iraq in 2004, makes no reference to the reasons for the U.S. occupation and offers no comment on the strategy guiding America's involvement.[19] Saddam Hussein, 9/11, and the war on terror are never mentioned, and the enemies confronting the GIs are never named. Whether the insurgents are Saddam loyalists, Shiite militants, or al-Qaeda zealots matters little to American troops with little understanding of the local people or their surroundings. They might as well be invaders on an alien planet, an image enhanced by the astronaut-like protective suit and helmet worn by the ordnance techs as they disarm IEDs.

The United States's attack on Iraq, the subsequent occupation, and the combat role of American forces through their withdrawal in 2011 were not the nation's first military intervention in the region. Under President George H. W. Bush the United States had led an international coalition that drove Saddam Hussein's forces from Kuwait with air raids and lightning-fast ground engagements in January and February 1991. The buildup of U.S. forces in Saudi Arabia took longer than the military action; the Persian Gulf War was too short to inspire many movies. The most successful, *Jarhead* (2005), is based on the memoir of Marine Corps private Anthony Swofford, part of the forces that drove Iraqi occupiers from Kuwait. The war was covered incessantly by cable news, and its enduring images were of pillars of fire rising from the desert as Hussein's retreating troops set Kuwait's oil fields ablaze.

The first President Bush presided over rancorous meetings pitting administration hawks, clustered around Defense Secretary Dick Cheney and his undersecretary, Paul Wolfowitz, who advocated toppling Hussein's regime, and Joint Chiefs of Staff chairman Colin Powell, who advised caution. Bush reasoned that tolerating Hussein's seizure of Kuwait would encourage other rogue leaders to help themselves to their neighbor's territory and give Iraq, with the fourth largest military in the world, license to snatch the rich oil fields of Saudi Arabia and the United Arab Emirates and to threaten Israel. The campaign to repulse Iraq, eventually named Operation Desert Storm, was executed by Gen. H. Norman Schwarzkopf, whose father had been a military advisor to the Shah of Iran. Schwarzkopf headed

Central Command, an empty shell until the Iraqi invasion of Kuwait, with no forces at its disposal, only a headquarters in Tampa.[20] The Iraqi army was humbled by American air superiority and driven back within its borders. Hussein's regime remained intact, albeit hampered by UN sanctions and restricted by a no-fly zone over the northern tier of Iraq, patrolled by U.S. warplanes to protect the regime's Kurdish citizens from chemical weapons.

Many names associated with the Persian Gulf War returned for the Iraq War in 2003. The second President Bush followed the hawkish counsel of Cheney and Wolfowitz as well as Defense Secretary Donald Rumsfeld, with Secretary of State Powell providing a cautious counterpoint. Central Command, under Gen. Tommy Franks, was charged with defeating Hussein's forces and occupying Iraq in preparation for installing a regime friendly to Western interests.

Unlike the Taliban, Hussein was an ideological foe of al-Qaeda and played no role in 9/11. The attack on Iraq followed the preemptive logic of Bush's January 2002 "Axis of Evil" speech. Like the Clinton administration and the United Nations (UN), the Bush administration had reason to suspect that Hussein had a viable nuclear weapons program, and the dictator's past behavior, including invasions of Iran and Kuwait, ethnic cleansing of Kurds, and missile strikes against Israel, supported the idea that he posed a threat in an already dangerous part of the world. Advisors to the first President Bush who felt the U.S. military had been too timid in the Persian Gulf War resurfaced in the circle of the second President Bush, determined to complete what they saw as unfinished business.

The U.S. military had no trouble overwhelming Hussein's forces when Operation Iraqi Freedom began on March 20, 2003. Rumsfeld based his strategy on a book by military theorists Harlan Ullman and James Wade, *Shock and Awe*, which argued for paralyzing the enemy with volleys of air- and sea-launched "precision weapons" to achieve "rapid dominance." With Iraqi targets softened by missile strikes and air raids, General Franks was given a relatively small number of troops to subdue Iraq, 145,000, including one British division. Coalition casualties were light, with fewer than 200 deaths in the initial assault, while Iraqi losses were estimated at 13,000 to 45,000 soldiers, plus 7,000 civilian deaths from air raids. Problems began after Iraq fell. The State Department warned that the "focus on primarily military objectives and reluctance to take on 'policing roles' was a recipe for disaster" marked by "serious planning gaps for post-conflict public security and humanitarian assistance."[21] Ignoring the example of Germany after World War II, in which high officials were tried by an international tribunal and low-level Nazis and functionaries continued the job of civil administration under the watchful eyes of Allied troops, the Bush administration insisted on "de-Baathification," meaning that all members of Hussein's ruling Baath Party were removed from their positions. The difficulty was that in a one-party dictatorship, every policeman, government employee, and professional was affiliated by necessity with the party. At the onset of the American occupation, Iraq fell into chaos. With the elimination of Hussein's organs of repression, sectarian violence erupted between Iraq's largest constituencies, the Kurds, Sunni Arabs, and Shiite Arabs.

The Hurt Locker jumps into Iraq at the nadir of the occupation, before a credible national government was installed and the "troop surge" of 2007 restored a semblance of order to the country. The film is intensely focused on its three-man bomb disposal team. Newcomer James is a little too brave and would, if not for the jewel cutter's precision he brings to his trade, ask the question of when courage turns to carelessness. He makes no effort to rationalize his actions in terms of patriotism or self-sacrifice. Kathryn Bigelow described James as "attracted to the adrenalin the combat provides." Sergeant Sanborn (Anthony Mackie) is a veteran, a professional doing his job and determined to survive. He "navigates in a very rational way through this chaos," Bigelow added.[22] Specialist Eldridge (Brian Geraghty) is young and impressionable, looking to his very different noncoms for plausible role models. The film occasionally inserts reminders of the passage of time: "38 Days Left in Bravo Company's Rotation," and so on, until only two days remain.

The soldiers' talk is rough and realistic, parsimonious with details about their lives back home and shot through with the gallows humor of men in constant danger. Even their base, optimistically renamed Camp Victory, provides only slight protection against mortar attacks at night. They entertain themselves at day's end with hard liquor, heavy metal music, and rough horseplay. An undercurrent of animosity cuts between James, who is white, and Sanborn, who is black. Racial tension is never alluded to, however, and might only be a half-conscious contributing factor in the dislike between two men whose emotional constitutions are incompatible.

The environment outside the gates of their prefabricated base is uncomforting. Baghdad was once among the world's greatest and storied cities; during the Middle Ages it boasted a population larger than Rome or London and was a center of learning. As recently as the 1970s, Baghdad was one of the jewels of the Middle East. As the capital of a nation sitting atop capacious oil reserves, Baghdad benefited from government largesse in education and health care. Food was subsidized, women's rights were upheld in law, and cultural life flourished. Soon after Hussein seized power in a bloody putsch in 1979, the dictator plunged Iraq into a devastating war with Iran, a World War I–style struggle complete with trench warfare and poison gas. Casualty estimates are unreliable, but perhaps as many as a half-million Iraqi soldiers and civilians died in the conflict. "When the fighting ground reluctantly to a halt in 1988, many in Baghdad, with only a hint of exaggeration, said the city they knew as children would never return," wrote the *Washington Post*'s Anthony Shadid.[23] By 2004 Baghdad was a sprawling city of cracked, dun-colored concrete. Public services deteriorated, leaving the streets strewn with the garbage that became ideal hiding places for IEDs.

Iraqi civilians posed a problem familiar to any army fighting a guerrilla war. Enemy combatants were unseen to the occupier until they struck, and with remotely detonated IEDs, they might remain hidden even then. The man with a friendly face who advances, asking "Where you from? California?" might be an innocent civilian besotted with

Hollywood movies or a suicide bomber with explosives strapped under his shirt. In *The Hurt Locker* the protagonists drive the streets in the war's characteristic vehicle, a Humvee vulnerable to mines and bombs, with a bilingual warning sign on its rear: "Caution: Stay 100 Meters Back or You Will Be Shot." Every encounter with the locals is fraught with the possibility of violence. The GIs of the ordnance disposal unit speak no Arabic, and a working knowledge of English is not universal among Baghdad's residents.

A plethora of documentaries on the Iraq war were released in the first decade of the twenty-first century, usually with limited circulation, but *The Hurt Locker* presents a more visceral portrait of the sputtering urban guerrilla war than any of them. Bigelow and cinematographer Barry Ackroyd strove for realism and achieved something more real than anything a documentary film crew could have captured. *The Hurt Locker* thrusts viewers into the heart of the action using actual explosives and with multiple cameras catching the protagonists from every angle. Filmed in Jordan, just across from the Iraqi border, *The Hurt Locker* picks up the texture of the land with its unforgiving heat, its windblown sand and scuttling scorpions. The sweat on the actors' faces is real. Bigelow's intention was for each audience member to feel like "the fourth man on the team."[24]

Like *All Quiet on the Western Front*, *The Hurt Locker* is primarily a story of frontline comradeship among fighting men, and like *Apocalypse Now*, the men are fighting in a war that can easily turn surreal. In contrast to both of these classic war movies, however, it is difficult to discern a message in *The Hurt Locker* beyond the psychological and physical destruction of war. Eldridge is maimed at the end of his tour of duty thanks to James's proclivity for tempting fate. Sanborn returns home safely. Unable to relate to civilian life, James volunteers for another tour in Iraq. Nothing is resolved.

The Hurt Locker won six Oscars in 2010, including Best Picture and Best Director for Bigelow, the first woman so honored. It was a dark horse coming out of the Motion Picture Academy's nomination process; the frontrunner was a special effects–driven, science fiction blockbuster, *Avatar*, directed by Bigelow's ex-husband, James Cameron. Cameron's hugely successful story of interplanetary exploitation drew praise and criticism as a metaphor for Iraq, with *Avatar*'s private military contracting firm standing in for Halliburton, the American company that provided security and other services during the Iraq occupation.[25] *The Hurt Locker* also earned Bigelow the distinction of being the first woman director to win a Directors Guild of America Award, a Critics Choice Award, and a BAFTA Award.

Kathryn Bigelow and screenwriter Mark Boal returned to the war on terror with her next film, *Zero Dark Thirty*, a compelling dramatization of the greatest manhunt of our time, the search for Osama bin Laden. The architect of 9/11 was the primary objective of the U.S. invasion of Afghanistan, but he slipped the net at the end of 2001. For years bin Laden was the world's most wanted fugitive. Some speculated that he was dead, even though he continued to communicate to the outside world in taped messages. Bigelow and Boal were planning a film around bin Laden's escape from the caves of Tora Bora, where he had retreated after U.S. forces landed in Afghanistan, when news broke that Navy SEAL Team 6 had killed al-Qaeda's leader. They immediately switched gears, instead making a film about the ten-year hunt for bin Laden.[26]

While "fact based," *Zero Dark Thirty* generated controversy over which facts were included and which were left out. Its scenes of torture, or "enhanced interrogation," at covert CIA "black sites" located beyond the reach of the Bill of Rights in cooperative foreign nations imply that the ends of justice can be served by cruel means. Although widely praised by critics, *Zero Dark Thirty* casts a disturbing shadow as it asks eternal questions about the morally correct response to evil.

The film's name derives from "oh-dark-thirty," military lingo for half-past midnight, and *Zero Dark Thirty* mirrors the Alejandro Gonzalez Inarritu short subject praised by Roger Ebert by opening with voices from 9/11 heard against a black screen, brilliantly recounting the event's horror without recourse to the familiar images of the World Trade Center's meltdown. It cuts from there to a black site, where

Dan (Jason Clarke), a CIA interrogator, is committing horror on a smaller scale. He appears to enjoy his work inside the soundproof chamber where prisoners are kept. "I own you — you belong to me," he taunts an al-Qaeda operative before hoisting him into the air on pulleys, knocking him to the floor, pouring gallons of water down his throat, fastening a collar to his neck, and walking him like a dog. Maya (Jessica Chastain) watches almost impassively, standing in the corner, wan as a candle in a dark church, her calm ruffled occasionally by a sick feeling. Maya becomes *Zero Dark Thirty*'s propulsive engine as qualms evaporate and nausea fades. In this telling bin Laden is located almost entirely through her efforts. "It was important to us not to advance any kind of political agenda," Boal said, "but just to, hopefully, put the audience in a position to be able to look behind the curtain."[27]

"Come on, let's get a coffee," Dan says after completing a torture session. The horrible is made banal to cushion the psychological damage to the torturers. In *Zero Dark Thirty* torture is an office job with blood on the floor, a far cry from the scholarly CIA analysts in Cold War films such as *Three Days of the Condor*. And yet analysis is the integral next step after interrogation. Maya watches videotaped sessions of dozens of prisoners, a gruesome visual library from which she pieces together fragments of useful information from broken men. The objective is to find people who know people who know where bin Laden might be hiding, and *Zero Dark Thirty* nails the essential problem facing intelligence agencies in a world awash in data: the valuable clues are needles in a haystack of leads.

The movie eludes any message on the ethics of torture but appears to support its efficacy. *Zero Dark Thirty* drew bipartisan criticism for its depiction of so-called enhanced interrogation. In December 2012 Senate Intelligence Committee chair Diane Feinstein, Armed Services Committee chair Carl Levin, and Armed Services Committee member John McCain wrote a letter to the chairman of Bigelow's studio, Sony Pictures, calling *Zero Dark Thirty* "grossly inaccurate and misleading in its suggestion that torture helped extract information that led to the death of Usama bin Laden." The CIA cooperated with Boal as he wrote the screenplay with May, Dan, and other characters as composites of real agents. After its release acting CIA director Michael Morell condemned the picture for creating "the strong impression that the enhanced interrogation techniques that were part of our former detention and interrogation program were the key to finding bin Laden." He insisted, "That impression is false."[28]

The *New Yorker*'s Jane Mayer, who has covered the CIA extensively, accused *Zero Dark Thirty* of "providing false advertising for water-boarding." She accused Bigelow and Boal of "ignoring the full weight of the dark history of torture" and of overlooking the FBI's refusal to cooperate with the CIA's enhanced interrogation program on the grounds that it was illegal and the controversy the program stirred within the military, the Justice Department, and the CIA itself, which eventually abandoned waterboarding.[29]

Bigelow and Boal defended the veracity of their depiction. To omit torture "would have been to whitewash history," Bigelow said.[30] She added: "I feel we got it right. I'm proud of the movie, and I stand behind it completely. I think that it's a deeply moral movie that questions the use of force. It questions what was done in the name of finding bin Laden." Jessica Chastain believed that Bigelow's intention was "to open a conversation. She ends it with an unanswered question, Where do you want to go? She's asking the audience, Where have we been and where do we go from here?"[31]

As the movie unfolds, Maya moves in stages from mildly shocked novice to America's avenging angel, her resolve stiffened by an ongoing chain of al-Qaeda outrages around the world, including the London mass transit bombings (2005), her own brush with death during the detonation of the Islamabad Marriott Hotel (2008), and the death of several colleagues in the suicide bombing of the CIA's Forward Operating Base Chapman at Bagram Airfield in Afghanistan (2009). Maya plays the relentless hero, a role Hollywood had until recently reserved for men.

Zero Dark Thirty shifts on its axis after Barack Obama's declaration that "America does not torture." The film seems to imply that progress toward catching bin Laden slows in light of policy changes, and yet Maya never stops sifting through data until she arrives at a plausible theory: a mysterious compound in Abbottabad, down the road from Pakistan's Military Academy, is bin Laden's lair. James Gandolfini plays CIA director Leon Panetta as a shrewd consigliore who weighs the odds and gives the go-ahead to the Navy SEALs.

The climactic helicopter raid on the bin Laden compound that kills the al-Qaeda leader on May 2, 2011, occupies a small part of the film. *Zero Dark Thirty* is not primarily a war movie or a thriller in form but a detective story in which the pursuers collect their clues by any means possible. Bigelow's skill as a director keeps all eyes on the screen, even when the audience would rather look the other way.

Zero Dark Thirty was number one at box offices on opening weekend and was nominated by the Motion Picture Academy for Best Picture and Best Screenplay but won only the Oscar for editing. Controversy over the torture scenes may have swayed some Academy members, but new voting deadlines and a strong field of contenders might also have played a role. Although honored with only one golden trophy, it was the year's most talked-about film.

The earliest movies produced by Thomas Edison were glimpsed by peering into a box, the Kinetoscope. Movie watching was a personal experience of small-scale images until 1895, when Auguste and Louis Lumière unveiled the motion picture projector and transformed movies into cinema, a shared public experience of stories on big screens. By the time of World War I, which coincided with the birth of Hollywood, movies attained formal sophistication as well as a mass audience; they became the greatest mirror and magnifier of world events in the twentieth century and were inseparable from the memories of the century's major wars.

In the twenty-first century motion pictures are receding into personal experience on the small screens of smartphones; topical feature films are hard-pressed to keep up with the rapid pace of changing events and the flood of images from other media. Movies have more competition for people's attention than ever, and yet movies on wars to come will still be made. The best of them will illuminate those conflicts more brightly than any newscast or documentary by harnessing the imaginative power of art in revealing the human condition.

Notes

1. WORLD WAR I (1914–1918)

1. John H. Morrow Jr., *The Great War: An Imperial History* (London: Routledge, 2004), xii.
2. J. A. Hobson, *Imperialism: A Study* (London: Allen & Unwin, 1902), 311–12.
3. Adolf Hitler, *Mein Kampf* (New York: Reynal & Hitchcock, 1941), 210.
4. Jean Moorcroft Wilson, *Siegfried Sassoon: The Making of a War Poet, A Biography, 1886–1918* (New York: Routledge, 1999), 182.
5. Morrow, *Great War*, 99.
6. Editorial, *Moving Picture World*, August 15, 1914.
7. Leslie Midkiff DeBauche, *Reel Patriotism: The Movies and World War I* (Madison: University of Wisconsin Press, 1997), xvi; Christel Schmidt, ed., *Mary Pickford: Queen of the Movies* (Lexington: Library of Congress / University Press of Kentucky, 2012), 152–58.
8. Jay Winter and Blaine Baggett, *The Great War and the Shaping of the 20th Century* (New York: Penguin Studio, 1996), 102.
9. Steven Philip Kramer, *Abel Gance* (Boston: Twayne, 1978), 66.
10. Andrew Sarris, *You Ain't Heard Nothin' Yet: The American Talking Film History and Memory, 1927–1949* (New York: Oxford University Press, 1998), 128.
11. Christian R. Barker and R. W. Last, *Erich Maria Remarque* (London: Oswald Wolf, 1979), 7–8.
12. Axel Eggebrecht, "Gesprach mit Remarque," *Die literarische Welt*, June 14, 1929.
13. Barker and Last, *Erich Maria Remarque*, 19–20, 41.
14. Joseph R. Millichap, *Lewis Milestone* (Boston: Twayne, 1981), 26–32.
15. Winter and Baggett, *Great War*, 241–45.
16. Scott and Barbara Siegel, *Encyclopedia of Hollywood* (New York: Facts on File, 1990), 26.

17. Jeremy Bernstein interview with Stanley Kubrick; Michael Parkinson interview with Kirk Douglas; James Naremore, "We Have Met the Enemy . . . ," *Paths of Glory* (Criterion Collection DVD, 2010).

18. Morrow, *Great War*, 186; Winter and Baggett, *Great War*, 241; Stéphane Audoin-Rouzeau and Annette Becker, *14–18: Understanding the Great War* (New York: Hill & Wang, 2000), 106–7.

19. Dave Thomson, *Have You Seen . . . ? A Personal Introduction to 1,000 Films* (New York: Knopf, 2008), 650.

20. Naremore, "We Have Met the Enemy."

21. Adam Hochschild, *To End All Wars: A Story of Loyalty and Rebellion, 1914–1918* (Boston: Houghton Mifflin Harcourt, 2011), xiv.

22. Paul Duncan, *Stanley Kubrick: The Complete Films* (Hong Kong: Taschen, 2003), 50.

23. William Pfaff, *The Bullet's Song: Romantic Violence and Utopia* (New York: Simon & Schuster, 2004), 52.

24. Andrew Kelly, James Pepper, and Jeffrey Richards, *Filming T. E. Lawrence: Korda's Lost Epics* (London: I. B. Tauris, 1997), 1–18.

25. Sandra Lean, with Barry Chattington, *David Lean: An Intimate Portrait* (New York: Universal, 2001), 20.

26. Gene D. Phillips, *Beyond the Epic: The Life and Films of David Lean* (Lexington: University Press of Kentucky, 2006), 258, 272–73.

27. Stanley and Rodelle Weintraub, *Lawrence of Arabia: The Literary Impulse* (Baton Rouge: Louisiana State University Press, 1975), 1–4.

28. T. E. Lawrence, *Seven Pillars of Wisdom: A Triumph* (Garden City NY: Garden City Publishing, 1938), 202.

29. Lawrence, *Seven Pillars of Wisdom*, 29.

30. Sean McMeekin, *The Berlin-Baghdad Express: The Ottoman Empire and Germany's Bid for World Power* (Cambridge: Harvard University Press, 2010), 141–79, 191–200.

31. Lawrence, *Seven Pillars of Wisdom*, 224.

32. For a recent attack on the mission's strategy, tactics, and execution, see Peter Hart, *Gallipoli* (New York: Oxford University Press, 2011).

33. Henry Morgenthau, *Ambassador Morgenthau's Story* (Garden City NY: Doubleday, Page, 1918), 161.

34. Jonathan Rayner, *The Films of Peter Weir* (London: Cassell, 1998), 99.

35. "Entrenched: The Making of *Gallipoli*," *Gallipoli* Special Collectors Edition DVD (Paramount, 2005); P. and C. Fonda-Bonard, "The Birth of a Nation: An Interview with Peter Weir," *Cineaste* 11 (1982).

36. Robert Rhodes James, *Gallipoli* (New York: Macmillan, 1965), 275.

37. C.E.W. Bean, *Anzac to Amiens* (Canberra: Australia War Memorial, 1981), 155.

38. "Entrenched"; Winter and Baggett, *Great War*, 113–17.

39. James, *Gallipoli*, 79.

2. WORLD WAR II (1939–1945)

1. Michael C. C. Adams, *The Best War Ever: America and World War II* (Baltimore: Johns Hopkins University Press, 1994), 2.

2. Ian Stephens, *Monsoon Morning* (London: Ernest Benn, 1966), 184.

3. Lizzie Collingham, *The Taste of War: World War II and the Battle for Food* (New York: Penguin Press, 2012).

4. Philippe Burrin, *France under the Nazis: Collaboration and Compromise* (New York: New Press, 1996).

5. Robert O. Paxton, *Vichy France: Old Guard and New Order, 1940–1944* (New York: Norton, 1975), 182–84; Marshall Lee Miller, *Bulgaria during the Second World War* (Stanford: Stanford University Press, 1975), 102.

6. Greg Annussek, *Hitler's Raid to Save Mussolini* (Cambridge MA: Da Capo, 2005).

7. Adams, *Best War Ever*, 9.

8. David Culbert, ed., *Film and Propaganda in America: A Documentary History II*, pt. 1 (New York: Greenwood Press, 1990), xvi–xvii.

9. Joe Morella, Edward Z. Epstein, and John Griggs, *The Films of World War II* (Secaucus NJ: Citadel Press, 1975), 11–13.

10. Paul Holsinger, ed., *War and American Popular Culture* (Westport CT: Greenwood Press, 1999), 246–47.

11. Howard Koch, ed., *Casablanca Script and Legend* (Woodstock NY: Overlook Press, 1992), 3.

12. Holsinger, *War and American Popular Culture*, 22.

13. Klaus Kreimeier, *The UFA Story: A History of Germany's Greatest Film Company, 1918–1945* (New York: New Press, 1996), 310.

14. Holsinger, *War and American Popular Culture*, 228–29; Morella, Epstein, and Griggs, *Films of World War II*, 11.

15. Koch, *Casablanca*, 250.

16. Koch, *Casablanca*, 16, 18, 19.

17. For an overview of the story's historicity, see Richard E. Osborne, *The Casablanca Companion: The Movie Classic and Its Place in History* (Indianapolis: Riebel-Roque, 1997).

18. "Casablanca," *Film Daily*, November 27, 1942.

19. John Toland, *Adolf Hitler* (Garden City NY: Doubleday, 1976), 729–30.

20. Michael Burleigh, *The Third Reich: A New History* (New York: Hill & Wang, 2000), 740–41.

21. Alistair Cooke, "Humphrey Bogart: Epitaph for a Tough Guy," *Atlantic Monthly*, May 1957.

22. Frank Miller, *Casablanca: As Time Goes By: 50th Anniversary Commemorative* (Atlanta: Turner Publishing, 1992), 184.

23. Anthony Rhodes, *Propaganda, The Art of Persuasion: World War II* (New York: Chelsea House, 1976), 147.

24. Bosley Crowther, "'Saboteur,' Alfred Hitchcock Melodrama, Starring Priscilla Lane, Robert Cummings and Otto Kruger, at Music Hall," *New York Times*, May 8, 1942.

25. Patrick McGilligan, *Alfred Hitchcock: A Life in Darkness* (New York: Regan Books, 2003), 301.

26. Testimony of John L. DeWitt, April 13, 1943, House Naval Affairs Subcommittee to Investigate Congested Areas, pt. 3, 739–40 (78th Cong., 1st sess.).

27. McGilligan, *Alfred Hitchcock*, 303.

28. Keith L. Nelson, ed., *The Impact of War on American Life: The Twentieth-Century Experience* (New York: Holt, Rinehart & Winston, 1971), 99, 108.

29. Adams, *Best War Ever*, 115, 119,123.

30. Nicholas Christopher, *Somewhere in the Night: Film Noir and the American City* (New York: Free Press, 1997), 208.

31. Richard Severo and Lewis Milford, *The Wages of War: When America's Soldiers Came Home—From Valley Forge to Vietnam* (New York: Simon & Schuster, 1990), 288–89; Adams, *Best War Ever*, 152.

32. Gary Fishgall, *Gregory Peck: A Biography* (New York: Scribner, 2002), 139–40; "Twelve O'Clock High (1950)," Notes, Turner Classic Movies (TCM) website, www.tcm.com/tcmdb/title/94088/Twelve-O-Clock-High/notes.html (last accessed on May 9, 2014); John T. Correll, "The Real Twelve O'Clock High," *Air Force Magazine* 94, no. 1 (January 2011).

33. Allan T. Duffin and Paul Matheis, *The 12 O'Clock High Logbook* (Albany GA: Bearmanor Media, 2005), 87.

34. Correll, "Real Twelve O'Clock High."

35. "Twelve O'Clock High," Notes, TCM.com.

36. Philip Kaplan and Rex Alan Smith, *One Last Look: A Sentimental Journey to the Eight Air Force Heavy Bomber Bases of World War II* (New York: Abbeville Press, 1983), 7, 23, 128, 136.

37. Stephen A. Garrett, *Ethics and Airpower* (New York: St. Martin's Press, 1993), 83–97.

38. Adolf Galland, *The First and the Last* (London: Methuen, 1955), 220–21.

39. Peter Young, *A Short History of World War II, 1939–1945* (New York: Crowell, 1966), 260; Burleigh, *Third Reich*, 746–47.

40. "Twelve O'Clock High," Notes, TCM.com.

41. Michael Schumacher, *Francis Ford Coppola: A Filmmaker's Life* (New York: Crown, 1999), 42.

42. Carlo D'Este, *Patton: Genius for War* (New York: HarperCollins, 1995), 454.

43. Schumacher, *Francis Ford Coppola*, 43; David Sheward, *Rage and Glory: The Volatile Life and Career of George C. Scott* (New York: Applause, 2008), 178, 179; Lawrence H. Suid, *Guts & Glory: Great American War Movies* (Reading MA: Addison-Wesley, 1978), 256.

44. Glen Jeansonne, Frank C. Haney, and David Luhrssen, "A Life Shaped by Dyslexia: The Positive and Negative Aspects of Dyslexia Made George S. Patton, Jr., Both a Great Military Commander and a Controversial Personality," *WWII History*, January 2008.

45. D'Este, *Patton*, 164.

46. D'Este, *Patton*, 233.

47. David Nichols, *Ernie's War: The Best of Ernie Pyle's World War II Dispatches* (New York: Simon & Schuster, 1986), 358.

48. Ladislas Farago, *Patton: Ordeal and Triumph* (London: Arthur Baker, 1966), 34–36.

49. D'Este, *Patton*, 481.

50. D'Este, *Patton*, 453, 522–25.

51. D'Este, *Patton*, 533–46.

52. Brenton G. Wallace, *Patton & His Third Army* (Harrisburg PA: Military Service Publishing, 1946), 194–95.

53. Sheward, *Rage and Glory*, 209; Tim Purtell, "Oscar Grouch," *Entertainment Weekly*, April 16, 1993.

54. Theodor Adorno, "Cultural Criticism and Society," *Prisms* (Cambridge MA: MIT Press, 1981), 34.

55. Elie Wiesel, "Trivializing the Holocaust: Semi-Fact and Semi-Fiction," *New York Times*, April 16, 1978.

56. Joseph McBride, *Steven Spielberg: A Biography* (New York: Simon & Schuster, 1997), 425.

57. Yosefa Loshitzky, *Spielberg's Holocaust: Critical Perspectives on Schindler's List* (Bloomington: Indiana University Press, 1997), 2–3.

58. McBride, *Steven Spielberg*, 414–16.

59. George Perry, *Steven Spielberg* (London: Orion House, 1998), 83–85.

60. Thomas Keneally, *Schindler's List* (New York: Touchstone Books, 1992), 292.

NOTES TO PAGES 67–80

61. David M. Crowe, *Oskar Schindler: The Untold Account of His Life, Wartime Activities, and the True Story behind the List* (Cambridge MA: Westview Press, 2004), 361–63.

62. Adolf Hitler, *Mein Kampf* (New York: Houghton Mifflin, 1943), 654.

63. Crowe, *Oskar Schindler*, 2–8.

64. Crowe, *Oskar Schindler*, 16.

65. Crowe, *Oskar Schindler*, 18, 40.

66. Joachim C. Fest, *The Faces of the Third Reich: Portraits of the Nazi Leadership* (New York: Pantheon, 1970), 214–15.

67. Ian Kershaw, *Hitler 1936–1945: Nemesis* (New York: Norton, 2000), 245–47.

68. Letter from Oskar Schindler to Fritz Lang, July 20, 1950, Bundesarchiv (Koblenz), Bestand 1493, Nachlass Oskar Schindler.

69. Crowe, *Oskar Schindler*, 193–94.

70. For a graphic account of a survivor of the Kraków ghetto, validating Spielberg's visualization, see Malvina Graf, *The Krakow Ghetto and the Plaszow Camp Revisited* (Tallahassee: Florida State University Press, 1989).

71. Alfred Katz, *Poland's Ghettos at War* (New York: Twayne, 1970), 76, 92–98.

72. Judith E. Doneson, "The Image Lingers: The Feminization of the Jew in Schindler's List," in Loshitzky, *Spielberg's Holocaust*, 145–46.

73. Quoted in Fest, *Faces of the Third Reich*, 118.

74. Robert S. Burrell, "Breaking the Cycle of Iwo Jima Mythology: A Strategic Study of Operation Detachment," *Journal of Military History* 68 (October 2004).

75. Burrell, *The Ghosts of Iwo Jima* (College Station: Texas A&M University Press, 2006), x.

76. "Red Sun, Black Sand: The Making of Letters from Iwo Jima," *Letters from Iwo Jima*: Two-Disc Special Edition (Warner Brothers, 2007).

77. Roger Ebert, "Tora! Tora! Tora!" *Chicago Sun Times*, October 12, 1970.

78. "Red Sun, Black Sand."

79. James A. Warren, *The Lions of Iwo Jima* (New York: Henry Holt, 2008), 45; David McNeill, "His Emperor's Reluctant Warrior," *Japan Times*, August 13, 2006.

80. Holland M. Smith and Percy Finch, *Coral and Brass* (New York: Scribner's, 1949), 255.

81. Karl Friday, "Bushidō or Bull? A Medieval Historian's Perspective on the Imperial Army and the Japanese Warrior Tradition," *History Teacher* 27, no. 3 (May 1994).

82. U.S. Army Historical Division, "Operations in the Central Pacific: Japanese Studies in World War II" (Japanese Monograph No. 48), 62.

3. THE COLD WAR (1947–1991), INCLUDING THE KOREAN WAR (1950–1953) AND THE VIETNAM WAR (1955–1975)

1. Yanek Mieczkowski, *Eisenhower's Sputnik Moment: The Race for Space and World Prestige* (Ithaca NY: Cornell University Press, 2013), 6.

2. Michael Beschloss, *Our Documents: 100 Milestone Documents from the National Archives* (New York: Oxford University Press, 2006), 194–99; X (pseud. George Kennan), "The Sources of Soviet Conduct," *Foreign Affairs* 24, no. 4 (July 1947).

3. "Unforgettable: The Korean War," PBS, June 2010, DVD.

4. Ralph B. Levering, *The Cold War: A Post–Cold War History* (Wheeling IL: Harland Davidson, 1994), 51.

5. Athan Theoharis, *Chasing Spies: How the FBI Failed in Counterintelligence but Promoted the Politics of McCarthyism in the Cold War* (Chicago: Ivan R. Dee, 2002), 3, 15–16.

6. Max Lerner, *The Unfinished Country: A Book of American Symbols* (New York: Simon & Schuster, 1959), 443.

7. For a comprehensive biography drawing from all available sources, see G. Edward White, *Alger Hiss's Looking-Glass Wars: The Covert Life of a Soviet Spy* (New York: Oxford University Press, 2004).

8. Lerner, *Unfinished Country*, 484.

9. For a thorough appraisal of the evidence against the Rosenbergs and the political agendas on both sides of the issue, see Ronald Radosh and Joyce Milton, *The Rosenberg File: A Search for the Truth* (New York: Holt, Rinehart & Winston, 1983).

10. Steven J. Ross, *Hollywood Left and Right: How Movie Stars Shaped American Politics* (New York: Oxford University Press, 2011), 108–11.

11. David A. Cook, *A History of Narrative Film* (New York: Norton, 1981), 410.

12. Theoharis, *Chasing Spies*, 155–59.

13. Richard Schickel, *Elia Kazan: A Biography* (New York: HarperCollins, 2005), 271–72.

14. For the screenplay's factual backdrop and composition, see James T. Fisher, *On the Irish Waterfront: The Crusader, the Movie, and the Soul of the Port of New York* (Ithaca NY: Cornell University Press, 2009).

15. Nicholas Christopher, *Somewhere in the Night: Film Noir and the American City* (New York: Free Press, 1997), 50–51.

16. For a firsthand account of the French war in Indochina, see Lucien Bodard, *The Quicksand War: Prelude to Vietnam* (London: Faber & Faber, 1967).

17. Bernard B. Fall, "Ho Chi Minh: July 1962," *Saturday Evening Post*, November 24, 1962.

18. With Soviet backing Zhou overruled objections from the Vietnamese Communists. See *The Pentagon Papers: The Senator Graves Edition; The Defense Department History of United States Decisionmaking on Vietnam* (Boston: Beacon Hill Press, 1971), 108–78.

19. *Pentagon Papers*, 82.

20. Stanley Karnow, *Vietnam: A History* (New York: Penguin, 1984), 238, 247.

21. James S. Olson and Randy Roberts, *My Lai: A Brief History with Documents* (Boston: Bedford St. Martin's, 1998), 44.

22. *Vietnam: The Ten Thousand Day War* (TimeLife DVD, 2013).

23. *Vietnam: The Ten Thousand Day War*.

24. Karnow, *Vietnam*, 545.

25. Karnow, *Vietnam*, 654–55.

26. Stephen E. Ambrose, *Nixon: The Triumph of a Politician 1962–1972* (New York: Simon & Schuster, 1989), 451–54.

27. Tamim Ansary, *Games without Rules: The Often Interrupted History of Afghanistan* (New York: PublicAffairs, 2012), 179–209.

28. John Marks, *The Search for the Manchurian Candidate: The CIA and Mind Control* (New York: New York Times Books, 1979), 9, 125–46, 183–87.

29. Lerner, *Unfinished Country*, 448–49.

30. Walt Kelly, *Ten Ever-Lovin', Blue-Eyed Years with Pogo* (New York: Simon & Schuster, 1959), 81.

31. Stephen J. Whitfield, *The Culture of the Cold War* (Baltimore: Johns Hopkins University Press, 1990), 20.

32. Pauline Kael, "Trash, Art, and the Movies," *Harper's*, February 1969.

33. Donald Clarke, *All or Nothing at All: A Life of Frank Sinatra* (New York: Freeman International, 1997), 192.

34. Thomas C. Reeves, *The Life and Times of Joe McCarthy: A Biography* (Lanham MD: Madison Books, 1997), 605.

35. Quoted in J. Hoberman, *The Magic Hour: Film at the Fin de Siècle* (Philadelphia: Temple University Press, 2003), 165.

36. Quoted in Reeves, *Life and Times of Joe McCarthy*, 588.

37. Chris Fujiwara, *The World and Its Double: The Life and Work of Otto Preminger* (New York: Faber & Faber, 2008), 239.

38. Fred J. Cook, *The Nightmare Decade: The Life and Times of Senator Joe McCarthy* (New York: Random House, 1971), 537.

39. Hoberman, *Magic Hour*, 167.

40. Samuel Fuller, *A Third Face* (New York: Knopf, 2002), 308. For a thorough examination of the FBI's efforts to monitor and influence the content of Hollywood movies, see John Sbardellati, *J. Edgar Hoover Goes to the Movies:*

The FBI and the Origins of Hollywood's Cold War (Ithaca NY: Cornell University Press, 2012).

41. John Pearson, *The Life of Ian Fleming* (New York: McGraw-Hill, 1966), 12, 18, 33.

42. Pearson, *Life of Ian Fleming*, 73–74, 79.

43. William Stevenson, *A Man Called Intrepid: The Secret War* (New York: Harcourt Brace Jovanovich, 1976), 54, 270–71; Pearson, *Life of Ian Fleming*, 93, 99–102, 108–9.

44. "Harry Saltzman: Showman" in *From Russia with Love*: Two-Disc Ultimate Edition (MGM, 2008)

45. Hugh Sidey, "The President's Voracious Reading Habits," *Life*, March 17, 1961.

46. Jeffrey S. Miller, *Something Completely Different: British Television and American Culture* (Minneapolis: University of Minnesota Press, 2000), 25–26.

47. Steven Jay Rubin, *The James Bond Films: A Behind the Scenes History* (Westport CT: Arlington House, 1981), 11.

48. Geoffrey Bocca, "The Spectacular Cult of Ian Fleming," *Saturday Evening Post*, June 22, 1963.

49. Rubin, *James Bond Films*, 12, 13.

50. Vincent Canby, "United Artists; Fort Knox: No Picture like Its 'Goldfinger,'" *Variety*, March 31, 1965.

51. "Inside *From Russia with Love*," Two-Disc Ultimate Edition.

52. "Ian Fleming: The CBC Interview," Two-Disc Ultimate Edition.

53. Miller, *Something Completely Different*, 35.

54. Tony Barley, *Taking Sides: The Fiction of John le Carré* (Milton Keynes UK: Open University Press, 1986), 1.

55. Barley, *Taking Sides*, 10.

56. H. V. Kaltenborn Papers, State Historical Society of Wisconsin, Madison; Anne O'Hare-McCormick, "The Promethean Role of the United States," *New York Times*, August 8, 1945; Paul Boyer, *By the Bomb's Early Light: American Thought and Culture at the Dawn of the Atomic Age* (New York: Pantheon, 1985), xiv, 4.

57. Jay Bergman, *Meeting the Demands of Reason: The Life and Thought of Andrei Sakharov* (Ithaca NY: Cornell University Press, 2009), 46–59.

58. *The Atomic Café*: Collector's Edition DVD (Docuramafilm, 2008), *Duck and Cover* bonus feature.

59. Boyer, *By the Bomb's Early Light*, 10–11.

60. Quoted in David McCullough, *Truman* (New York: Simon & Schuster, 1992), 442.

61. Harrison Brown, "The Beginning or the End: A Review," *Bulletin of Atomic Scientists*, March 1947.

62. Boyer, *By the Bomb's Early Light*, 257.

63. Kael, "Bonnie and Clyde," *New Yorker*, October 21, 1967.

64. David A. Rosenberg, "The Origins of Overkill: Nuclear Weapons and American Strategy, 1945–1960," *International Security* 7, no. 4 (Spring 1983).

65. Robert D. Johnston, *The Politics of Healing* (New York: Routledge, 2004), 136.

66. Vincent LoBrutto, *Stanley Kramer: A Biography* (New York: Donald I. Fine Books, 1997), 239.

67. Henry Kissinger, *Nuclear Weapons and Foreign Policy* (New York: Harper & Brothers, 1957), 25.

68. LoBrutto, *Stanley Kramer*, 231, 239, 240.

69. LoBrutto, *Stanley Kramer*, 237.

70. LoBrutto, *Stanley Kramer*, 248; Patsy Guy Hammontree, *Elvis Presley: A Bio-Bibliography* (Westport CT: Greenwood Press, 1985), 156–57.

71. LoBrutto, *Stanley Kramer*, 242; Joanna E. Rapf, ed., *Sidney Lumet Interviews* (Jackson: University Press of Mississippi, 2006), 60.

72. Ronald L. Davis, *Duke: The Life and Image of John Wayne* (Norman: University of Oklahoma Press, 1998), 278–79.

73. Davis, *Duke*, 279–81.

74. Davis, *Duke*, 281.

75. Jane Fonda, *My Life So Far* (New York: Random House, 2005), 318.

76. Ronald Brownstein, *The Power and the Glitter: The Hollywood-Washington Connection* (New York: Pantheon, 1992), 255.

77. William Greider, "Viet Vets: A Sad Reminder," *Washington Post*, March 30, 1974; Philip Caputo, "Running Again — The Last Retreat," *Chicago Tribune*, April 28, 1975; Keyes Beech, "We Clawed for Our Lives!" *Chicago Daily News*, May 1, 1975.

78. David Thomson, *"Have You Seen . . . ? A Personal Introduction to 1,000 Films* (New York: Knopf, 2008), 209.

79. Michael Schumacher, *Francis Ford Coppola* (New York: Crown Publishers, 1999), 184, 193.

80. Schumacher, *Francis Ford Coppola*, 185; William Murray, "The Playboy Interview: Francis Ford Coppola," *Playboy*, July 1975; "Watch Apocalypse Now with Francis Ford Coppola," special feature in *Apocalypse Now*: The Complete Dossier Dual Feature (Paramount Pictures DVD, 2006).

81. Schumacher, *Francis Ford Coppola*, 193; "Watch Apocalypse Now with Francis Ford Coppola."

82. Lawrence H. Suid, *Guts and Glory: Great American War Movies* (Reading MA: Addison-Wesley Publishing, 1978), 310–11.

83. Peter Cowie, *Coppola* (New York: Da Capo, 1990), 123. For revealing footage shot in the Philippines during the production by the director's wife, Eleanor Coppola, see the documentary *Hearts of Darkness: A Filmmaker's Apocalypse* (1991).

84. Cowie, *Coppola*, 125.

85. "Movies: The Greatest Films Ever," *Entertainment Weekly*, July 5, 2013.

86. "Watch Apocalypse Now with Francis Ford Coppola."

87. "Watch Apocalypse Now with Francis Ford Coppola"; Schumacher, *Francis Ford Coppola*, 207, 242.

88. Norman Friedman, *U.S. Small Combatants, Including PT-Boats, Subchasers, and the Brown-Water Navy: An Illustrated Design History* (Annapolis: Naval Institute Press, 1987).

89. "Watch Apocalypse Now with Francis Ford Coppola."

90. Schumacher, *Francis Ford Coppola*, 221.

91. Marlon Brando with Robert Lindsey, *Brando: Songs My Mother Taught Me* (New York: Random House, 1994), 431.

92. Schumacher, *Francis Ford Coppola*, 216–19.

93. G. Roy Levin, "Francis Coppola Discusses *Apocalypse Now*," *Millimeter*, October 1979.

94. "Watching *Apocalypse Now* with Francis Ford Coppola."

95. Gene Siskell, "Coppola's Sales Tactics Fuel His 'Apocalypse' Launching," *Chicago Tribune*, October 14, 1979.

96. Cowie, *Coppola*, 132; Roger Ebert, "Great Movies: Apocalypse Now," *Chicago Sun-Times*, November 28, 1999.

97. Randy Roberts and David Welky, "A Sacred Mission: Oliver Stone and Vietnam," in *Oliver Stone's USA*, edited by Robert Brent Toplin (Lawrence: University Press of Kansas, 2000), 66–67.

98. Roberts and Welky, "Sacred Mission," 70–72.

99. Tim Cahill, "The *Rolling Stone* Interview: Stanley Kubrick," *Rolling Stone*, August 27, 1987.

100. Cahill, "*Rolling Stone* Interview."

101. Yang Jisheng, *Tombstone: The Great Chinese Famine, 1958–1962* (New York: Farrar, Straus & Giroux, 2012), 3.

102. Ben Kiernan, *The Pol Pot Regime: Race, Power, and Genocide in Cambodia under the Khmer Rouge, 1970–79* (New Haven: Yale University Press, 1996), 16.

103. François Bizot, *The Gate* (New York: Knopf, 2003), 5.

104. Patrick Heuveline, "Between One and Three Million: Towards the Demographic Reconstruction of a Decade of Cambodian History (1970–79)," *Population Studies* 52, no. 1 (March 1998).

105. David P. Chandler, *Brother Number One: A Political Biography of Pol Pot* (Boulder: Westview Press, 1992), 28.

106. George Crile, *Charlie Wilson's War: The Extraordinary Story of the Largest Covert Operation in History* (New York: Atlantic Monthly Press, 2003), 20.

107. Ansary, *Games without Rules*, 180–82; Giles Dorronsoro, *Revolution Unending: Afghanistan, 1979 to the Present* (London: Hurst & Co., 2005), 80–87.

108. Ansary, *Games without Rules*, 186–87; Dorronsoro, *Revolution Unending*, 98–101.

109. Dorronsoro, *Revolution Unending*, 92.

110. Nikolai Inozemtsev, "Policy of Peace: Theory and Practice — 106th Anniversary of Vladimir Lenin's Birth," *Soviet Life*, April 1976.

111. Tony Judt, *Postwar: A History of Europe since 1945* (New York: Penguin Press, 2005), 551.

112. Crile, *Charlie Wilson's War*, 14.

113. Crile, *Charlie Wilson's War*, 42–43; John H. Cushman Jr., "The Stinger Missile: Helping to Change the Course of a War," *New York Times*, January 17, 1988.

114. Judt, *Postwar*, 593.

4. THE WAR ON TERROR (2001–)

1. Sarah Anderson, Phyllis Bennis, and John Cavanagh, "Coalition of the Willing or Coalition of the Coerced?" *Institute for Policy Studies,* February 26, 2003.

2. Peter Baker, "A Pivot from War: Seeks Curb on Powers — GOP Labels Steps Premature," *New York Times*, May 24, 2013.

3. David Thomson, *The Big Screen: The Story of Movies* (New York: Farrar, Straus & Giroux, 2012), 3–4.

4. Brett Martin, *Difficult Men: Behind the Scenes of a Creative Revolution from "The Sopranos" and "The Wire" to "Mad Men" and "Breaking Bad"* (New York: Penguin, 2013).

5. Jane Mayer, "The Politics of the Man Behind *24*," *New Yorker*, February 22, 2007.

6. Paul A. Cantor, *The Invisible Hand in Popular Culture: Liberty vs. Authority in American Film and TV* (Lexington: University Press of Kentucky, 2012), 296.

7. Robert Sullivan, ed., *One Nation: America Remembers September 11, 2001* (Boston: Little, Brown, 2001), 71.

8. Beverly Gage, *The Day Wall Street Exploded* (Oxford: Oxford University Press, 2009).

9. Debra Burlingame, "The Clintons' Terror Pardons," *Wall Street Journal*, February 12, 2008.

10. Paul Berman, "The Philosopher of Islamic Terror," *New York Times Magazine*, March 23, 2003. For a less polemical interpretation of Qutb's views, see James Toth, *Sayyid Qutb: The Life and Legacy of a Radical Islamic Intellectual* (Oxford: Oxford University Press, 2013.

11. Alexander Moens, *The Foreign Policy of George W. Bush: Values, Strategy, and Loyalty* (Aldershot UK: Ashgate, 2004), 123, 124; Shaul Shay, *The Endless Jihad: The Mujahidin, the Taliban and Bin Laden* (Herzliya, Israel: International Policy Institute for Counter-Terrorism, 2002), 140–41.

12. Moens, *Foreign Policy of George W. Bush*, 124–25; James Kitfield, "A New and Colder War," *National Journal*, September 21, 2001.

13. Bob Woodward, *Bush at War* (New York: Simon & Schuster, 2002), 4, 34.

14. National Commission on Terrorist Attacks upon the United States, *The 9/11 Commission Report: Final Report of the National Commission on Terrorist Attacks upon the United States* (Washington DC: Government Printing Office, 2004), "Foresight and Hindsight."

15. Sullivan, *One Nation*, 169.

16. Roger Ebert, "9/11 Dwarfed the Films about It," *Roger Ebert's Journal*, September 11, 2011, www.rogerebert.com/rogers-journal/911-dwarfed-the-films-about-it (last accessed on May 9, 2014).

17. Ebert, "9/11."

18. "United 93: The Families and the Film," *United 93*, DVD (Universal Studios, 2006).

19. Christopher Goodwin, "Kathryn Bigelow Is Back with *The Hurt Locker*," *Sunday Times*, August 16, 2009.

20. Geoffrey Wawro, *Quicksand: America's Pursuit of Power in the Middle East* (New York: Penguin Press, 2010), 412–27.

21. Ivo H. Daalder and I. M. Destler, *In the Shadow of the Oval Office: Profiles of the National Security Advisers and the Presidents They Served—From JFK to George W. Bush* (New York: Simon & Schuster, 2009), 349–50.

22. "*The Hurt Locker*: Behind the Scenes," *The Hurt Locker* (Summit Entertainment, DVD bonus feature, 2010).

23. Anthony Shadid, *Night Draws Near: Iraq's People in the Shadow of America's War* (New York: Henry Holt, 2005), 23.

24. "*Hurt Locker*: Behind the Scenes."

25. Nile Gardiner, "Avatar: The Most Expensive Piece of Anti-American Propaganda Ever Made," *Telegraph*, December 25, 2009.
26. Jessica Winter, "Art of Darkness: To Understand the Controversy around Kathryn Bigelow's Hit Film *Zero Dark Thirty*, It Helps to Understand Kathryn Bigelow's Kind of Movie," *Time*, February 4, 2013.
27. Deborah Wilson, "Gunsmoke and Mirrors: Integrity of Groundbreaking *Zero Dark Thirty* Director Runs Much Deeper than a Patina," *Movie Entertainment*, July 2013.
28. Winter, "Art of Darkness."
29. Jane Mayer, "Zero Conscience in 'Zero Dark Thirty,'" *New Yorker*, December 14, 2012.
30. Wilson, "Gunsmoke and Mirrors."
31. Winter, "Art of Darkness."

Bibliography

Adams, Michael C. C. *The Best War Ever: America and World War II*. Baltimore: Johns Hopkins University Press, 1994.

Adorno, Theodor. *Prisms*. Cambridge MA: MIT Press, 1981.

Ambrose, Stephen E. *Nixon: The Triumph of a Politician, 1962–1972*. New York: Simon & Schuster, 1989.

Annussek, Greg. *Hitler's Raid to Save Mussolini: The Most Infamous Commando Operation of World War II*. Cambridge MA: Da Capo, 2005.

Ansary, Tamim. *Games without Rules: The Often Interrupted History of Afghanistan*. New York: PublicAffairs, 2012.

Audoin-Rouzeau, Stéphane, and Annette Becker. *14–18: Understanding the Great War*. Translated by Catherine Temerson. New York: Hill & Wang, 2000.

Barker, Christian R., and R. W. Last. *Erich Maria Remarque*. London: Oswald Wolf, 1979.

Barley, Tony. *Taking Sides: The Fiction of John le Carré*. Milton Keynes UK: Open University Press, 1986.

Bean, C.E.W. *Anzac to Amiens*. Canberra: Australia War Memorial, 1981.

Bergman, Jay. *Meeting the Demands of Reason: The Life and Thought of Andrei Sakharov*. Ithaca: Cornell University Press, 2009.

Beschloss, Michael. *Our Documents: 100 Milestone Documents from the National Archives*. New York: Oxford University Press, 2006.

Bizot, François. *The Gate*. New York: Knopf, 2003.

Bodard, Lucien. *The Quicksand War: Prelude to Vietnam*. London: Faber & Faber, 1967.

Boyer, Paul. *By the Bomb's Early Light: American Thought and Culture at the Dawn of the Atomic Age*. New York: Pantheon, 1985.

Brando, Marlon, with Robert Lindsey. *Brando: Songs My Mother Taught Me*. New York: Random House, 1994.

Brownstein, Ronald. *The Power and the Glitter: The Hollywood-Washington Connection*. New York: Pantheon, 1992.

Burleigh, Michael. *The Third Reich: A New History*. New York: Hill & Wang, 2000.

Burrell, Robert S. *The Ghosts of Iwo Jima*. College Station: Texas A&M University Press, 2006.

Burrin, Philippe. *France under the Nazis: Collaboration and Compromise*. New York: New Press, 1996.

Cantor, Paul A. *The Invisible Hand in Popular Culture: Liberty vs. Authority in American Film and TV*. Lexington: University Press of Kentucky, 2012.

Chandler, David P. *Brother Number One: A Political Biography of Pol Pot*. Boulder: Westview Press, 1992.

Christopher, Nicholas. *The Somewhere in the Night: Film Noir and the American City*. New York: Free Press, 1997.

Clarke, Donald. *All or Nothing at All: A Life of Frank Sinatra*. New York: Freeman International, 1997.

Collingham, Lizzie. *The Taste of War: World War II and the Battle for Food*. New York: Penguin Press, 2012.

Cook, David A. *A History of Narrative Film*. New York: Norton, 1981.

Cook, Fred J. *The Nightmare Decade: The Life and Times of Senator Joe McCarthy*. New York: Random House, 1971.

Cowie, Peter. *Coppola*. New York: Scribner, 1990.

Crile, George. *Charlie Wilson's War: The Extraordinary Story of the Largest Covert Operation in History*. New York: Atlantic Monthly Press, 2003.

Crowe, David M. *Oskar Schindler: The Untold Account of His Life, Wartime Activities, and the True Story behind the List*. Cambridge MA: Westview Press, 2004.

Culbert, David, ed. *Film and Propaganda in America: A Documentary History*. New York: Greenwood Press, 1990.

Daalder, Ivo H., and I. M. Destler. *In the Shadow of the Oval Office: Profiles of the National Security Advisers and the Presidents They Served — From JFK to George W. Bush*. New York: Simon & Schuster, 2009.

Davis, Ronald L. *Duke: The Life and Image of John Wayne*. Norman: University of Oklahoma Press, 1998.

DeBauche, Leslie Midkiff. *Reel Patriotism: The Movies and World War I*. Madison: University of Wisconsin Press, 1997.

D'Este, Carlo. *Patton: Genius for War*. New York: HarperCollins, 1995.

Dorronsoro, Giles. *Revolution Unending: Afghanistan, 1979 to the Present*. London: Hurst & Co., 2005.

Duffin, Allan T., and Paul Matheis. *The 12 O'Clock High Logbook*. Albany GA: Bearmanor Media, 2005.

Duncan, Paul. *Stanley Kubrick: The Complete Films*. Hong Kong: Taschen, 2003.

Farago, Ladislas. *Patton: Ordeal and Triumph*. London: Arthur Baker, 1966.

Fest, Joachim C. *The Faces of the Third Reich: Portraits of the Nazi Leadership*. New York: Pantheon, 1970.

Fisher, James T. *On the Irish Waterfront: The Crusader, the Movie, and the Soul of the Port of New York*. Ithaca NY: Cornell University Press, 2009.

Fishgall, Gary. *Gregory Peck: A Biography*. New York: Scribner, 2002.

Fonda, Jane. *My Life So Far*. New York: Random House, 2005.

Friedman, Norman. *U.S. Small Combatants, Including PT-Boats, Subchasers, and the Brown-Water Navy: An Illustrated Design History*. Annapolis: Naval Institute Press, 1987.

Fujiwara, Chris. *The World and Its Double: The Life and Work of Otto Preminger*. New York: Faber & Faber, 2008.

Fuller, Samuel. *A Third Face*. New York: Knopf, 2002.

Gage, Beverly. *The Day Wall Street Exploded*. Oxford: Oxford University Press, 2009.

Garrett, Stephen A. *Ethics and Airpower*. New York: St. Martin's Press, 1993.

Graf, Malvina. *The Krakow Ghetto and the Plaszow Camp Revisited*. Tallahassee: Florida State University Press, 1989.

Hammontree, Patsy Guy. *Elvis Presley: A Bio-Bibliography*. Westport CT: Greenwood Press, 1985.

Hart, Peter. *Gallipoli*. New York: Oxford University Press, 2011.

Hitler, Adolf. *Mein Kampf*. New York: Reynal & Hitchcock, 1941

Hoberman, J. *The Magic Hour: Film at the Fin de Siècle*. Philadelphia: Temple University Press, 2003.

Hobson, J. A. *Imperialism: A Study*. London: Allen & Unwin, 1902.

Hochschild, Adam. *To End All Wars: A Story of Loyalty and Rebellion, 1914–1918*. Boston: Houghton Mifflin Harcourt, 2011.

Holsinger, Paul, ed. *War and American Popular Culture*. Westport CT: Greenwood Press, 1999.

James, Robert Rhodes. *Gallipoli*. New York: Macmillan, 1965.

Jeansonne, Glenn, with David Luhrssen. *A Time of Paradox: America since 1890*. Lanham MD: Rowman & Littlefield, 2006.

Jisheng, Yang. *Tombstone: The Great Chinese Famine, 1958–1962*. New York: Farrar Straus & Giroux, 2012.

Johnston, Robert D. *The Politics of Healing*. New York: Routledge, 2004.

Judt, Tony. *Postwar: A History of Europe since 1945*. New York: Penguin Press, 2005.

Kael, Pauline. *For Keeps: 30 Years at the Movies*. New York: Dutton, 1994.

Kaplan Philip, and Rex Alan Smith. *One Last Look: A Sentimental Journey to the Eight Air Force Heavy Bomber Bases of World War II in England*. New York: Abbeville Press, 1983.

Karnow, Stanley. *Vietnam: A History*. New York: Penguin, 1984.

Katz, Alfred. *Poland's Ghettos at War*. New York: Twayne, 1970.

Kelly, Andrew, James Pepper, and Jeffrey Richards. *Filming T. E. Lawrence: Korda's Lost Epics*. London: I. B. Tauris, 1997.

Kelly, Walt. *Ten Ever-Lovin' Blue-Eyed Years with Pogo*. New York: Simon & Schuster, 1959.

Keneally, Thomas. *Schindler's List*. New York: Touchstone Books, 1992.

Kershaw, Ian. *Hitler, 1936–1945: Nemesis*. New York: Norton, 2000.

Kiernan, Ben. *The Pol Pot Regime: Race, Power, and Genocide in Cambodia under the Khmer Rouge, 1970–79*. New Haven: Yale University Press, 1996.

Kissinger, Henry. *Nuclear Weapons and Foreign Policy*. New York: Harper & Brothers, 1957.

Koch, Howard, ed. *Casablanca Script and Legend*. Woodstock NY: Overlook Press, 1992.

Kramer, Steven Philip. *Abel Gance*. Boston: Twayne, 1978.

Kreimeier, Klaus. *The UFA Story: A History of Germany's Greatest Film Company, 1918–1945*. New York: New Press, 1996.

Lawrence, T. E. *Seven Pillars of Wisdom: A Triumph*. Garden City NY: Garden City Publishing, 1938.

Lean, Sandra, with Barry Chattington. *David Lean: An Intimate Portrait*. New York: Universal, 2001.

Lerner, Max. *The Unfinished Country: A Book of American Symbols*. New York: Simon & Schuster, 1959.

Levering, Ralph B. *The Cold War: A Post-Cold War History*. Wheeling IL: Harland Davidson, 1994.

LoBrutto, Vincent. *Stanley Kramer: A Biography*. New York: Donald I. Fine Books, 1997.

Loshitzky, Yosefa. *Spielberg's Holocaust: Critical Perspectives on Schindler's List*. Bloomington: Indiana University Press, 1997.

Marks, John. *The Search for the Manchurian Candidate: The CIA and Mind Control*. New York: New York Times Books, 1979.

Martin, Brett. *Difficult Men: Behind the Scenes of a Creative Revolution from "The Sopranos" and "The Wire" to "Mad Men" and "Breaking Bad."* New York: Penguin, 2013.

McBride, Joseph. *Steven Spielberg*. New York: Simon & Schuster, 1997.

McCullough, David. *Truman*. New York: Simon & Schuster, 1992.

McGilligan, Patrick. *Alfred Hitchcock: A Life in Darkness*. New York: Regan Books, 2003.

McMeekin, Sean. *The Berlin-Baghdad Express: The Ottoman Empire and Germany's Bid for World Power*. Cambridge: Harvard University Press, 2010.

Mieczkowski, Yanek. *Eisenhower's Sputnik Moment: The Race for Space and World Prestige*. Ithaca NY: Cornell University Press, 2013.

Miller, Frank. *Casablanca as Time Goes By: 50th Anniversary Commemorative*. Atlanta: Turner Publishing, 1992.

Miller, Jeffrey S. *Something Completely Different: British Television and American Culture*. Minneapolis: University of Minnesota Press, 2000.

Miller, Marshall Lee. *Bulgaria during the Second World War*. Stanford: Stanford University Press, 1975.

Millichap, Joseph R. *Lewis Milestone*. Boston: Twayne, 1981.

Moens, Alexander. *The Foreign Policy of the George W. Bush: Values, Strategy, and Loyalty*. Aldershot UK: Ashgate, 2004.

Morella, Joe, Edward Z. Epstein, and John Griggs. *The Films of World War II*. Secaucus NJ: Citadel Press, 1975.

Morgenthau, Henry. *Ambassador Morgenthau's Story*. Garden City NY: Doubleday, Page, 1918.

Morrow, John H., Jr. *The Great War: An Imperial History*. London: Routledge, 2004.

Nelson, Keith L., ed. *The Impact of War on American Life: The Twentieth-Century Experience*. New York: Holt, Rinehart & Winston, 1971.

Nichols, David. *Ernie's War: The Best of Ernie Pyle's World War II Dispatches*. New York: Simon & Schuster, 1986.

O'Brien, Geoffrey. *The Phantom Empire*. New York: Norton, 1993.

Olson, James S., and Randy Roberts. *My Lai: A Brief History with Documents*. Boston: Bedford St. Martin's, 1998.

Osborne, Richard E. *The Casablanca Companion: The Movie Classic and its Place in History*. Indianapolis: Riebel-Roque, 1997.

Paxton, Robert O. *Vichy France: Old Guard and New Order 1940–1944*. New York: Norton, 1975.

Pearson, John. *The Life of Ian Fleming*. New York: McGraw-Hill, 1966.

Perry, George. *Steven Spielberg*. London: Orion House, 1998.

Pfaff, William. *The Bullet's Song: Romantic Violence and Utopia*. New York: Simon & Schuster, 2004.

Phillips, Gene D. *Beyond the Epic: The Life and Films of David Lean*. Lexington: University Press of Kentucky, 2006.

Radosh, Ronald, and Joyce Milton. *The Rosenberg File: A Search for the Truth*. New York: Holt, Rinehart & Winston, 1983.

Rapf, Joanna E., ed. *Sidney Lumet Interviews*. Jackson: University Press of Mississippi, 2006.

Rayner, Jonathan. *The Films of Peter Weir*. London: Cassell, 1998.

Reeves, Thomas C. *The Life and Times of Joe McCarthy: A Biography*. Lanham MD: Madison Books, 1997.

Rhodes, Anthony. *Propaganda, The Art of Persuasion: World War II*. New York: Chelsea House, 1976.

Ross, Steven J. *Hollywood Left and Right: How Movie Stars Shaped American Politics*. New York: Oxford University Press, 2011.

Rubin, Steven Jay. *The James Bond Films: A Behind the Scenes History*. Westport CT: Arlington House, 1981.

Sarris, Andrew. *"You Ain't Heard Nothin' Yet": Talking Film History and Memory, 1927–1949*. New York: Oxford University Press, 1998.

Sbardellati, John. *J. Edgar Hoover Goes to the Movies: The FBI and the Origins of Hollywood's Cold War*. Ithaca NY: Cornell University Press, 2012.

Schickel, Richard. *Elia Kazan: A Biography*. New York: HarperCollins, 2005.

Schmidt, Christel, ed. *Mary Pickford: Queen of the Movies*. Lexington: Library of Congress / University Press of Kentucky, 2012.

Schumacher, Michael. *Francis Ford Coppola*. New York: Crown Publishers, 1999.

Severo, Richard, and Lewis Milford. *The Wages of War: When America's Soldiers Came Home — From Valley Forge to Vietnam*. New York: Simon & Schuster, 1990.

Shadid, Anthony. *Night Draws Near: Iraq's People in the Shadow of America's War*. New York: Henry Holt, 2005.

Shay, Shaul. *The Endless Jihad: The Mujahidin, the Taliban and Bin Laden*. Herzliya, Israel: International Policy Institute for Counter-Terrorism, 2002.

Sheward, David. *Rage and Glory: The Volatile Life and Career of George C. Scott*. New York: Applause, 2008.

Siegel, Scott, and Barbara Siegel. *Encyclopedia of Hollywood*. New York: Facts on File, 1990.

Smith, Holland M., and Percy Finch. *Coral and Brass*. New York: Charles Scribner's Sons, 1949.

Stephens, Ian. *Monsoon Morning*. London: Ernest Benn, 1966.

Stevenson, William. *A Man Called Intrepid: The Secret War*. New York: Harcourt Brace Jovanovich, 1976.

Suid, Lawrence H. *Guts and Glory: Great American War Movies*. Reading MA: Addison-Wesley, 1978.

Sullivan, Robert, ed. *One Nation: America Remembers September 11, 2001*. Boston: Little, Brown, 2001.

Theoharis, Athan. *Chasing Spies: How the FBI Failed in Counterintelligence but Promoted the Politics of McCarthyism in the Cold War.* Chicago: Ivan R. Dee, 2002.

Thomson, David. *"Have You Seen . . . ? A Personal Introduction to 1,000 Films.* New York: Knopf, 2008.

Thomson, David. *The Big Screen: The Story of Movies.* New York: Farrar, Straus & Giroux, 2012.

Toland, John. *Adolf Hitler.* Garden City NY: Doubleday, 1976.

Toplin, Robert Brent, ed. *Oliver Stone's USA.* Lawrence: University Press of Kansas, 2000.

Toth, James. *Sayyid Qutb: The Life and Legacy of a Radical Islamic Intellectual.* Oxford: Oxford University Press, 2013.

Wallace, Brenton G. *Patton & His Third Army.* Harrisburg PA: Military Service Publishing, 1946.

Warren, James A. *The Lions of Iwo Jima.* New York: Henry Holt, 2008.

Wawro, Geoffrey. *Quicksand: America's Pursuit of Power in the Middle East.* New York: Penguin Press, 2010.

Weintraub, Stanley, and Rodelle Weintraub. *Lawrence of Arabia: The Literary Impulse.* Baton Rouge: Louisiana State University Press, 1975.

White, G. Edward. *Alger Hiss's Looking-Glass Wars: The Covert Life of a Soviet Spy.* New York: Oxford University Press, 2004.

Whitfield, Stephen J. *The Culture of the Cold War.* Baltimore: Johns Hopkins University Press, 1990.

Wilson, Jean Moorcroft. *Siegfried Sassoon: The Making of a War Poet, A Biography, 1886–1918.* New York: Routledge, 1999.

Winter, Jay, and Blaine Baggett. *The Great War and the Shaping of the 20th Century.* New York: Penguin Studio, 1996.

Woodward, Bob. *Bush at War.* New York: Simon & Schuster, 2002

Young, Peter. *A Short History of World War II, 1939–1945.* New York: Crowell, 1966.

*The Life of Herbert Hoover:
Fighting Quaker, 1928–1933*

*Elvis Presley: Reluctant Rebel: His
Life and Our Times* (with David
Luhrssen and Dan Sokolovic)

*Changing Times: The Life of Barack
Obama* (with David Luhrssen)

A Time of Paradox: America since 1890

*A Time of Paradox: America from
Awakening to Superpower, 1890–1945*

*A Time of Paradox: From the Cold War
to the Third Millennium, 1945–Present*

*Women of the Far Right: The Mothers
Movement and World War II*

*Transformation and Reaction:
America, 1921–1945*

*Messiah of the Masses: Huey P.
Long and the Great Depression*

Gerald L. K. Smith: Minister of Hate

Leander Perez: Boss of the Delta

*Race, Religion, and Politics: The Louisiana
Gubernatorial Elections of 1959–1960*

Editor, *Huey at 100: Centennial
Essays on Huey P. Long*

Editor, *A Guide to the History of Louisiana*